Overdue items may incur
charges as published in the
current Schedule of Charges.

L21

GUARDRAILS

GUARDRAILS

GUIDING HUMAN DECISIONS
IN THE AGE OF AI

URS GASSER
VIKTOR MAYER-SCHÖNBERGER

PRINCETON UNIVERSITY PRESS

PRINCETON & OXFORD

Published by Princeton University Press
41 William Street, Princeton, New Jersey 08540
99 Banbury Road, Oxford OX2 6JX

press.princeton.edu

All Rights Reserved

ISBN 9780691150680
ISBN (e-book) 9780691256351

British Library Cataloging-in-Publication Data is available

Editorial: Bridget Flannery-McCoy and Alena Chekanov
Production Editorial: Sara Lerner
Text and Jacket Design: Karl Spurzem
Production: Erin Suydam
Publicity: James Schneider and Kathryn Stevens
Copyeditor: Karen Verde

This book has been composed in Arno Pro with Acumin Pro Extra Condensed Bold

Printed on acid-free paper. ∞

Printed and bound by CPI Group (UK) Ltd, Croydon, CRO 4YY

10 9 8 7 6 5 4 3 2 1

To our teachers
Herbert Burkert and Hannes Pichler

CONTENTS

GUARDRAILS

1

DECISIONS

July 1, 2002, was a dark summer night at the German/Swiss border. Well above the clouds, a Russian Tupolev 154 airliner was cruising westward. Inside it, dozens of gifted children from Ufa, southwest of the Ural Mountains, were looking forward to a holiday in Spain. In the cockpit, highly experienced captain Alexander Gross had the controls, assisted by four colleagues. Not far away, a Boeing 757 freighter was flying northward to Brussels at the same altitude.

Noticing the converging flight trajectories, an air traffic controller for Swiss air space contacted the Tupolev crew to resolve the issue. He instructed Gross to descend and the Tupolev's crew complied.

However, both airplanes were equipped with automatic collision warning systems. Just after the air traffic controller had issued his command to descend, the collision warning systems instructed both crews to take evasive maneuvers—but it ordered the freighter to descend, and the Tupolev to climb.

Having received conflicting information from the human air traffic controller and the automated collision warning system, the Tupolev crew debated whether to continue its descent or climb instead. Their discussion was interrupted by the air traffic controller instructing them again and this time urgently to reduce its altitude, unaware that the automated system was now issuing contradictory instructions. As the crew continued on its downward trajectory—heading straight for the freighter which, following the orders of the automated system, was also descending—the warning system in the Tupolev more strongly commanded Gross to climb.

Collision warning systems in airplanes close to each other get in touch automatically and hash out which airplane is to climb and which to sink, to guarantee sufficient spatial separation between them as long as the system's commands are followed strictly. Hence, today standard operating procedures mandate that commands of the collision warning system must be complied with immediately, even if contradicting human air traffic controllers. But at the time, the pilots' training was not entirely clear on this matter. Forced to choose between human and machine, Gross chose to rely on the human controller. Shortly thereafter, at around 35,000 feet, the Tupolev collided at full speed with the Boeing freighter. Everyone on board both planes perished that night, high above the German city of Überlingen.[1]

The accident was quickly blamed on the air traffic controller, who was overworked and with some equipment not fully functional. But there is a more fundamental issue at play. On that fateful night, the Tupolev crew faced a consequential decision: Should they trust the information coming from the human controller or the collision warning system?

True, without the air traffic controller's mistaken information to descend, the crash would not have happened. But the midair collision wasn't caused only by bad information. Gross knew he had to *choose* between good and bad information, he just was unsure which was which. Rather than asking the air traffic controller for clarification or following the warning system's advice, he *chose* to descend.

Like pilots, we too face many decisions every single day, although few of them are similarly consequential. In deciding, we rely not only on information and our own thinking. Our decision-making is also shaped by external forces, especially society, prodding, nudging, or pushing us toward a particular option, like the collision warning system. We call these *guardrails*—and that's what this book is about, from the enablers and constraints of the information we receive to rules and norms that shape how we choose among our options and how bound we are by the choices we make.

The concept of such societal guardrails is a metaphor borrowed from the kind of physical structures you see along the sides of roads or boats. Done well, these structures offer the best of both worlds. They show you where the edge is, making it less likely that you'll step over without meaning to. But they aren't like prison walls, which make it impossible to climb over if you want. You can still go off road or take a swim if you desire. Guardrails are more about marking zones of desirable behavior rather than pushing narrowly for a single "right" choice.[2]

Decisional guardrails are the interface between a person's choice and the input of society. They link the individual and the collective. Decisions taken by individuals or small groups can shape the lives of many others, as the midair crash above Überlingen so horrifically exemplifies. In a world in which decision-making is largely individual, decisional guardrails are society's most direct way to influence our mutual trajectory. This book details how, collectively, we aim to alter the decisions that are being made. It is about how society governs the contexts in which individuals make decisions—a topic both powerful and ubiquitous, yet rarely understood comprehensively.

Selecting the appropriate qualities for these decision guardrails is critical. But we will argue that in our digital age we are too quick to opt for certain types of guardrails. Without much reflection, we amplify some guardrail qualities as we overemphasize the role of technology, reflecting a widespread trend for technology to increasingly govern all kinds of human decision-making. The 2002 midair collision over Überlingen seems to confirm these beliefs: If only humans follow machines, disasters are avoided.

In this book, we suggest that such a strategy is deeply flawed. This is not because technology is somehow unable or unfit to provide effective decision governance, but because the real issue is not the nature of the decision guardrails—whether they are technical or social—but the principles underlying their design. The real question is: What kind of decisions do guardrails facilitate and what decisions should they enable?

In the nine chapters that follow we examine guardrails in a variety of challenges, contexts, and cases. But our aim is not to examine every aspect or offer a detailed blueprint; we train our eye on what we think is an emerging bigger picture—a crucial red thread in appreciating the importance of designing good guardrails. Our goal is twofold: to broaden our normative horizons, so that we realize the breadth and depths of the solution space of possible guardrails; and to offer guidance that can help us craft and select guardrails that are fitting for our challenging times—to ensure not just human agency, but human progress.

Before we can fashion a solution, however, we need to better understand what's at stake and why.

Choices, Choices Everywhere

We all make decisions—hundreds, even thousands of times every day.[3] Most of these decisions are trivial. We make them quickly and without much thinking. For others, often more consequential ones, we spend hours agonizing. Each decision shapes our future. The academic field of decision science is relatively young, having formally been established in the twentieth century. The quest to make good decisions, however, is as old as the human capacity to reflect on the choices we face.[4]

Relevant information is an obvious and crucial element of good decision-making. We glean insights from our social interactions with others, aided by the evolution of language. Script made it possible to preserve knowledge across time and space. Libraries, a cultural invention built on reading and writing, have served for many centuries as crucial social institutions enabling us to collect information, learn from it, and use it to make life better.[5] The information stored and curated in these vast collections shaped decisions that led to important advances in areas as diverse as agriculture, architecture, medicine, art, manufacturing, and war. In the United States, libraries were assigned a crucial role at the birth of the nation: The Library of Congress was tasked with collecting the world's knowledge, and a nationwide system of public libraries aimed to bring this knowledge to the people.[6] The US Constitution makes clear that information is preserved and made available for a purpose, much as patents are granted not to reward the inventor, but "to promote the progress of science and useful arts."[7] It recognizes that the role of information, in all its mediated forms, is deeply utilitarian—improving individual and societal decisions.

More recently, digital technologies have dramatically promised to lay the groundwork for better decisions by unlocking the power of computing, data, and algorithms. More than ever before, information is at the center of our daily decision-making: We consult Siri about the weather forecast, ask ChatGPT for a couple of dinner jokes, and heed Tinder's recommendations for our next date. And indeed, in the grand scheme of things digital tools have improved the conditions for decision-making, from search engines to forecasting the spread of a virus to detecting credit card fraud from subtle anomalies in transaction data.

Information we receive needs to be analyzed and evaluated. We constantly "frame" information through our mental models about how the world works, often without much conscious thought. This is what we mean when we say that we put information into perspective. This process enables us to generate and compare options.[8] We tend to evaluate options for hugely consequential decisions more carefully, although our judgment isn't perfect—but sometimes we also fret over trivial decisions or choose bluntly without much consideration. As we ponder options, we wonder how irrevocable our actions will be. Are we bound by them, or could we reverse course if necessary?

Pop psych literature and management training courses offer a plethora of tools and tricks to help us in this process of generating and evaluating options. We are told to "think outside the box," or make a list of pros and cons. Not every such suggestion is backed up by solid research. We can't think outside the box, for instance, in the sense that we are always thinking within mental models (and decide badly if we try without them).[9] But many suggestions may be useful in appropriate contexts.

At this point some notes of caution are in order. We are focusing here on the elements of human decision-making and how to improve that process. But we are not suggesting that all our decisions are carefully thought through. While much of our argument applies for all decision contexts, it is strongest and most valuable when we decide deliberately.

Neither are we implying that decision-making is a clean linear process, with one step followed logically after the other: collect information, analyze it using our mental models to generate decision options, compare, and choose between them. On the contrary, these elements are linked in many ways. Even deliberate decision-making is often messy and iterant. For instance, as we compare options, we may realize we missed an important dimension and must go back and gather additional information.

Nor are we suggesting that even deliberate decisions are entirely rational. Research has impressively shown that our decision-making is shaped by cognitive biases that influence our thinking. We cannot switch them off—at least not easily and at will.[10] This realization may shatter any simplistic hope that we can achieve objective rationality in the choices we make, but it isn't fatal to the idea that the decision process is open to improvement toward better reasoning.

Decisions are important because they prepare us to take actions that shape the world. But it's not just that decisions change the world—it's that *we* change the world that way. Decisions are expressions of human agency—of our ability to influence the trajectory of our own existence and that of our species, even if only slightly. Human agency makes us matter. Without it, there would be no motivation to act. Agency is the source of energy that gets us out of bed in the morning to weather the storms of our daily lives.

Of course, we do not know whether we really have agency. Perhaps, from the vantage point of an omniscient objective bystander, both our actions and our sense of agency are just the results of biochemical processes over which we have no control.[11] But for us, the view of the nonexistent bystander is largely irrelevant. What matters, pragmatically speaking, is what we perceive every time we select an action and take it. Consequently, in this book we embrace human agency as something that we experience as existing.

Guardrails as Governance

Decisions are the cognitive mechanisms through which we interact with the world. Much hinges on them. Understandably, society has taken a keen interest in facilitating that we decide well.

Information is an important ingredient for good decision-making. And so, a variety of guardrails exist that shape what information is available. For instance, in the United States, corporate disclosure laws limit what a company's executives can share publicly and when.[12] Share too much information and you risk being fined, as Elon Musk found out when he tweeted about taking Tesla, a listed company, private in 2018.[13] In other contexts, the reverse is true, and one is required to make public certain information. Pharma companies need to disclose possible side effects for the drugs they manufacture, car companies need to publish emissions and fuel efficiency figures, and the food industry needs to put nutritional labels on most of their products.[14] Sometimes, such a *l'obligation d'information*, as the French call it poetically, may apply to a company's clients. Insurance policies are an example. The insured is typically under a duty to disclose material facts that affect the risk to the insurer. In a similar vein, the state itself makes available a wide variety of information to help individuals make better decisions.[15] Laws are made public so that citizens can obey them, at least in democratic states. Public registers, such as for corporations or landownership, help people decide whether to engage in a business transaction.

It is not only legal rules or government policies that mandate the sharing of information. It could also be a social norm, rooted in culture and custom, such as conflict-of-interest statements in academic publications. Or it could be a practice an organization voluntarily submits to. Think, for instance, of corporate disclosure of social and environmental responsibility metrics.[16]

The hope behind all such interventions is that providing relevant information leads to better choices. When IKEA provides detailed instructions on how to assemble their furniture, they hope it will lead to decisions that make one's sofa bed more stable. When regulators mandate labels on food wrappers, they hope information about high calories and excessive amounts of sugar will lead people to make nutritious choices—though the chocolate bar might still be too hard to resist.

In the preceding examples, information is required in situations where a decision is imminent. In other contexts, information is meant to serve as a foundation for actions further down the road. It becomes an accountability tool with a longer shelf life. For instance, freedom of information mandates, so the theory goes (as usual, myriads of practical issues mess with the theory), enable citizens to make better decisions about the policies that affect their lives and, ultimately, give a thumbs up or down when the government is up for reelection.[17] Ralph Nader, the famous US government reform and consumer protection advocate, summarized it succinctly: "Information is the currency of democracy."[18]

Beyond facilitating the flow of information, guardrails extend to the process of creating and weighing decision options. For example, numerous legal rules aim to ensure that individuals can decide without undue duress, including making extortion and coercion criminal offenses.[19] In some countries, certain particularly consequential transactions must be done before public authorities or involve testimony from experts to make sure that all parties are aware of and have considered all effects.[20] Nowhere is this more evident than in the growing number of nations that have chosen to permit assisted suicide. The decision to end one's life is so grave that these societies require multiple formal steps to confirm that the decision is deliberate, free of duress, and often in the context of a terminal and painful illness.[21]

Sometimes long-term decisions come with waiting times or "cooling-off" periods to give people ample opportunity to carefully think through their choices.[22] Being bound by a decision for a long time may have benefits—it offers stability. But we might want to think harder about whether it is the right option—and we may need more time to do so. In numerous other instances, societal guardrails explicitly enable decisions to be retracted and minds to be changed, even if that causes headaches for other parties involved.[23]

As with guardrails on information flow, guardrails on weighing options cover a spectrum from community practices to formal legal requirements. The standard operating procedures for aircraft pilots we mentioned at the start of this chapter—including whether to follow the commands of the collision warning system or the air traffic controller—are not formal law, but airlines require their flight crews to adhere to them. Similarly, emergency doctors in many hospitals must work through standard protocols of diagnosing and treating patients. It's not the law, but part of the organizational and professional culture—and it has been shown to be highly effective.

Such codes of conduct exist for many professions and organizations. Ever wondered how Amazon or McDonald's handles transaction complaints? They have detailed rules for how a customer service rep may decide and under what circumstances. Among merchants more generally, rules evolved over centuries that set out how they ought to behave when interacting with each other. Stemming from annual trade fairs in European cities from the thirteenth century, these rules, sometimes called "lex mercatoria," aimed to enhance trust in the market overall.[24]

A far more subtle shaping of individual decision processes has become popular lately in some policy circles. Called "nudging," the idea is to delicately prompt people to choose the option that will be most beneficial for them. For example, when it is judged that not enough individuals opt into a retirement savings plan, one could make participation the default and require those who do not want to partake to actively opt out instead.[25] Advocates tout nudging as less limiting than more outright restrictions, but skeptics point out that nudges are opaque, creating an illusion of choice while manipulating the decision process.[26]

Similar techniques can be used to shape decisions in ways that further the interests of people other than the decision-maker. Ads and salespeople use a wide variety of cognitive tricks to influence transaction decisions.[27] Even the layout of supermarkets is carefully designed to affect our purchasing choices.[28] Deep-rooted social and cultural practices can be deliberately repurposed to shape our decisions. In the early years of eBay, sellers often rated buyers highly *before* a transaction had been completed. That didn't make sense. Why should you rate somebody before you know whether she did as promised? Researchers took a closer look and discovered that such a premature positive rating was perceived by the buyer as a gift, which gave rise to a social expectation to reciprocate.[29] Those who quickly rated the other side in positive terms got more favorable ratings in return, which somewhat divorced ratings from the underlying transaction and prompted eBay to change its rating system.

So far, we have drawn a distinction between measures that shape the information we receive and measures that influence how we evaluate decision options. The distinction is artificial, in the sense that all measures that shape our decision processes involve information—otherwise they would not be able to reach into our mind. Airlines' standard operating procedures shape how pilots weigh their options, but they are also information that pilots read and digest. When a nudge shifts a decision default, it's also information about how easy or hard it is to decide on a particular option. However, we find the distinction between "informational" and "decisional" guardrails useful because it helps us comprehend the wide spectrum of possibilities.

As will be clear from the examples above, by guardrails we mean more than a simple norm or rule. Guardrails often include processes and institutions, mechanisms and tools, even a "culture" or "way of thinking." For instance, emergency doctors have internalized checklists, while standard operating procedures can take on material form in safety mechanisms in factory machinery. Programmers at large software companies live by a "software development life cycle," a combination of rules, processes, and organizational structures to help ensure good coding.[30] It is the "system" around a naked norm—the processes and institutions—that makes guardrails work. Hence, when we write here about guardrails we see beyond single rules and include the reality around them that makes them work (or not).

Because our notion of guardrails isn't limited to formal legal rules and because we include the structures around them, we see them in a very wide variety of contexts and circumstances. Dynamics like globalization have, some scholars maintain, proliferated the types and kinds of guardrails, leading to a pluralization of regulation.[31] Others, like Gillian Hadfield, agree—and turn the analysis into a prescription, suggesting we need to think more in terms of markets of rules than a hierarchy of them.[32] Whatever the concrete causes and consequences, what matters in our context is simply that guardrails shaping our decisions are plentiful and diverse. But if decision-making is the expression of an individual's volition, why are others—communities, society—so interested in shaping individual choices?

The Social and Externalities

The obvious answer is that as social beings, we care for each other. Helping each other is something we practice right from early childhood, so why should we not want to help each other to make good decisions? A friend, colleague, or a complete stranger may benefit from measures that improve their individual decision-making today—but we may be the lucky recipients of guidance tomorrow.

Anthropologists offer another compelling argument. Humans have made stunning progress over the past few millennia—compared to other species, but also to earlier phases of human existence. This cannot be explained by biological evolution, as the cogwheels of natural selection do not operate fast enough. Instead, what has propelled us forward so dramatically is some form of *cultural* evolution that involves learning things from each other, rather than having to learn everything for ourselves.[33] It's a marvelous cognitive shortcut to discovery: Insights can be passed on. We can stand on the shoulders of those who came before us. The key is our ability to learn abstractly, to let our minds wander instead of our bodies. When it comes to decision-making, too, communities want to ensure that good insights spread. We are eager to share suitable guardrails and are open to accept them—at least to an extent.

Economists put forward a related but distinct reason for societal guardrails. When people make decisions that affect other people, economists call those effects externalities. Implementing guardrails can serve a utilitarian purpose, as shaping an individual's decision influences the externalities the decision causes. For example, in 2015, the US Environmental Protection Agency (EPA) discovered that Volkswagen, one of the world's largest car manufacturers, had illegally deployed software in more than ten million of its cars to deceive emissions tests—thereby evading a requirement to provide truthful information that will help car buyers make good decisions. Top managers and engineers at the car company had known about the illegal scheme for years.[34] As a result, millions of consumers bought cars erroneously certified as green and powerful, which caused huge amounts of unhealthy emissions. When the deception became clear, millions of affected cars lost much of their residual value overnight.

Externalities can be positive as well as negative, of course. The decision of a well-known coffee chain to open a shop in a troubled neighborhood can be seen as a signal of confidence in the neighborhood's future, attracting others to invest and creating new opportunities for people nearby.

Decisions can have consequences that impact groups and institutions as well as other individuals. This idea is illustrated by the textbook example of used car sales.[35] A car's history—such as whether it has been in accidents or has serious mechanical problems—is not always evident from looking at it. Absent any requirement to disclose such information, buyers tend to distrust used cars. They bid less than they would if they knew the car was good, because they factor in the risk that the car may be a "lemon." This is unfortunate for the honest seller, who will not get the car's actual worth from a sale.

There is a bigger and more pernicious consequence, though. Discouraged by not being able to sell their good cars for a fair price, honest sellers exit the market. As economists have shown, this leads to a vicious cycle: As lemons account for more of the market, buyers become even more reluctant to transact. This makes the *market* ineffective. The societal intervention in many nations in response is to require sellers to disclose whether their car had previously been in an accident. This not only helps buyers make the right decision, it helps honest sellers to find buyers—which increases the average quality of cars on offer in the market, and enables the market to do what markets should: help allocate a scarce resource.

Because collectively we benefit from better decisions, for society it makes sense to establish guardrails to inform and affect decision-making. By influencing individual decisions, guardrails enable society to chart a middle path between two extremes: full individualism, unencumbered by collective needs, or complete control through the collective without regard for individual preferences. Instead of a choice between Ayn Rand's *Atlas Shrugged* and George Orwell's *1984*, good societal guardrails offer the best of both worlds—exercising societal control without negating individual volition.

Good guardrails are a sweet spot that is challenging to find. In the abstract, they effectively guide appropriate individual decision processes—but in concrete contexts, defining effective and appropriate is a difficult if worthy challenge. Guardrails are not only, to quote political scientist Friedrich Kratochwil, "guidance devices" shaping individual decisions, but "also means which allow people to pursue goals, share meanings, communicate with each other, criticize assertions and justify actions."[36] They signify that individuals are being taken seriously not only as decision-makers, but as members of the society they live in.[37] There are a lot of moving parts to keep in mind when crafting a good guardrail. But rather than tackling this challenge head on, in recent years we have become sidetracked by technology.

The Technological Digression

Humans have used technical tools to aid their decision-making for centuries, but digital technologies now promise to be an unprecedented turbo for improving our decision-making—unlocking information bottlenecks and offering humans comprehensive access to knowledge.

Take only generative artificial intelligence systems like GPT (Generative Pre-trained Transformer). Trained by ingesting more than half a trillion almost entirely human-written words from millions of digitized books as well as billions of web pages, GPT is built on the collective knowledge and experience of humanity (or at least a significant slice of it).[38] It is being used to retrieve decision-relevant facts and information, but also to provide a wide variety of known decision options and to even offer decision recommendations.

However, these technologies have given rise to new and urgent questions about who controls digital information flows and the algorithms that power them. Data-driven machine learning models, such as GPT, are black boxes; we can interact with them but not peek into them easily. It's not just cutting-edge AI that is incomprehensible, however. Infamously, it is said that not even Google's own engineers can fully understand the inner workings of their search engine, upon which so many of us rely to inform our daily decisions.[39] Nor do we know what exactly determines the news feed on our favorite social media channels, or what shapes which ads we get to see when browsing the web.

Faced with questions about the complexity of such systems, the response often is that we need *more technology, not less.* AI is touted as capable of making better-than-human decisions. More data, improved algorithms, and more computing power promise to govern decision-making processes of the future. From smart contracts to autonomous vehicles, decisions are increasingly prepared, performed, and executed within technical systems.

In part, this focus on technology is also a consequence of the rise of "Big Tech"—companies operating digital platforms that have accrued enormous power to shape information flows for billions of users. However, it also reflects a process that has been going on for many decades, even centuries.[40] To describe this process, historian Lorraine Daston differentiates between "thick" and "thin" rules. Thick rules require interpretation and social acceptance. This means they may not be perfectly enforced, but their flexibility often makes them effective. In contrast, thin rules are stepwise instructions that are set and fixed. It's hard to derail them, so they can be relied on—but they can't be adapted easily.

Daston argues that in Western societies thin rules have risen, while thick rules have declined. She points to the rise of the administrative state and detailed and comprehensive regulatory rules that try to cover all eventualities in advance. This brings more predictability and lowers risk; but it also means that there is less room for discretion, change, and flexibility. Algorithms are an example of thin rules. Their increasingly extensive use as guardrails can be seen as a continuation of a process that started long ago.

In this book we challenge the mantra that more technology is the best answer to problems of human decision-making. Of course, we acknowledge that technology has the capacity to empower individuals, institutions, and society at large to make better decisions.[41] We also recognize that technology is never neutral: What technology is chosen has consequences for what can be achieved with it and how.[42] And we agree that the link between technologies and commercial control ought to be scrutinized: Opaque values baked into crucial technical bottlenecks of global information flows that influence billions of individual decisions need our critical questioning.[43]

But our concern is more fundamental. We argue that the focus on technology is distracting because it shifts our attention to a discussion over operational mechanisms and their implications when instead we should be engaging in a normative debate about the right qualities of guardrails.

Qualities for Times of Uncertainty

Every shift of our focus comes at a cost. When light is shone on one feature, others remain in the dark—understudied and overlooked. And so, by focusing on technology, we lose sight of what we suggest matters most in our times: defining the qualities and features of our society's decision governance.

Our starting point is the proposition that our world is becoming more volatile and uncertain. Challenges as diverse as social justice, public health, geopolitical disorder, and climate change will persist and deepen in the decades to come. The frameworks we put in place today to guide our decisions must be able to strategically embrace uncertainty. But the technologies that promise to improve decision-making regularly seek to negate flexibility and uncertainty, as we will discuss in chapters 3, 4, and 5.

So what are the alternatives? How can we create and employ guardrails that support and guide our decision-making in a world marked by increased uncertainty?

We argue that we need to understand our situation as one that requires less *technical* innovation than *social* innovation. We need to build on existing processes and institutions. The real challenge lies less in the concrete mechanics of guardrails than in getting the foundations right. We know this from our everyday practices. Before a driver revs up her engine, she needs to clarify where she wants to go, and what aspects of the journey—speed, safety, cost—she most cares about. We, too, must first clarify not just what our goals are, but also what qualities we want to have embedded in the mechanisms we employ to reach these goals.

We need to choose the decision qualities we want our guardrails to further and facilitate. This necessitates analysis and critique, but also normative thinking, both about society's role in providing these guardrails
and what environment for individual decision-making we envision. We
map out a suitable process and develop three concrete design rules for
good guardrails in chapter 6. We then add an important, perhaps crucial, constraint to guardrail design in chapter 7.

As we do this, we will realize that we already have solid foundations
on which we can build. We recognize these qualities in some of the
governance mechanisms we already employ—with positive results. And
we will see that the space for governance mechanisms to incorporate
some (or all) of these desired qualities is far larger than we initially
might have believed. A fresh but detailed look at the qualities inherent
in various kinds of guardrails can help us see a broader spectrum of
possibilities. By combining mechanisms and institutions, we can establish the innovative governance framework we need. In chapter 8 we'll
map this diverse governance landscape in greater detail.

Implementing this governance framework may involve the use of
technology, but only to the extent that it advances our goals and reflects
the qualities we seek; we show how in greater detail in chapter 9. To
foreshadow, we need to be less impressed by superfast bits traversing
cutting-edge hardware than by existing social mechanisms that have
proven their use. Rather than supplanting existing governance setups,
technology should support them as a tool.

Widening the Aperture

Decisions prepare us to take actions. Through our actions we change
reality. Humans aren't the strongest or fastest species. We may have mas-
tered arithmetic, but computers calculate faster than we can. We may
be excellent at recognizing shapes and patterns, but AI turns out to be
even better. So, what's left for us?

As humans we believe in agency—in our ability to choose and shape
the lives we live. Steve Jobs referred to it as the desire to "leave a little
dent in the universe."[44] But the desire to make a difference manifests

itself not just on the individual level. As a society, even as a species, we want to effect change. When Neil Armstrong stepped on the moon, he said it was a "giant leap for mankind" because it showed how humanity could accomplish that little dent in the universe.

Societal guardrails to individual decision-making are where the collective and the individual meet. Considering what decision qualities they should enable means asking what is right for both the "I" and the "we." We cannot define society's goals without conceptualizing what we want individuals to aim for. Through guardrails, society may express itself by injecting its values into individual decision-making.

Thinking normatively about societal guardrails also entails pondering the role of the individual in society. Four decades ago, US constitutional scholar Kenneth Karst suggested the metaphor of "equal citizenship," capturing an individual's equal agency as part of a greater compact.[45] Around the same time, but across the Atlantic, the German Constitutional Court opined eloquently about "informational self-determination" as an "I" that is always contextualized and anchored in a "we."[46] Harvard's Human Flourishing Program emphasizes the human need to evolve along five dimensions, from the highly individual to the deeply collective.[47] The message of these three and many others is clear: We are individuals, but we also are a part of something larger.

So as we write about the qualities of guardrails in the chapters that follow, we are not only opining about society and its role. We are also writing normatively about the individual: the place she ought to occupy, the values she ought to cherish, and the goals she ought to attain. Guardrails are, to paraphrase sociologist Anthony Giddens, "social practices"—structural mechanisms that reconfigure and reshape society.[48] If our initial focus may seem narrow, the implications are far bigger. Because through the decisions we make, we become not only agents of our destiny, but fellows of our society.

2

RULES

One evening in March 1993, dozens of people congregated in LambdaMOO, an online virtual space. Some chatted with their peers, others explored the space or worked on expanding and extending it. The "Lambda," as its users affectionately called it, was the brainchild of Pavel Curtis, a software engineer working at Xerox PARC, the famous Palo Alto Research Center of the Xerox corporation. Many digital innovations originated at PARC, from the personal computer and graphical user interface to word processing, laser printing, and digital office networks. Research at PARC laid the groundwork for object-oriented programming and during a visit helped a young Steve Jobs realize the future of computing.[1]

The Lambda was yet another idea that found a natural home at PARC. At a time when telco heads were still dreaming of digital pipes across the United States and beyond, Lambda users already experienced virtual space—a new, uncharted realm connected with our world through text and human imagination. Lambda could be not only inhabited, but also designed, extended, and enlarged. It was not demarcated by mountain ranges and seashores, only by the constraints of our minds (and of Curtis's code and PARC's hardware). It beckoned opportunity, like the Oklahoma land rush in the 1890s. It was a metaverse long before Neal Stephenson coined the term or Mark Zuckerberg usurped it to reorient his digital empire (and perhaps disorient some regulators).[2] Those who looked at the Lambda got a peek into the future, not just of cyberspace but of the information age and the challenges it posed.

That fateful Monday evening, something terrible unfolded in one of Lambda's virtual rooms.[3] A user exploited a weakness in the software to take control of other people's virtual characters and have them engage in (virtual) sexual acts, over multiple hours. The humans behind these characters felt emotionally traumatized to be turned into objectified characters in a horrific narrative, while being watched by others. It was powerful evidence that, while no physical coercion took place, bits can hurt—much like words can wound. The Lambda community wasn't used to such blatant violations of basic human dignity.

As Lambda users picked up the pieces of their rattled community and discussed what had happened, they wondered how to respond to the incident and how to prevent future ones from happening. Many thought that a set of social norms existed in the community. Most users lived by these norms, were careful not to break them, and apologized if they accidentally did so. But the norms were not written down, nor were transgressors penalized in a formal process. It was all bottom-up and pragmatic. Tussles tended to be resolved through informal social mechanisms. So, this was new territory for the Lambda community—as it would soon be for society at large.

In this chapter, we look back in time at how debates in the 1990s over how to govern cyberspace—including following the tragic incident in 1993—presaged wider discussions about what kind of guardrails our informational interactions require to flourish, which phenomena to focus on, and through which mechanisms to govern. We do so for three reasons. First, many of the underlying themes of the governance debates then are still pertinent today and point toward issues and challenges that transcend a particular technology or phase of technological evolution. Second, the later years of the 1990s and the early years of the new millennium saw a global push for societal guardrails to govern cyberspace, providing us with a fresh sample of guardrails to examine. And third, despite innovative ideas and concepts, this initial push to govern the digital information space ended without a breakthrough. It prompts us to investigate why.

Our analysis is not just looking at historical facts, it also traces the progression of ideas and frameworks, laying the foundation (we hope) for the three chapters that follow, in which we'll look at distinct but related *current* governance challenges and the difficulties of crafting appropriate guardrails to address them. All this points toward a fundamental flaw in our understanding of the nature of the governance challenges we face.

The Real in the Virtual

As the public became aware of the Lambda incident and similar cases, they began to discuss their implications and consequences. Some experts quickly suggested that governance in cyberspace isn't as difficult or challenging as it might look. Every social interaction in every community is based on concrete human behavior. Somebody must work the keyboard, make bits travel across the Internet. Bits might inflict pain, but there is concrete human action at the end of the pipes that created them.

These experts reasoned that rules and norms shape human behavior in numerous ways—some prescribe, others incentivize. But the rules always target our actions. So, the reasoning continues, if interactions in cyberspace are the result of human behavior in real space—a real being at the keyboard—and our society already has rules in place for human behavior, the answer to the governance challenge in cyberspace is straightforward: All we need to do is to apply and enforce our existing rules. Case closed. There is no need to discuss governance, no reason to ponder new rules, no requirement for novel institutions or processes. The wheel has already been invented; what's required is simply to use it.

In 1996, Frank Easterbrook, a smart and well-known conservative US federal judge, spoke at what would turn out to be one of the most influential cyberspace governance conferences. Easterbrook ridiculed those who called for governance debates.[4] New laws, he said, would be as necessary as a "law of horses"—a verdict quoted many times thereafter. In fairness, Easterbrook did list three exceptions to his general statement, but these were comparatively technical. The message was clear (if you forgive the lame joke): Don't beat a dead horse.

There is some truth to Easterbrook's viewpoint. Humans, not bits, were abusing in the Lambda that night. The bits were simply the means through which that horrible interaction took place. More generally, humans typically react initially to novel challenges by framing them in familiar terms.[5] This may make evolutionary sense, by enabling us to apply existing solutions. That reduces the cognitive burden and offers a strategy for action.

Others, however, disagreed with Easterbrook's characterization. They offered two main arguments. First, all interactions in cyberspace are informational, because bits travel back and forth—and information has properties that are not shared by many physical objects.[6] For instance, information is (mostly) "non-rivalrous"—while two people cannot sit on the same chair at the same time, one individual reading a web page does not diminish the pleasure of another person doing the same. If our societal rules are made for humans living in a world of material objects, the rules may not translate directly into a purely informational realm.

The communications scholar Rohan Samarajiva once summarized this point nicely. Neither physical space nor cyberspace, he said, is a "neutral container," governance needs to reflect the specific qualities of the world it wants to shape.[7] William Mitchell, then a professor of architecture at MIT and the director of MIT's Media Lab, similarly highlighted the informational quality of this virtual space. He aptly titled his book on the subject *City of Bits* and suggested that those who build the informational foundations for virtual cities define what virtual interactions are possible and what aren't.[8]

The second argument builds on these informational qualities. Cyberspace is a construct of our minds; we need to imagine it because it does not physically exist. Our mental construction of cyberspace depends on our individual interpretation of information. Far more so than with physical reality, virtual reality is individualized in how we perceive it— despite the social interactions happening in it. This may make it more challenging to agree on a shared experience. It may lead to differences in appropriately interpreting information received. It may make it harder to be clear enough in one's communications for others to understand. Taken together, these effects decrease predictability and increase uncertainty compared to the real world, which complicates the application of real-world rules.

Perhaps, to extend these arguments, some of these features—unpredictability combined with a highly individualized experience—are hugely appealing to participants. This implies that attempts to infuse real-world rules into cyberspace might drain it of the very qualities its users crave. Such a line of reasoning is backed up by the popularity of many virtual spaces that were subsequently created, from Second Life in the early 2000s to massive multiplayer games such as World of Warcraft, and the addictive power of the fairly abstract virtual spaces enabled by platforms like Facebook and Instagram.

Governance Features, Not Templates

The idea of applying physical-world rules unmodified in cyberspace offered one huge advantage: cognitive efficiency. If we already know that we want the kind of governance we have in the offline world, we need only apply that template online. In contrast, the moment we concede that governance of bits may be different from the governance of atoms, we face a fundamental normative question: What kind of governance do we want? A wide variety of governance regimes are conceivable on multiple dimensions, starting with rules, processes, and institutions. How do we choose?

Of course, we want governance to further certain values. Some of these might be the same in the worlds of atoms and of bits, but others might differ. For instance, perhaps in the world of atoms we want to own certain things. This desire is reflected in an exclusion right we call property. Economists explain that exclusion rights enable markets, which are excellent coordination mechanisms.[9] But in a world of information, the case for a similar exclusion right is less obvious. What would be its purpose? Much information is a reflection of reality; would we really want somebody to "own" that reflection? It wouldn't necessarily enable markets, nor is there a scarce resource to allocate. On the contrary: The non-rivalrous nature of information makes it possible for multiple parties to use it, which potentially furthers efficiency and sustainability.

Intellectual property rights are not an appropriate template either. Copyright laws aim at incentivizing production of intellectual creations, such as books, songs, or paintings. But information often doesn't need to be produced; at best, it needs to be collected, which is increasingly cheap and easy due to the plummeting costs of sensors and storage devices. Far more information is collected than is ever used—six times more, by some measure.[10] If there is no need to incentivize collecting information, the analogy to intellectual property is simply not straightforwardly applicable to more general information governance.

Debates about values are crucial; they ensure that we devise governance regimes that capture the normative spirit of society. But values are not the only variable when designing governance. Equally important are features of governance that don't embed a single goal—like civility, trust, free speech, or individual privacy—but that capture a more abstract governance quality. These are the features that in the mid-1990s caught the interest of a young and unusually accomplished academic, who would turn arcane questions of cyberspace governance into public issues debated around the world.

Lessig's Dot

With his small round spectacles and boyish look, Lawrence Lessig could have been mistaken for a graduate student. His appearance belied his academic pedigree. Ivy League–educated, Lessig had clerked for some of the best-known judges in America. As an aspiring law professor, first at the University of Chicago, then at Harvard, he focused his research on the governance of cyberspace—a bold and risky step for an academic out to make his mark.

As a legal scholar, Lessig had researched how different layers of rules and their associated procedural and institutional structures govern societies; he was interested in how polities organize themselves. In the early 1990s he advised nations previously in Russia's political orbit on setting out their own constitutional paths.[11] But, for Lessig, virtual space presented a far larger opportunity to think about governance. Because software can be bent many ways, we potentially have far more freedom to shape virtual space than physical space. It could shape the trajectory of our future.

Lessig wanted to understand the structures and processes that bring about the rules that influence human behavior. In the physical world, these are not always easy to identify; in the informational realm it is even harder. But where others saw individual cases of digital information flowing and people engaging with it, Lessig saw patterns—and the need for governance of information.

In the digital realm, human interactions are mediated through bits. In turn, the way these bits are processed and made accessible to others is how cyberspace is shaped. The governance of bits is the primary mechanism governing cyberspace. For instance, if certain information is filtered out before it reaches its intended audience, no discussion in virtual space will ensue. It's as if the information was never uttered.

In his book *The Future of Ideas*, Lessig portrays cyberspace governance as a battle between those who value free flows of information and those who push for constraints, commercialization, and control.[12] In his next book, *Free Culture*, Lessig describes the formal appropriation of ever-increasing amounts of information: As less information is "free" to be shared, culture becomes less "free," too.[13]

The metaphors Lessig uses deliberately relate what's happening to historical precedent. The United States began as a nation with vast open spaces inhabited by indigenous people. But throughout the nineteenth century, land became increasingly demarcated, parceled, and appropriated.[14] Something similar had happened in Britain a couple of centuries earlier, when tracts of land were "enclosed" to be controlled by landowners. In Britain this had changed society, turning free farmers grazing their cattle on common land into dependent tenants.[15] In the United States, it erased much of the commons and turned the idea of private property into a quasi-religious belief.

The enclosure movement in the United States continued in the twentieth century, as chronicled by Lessig's Harvard colleague, Gerald Frug. Open streets of shops in towns were replaced by privately owned shopping malls. Institutions of knowledge—schools and universities—turned commercial. Increasingly, pieces of infrastructure were held by private investors and rented back to society. These acts of "enclosure" often had troubling consequences.[16] Now Lessig saw a similar dynamic play out in cyberspace—with potentially similarly troublesome long-term effects.[17]

Lessig's perspective offered more than a fresh look at governance in the early twenty-first century. It helped our imaginations to break free from their focus on human behavior in the physical world. Lessig was blazing a conceptual trail that encouraged researchers, policymakers, businesses, and the public to see the bit as the object of governance, and the struggle to influence its flow as the primary governance challenge of our times.

The Internet Turns to Law

To be effective, governance of information must reflect not only the values and goals policymakers want to achieve, but also the nature of what is being governed. This includes how digital information flows: almost instantaneously across great distances; and cheaply, with cost unrelated to the distance traveled.

Before the digital age, information governance often relied on local norms and views. For example, in the United States, obscenity was assessed using "community standards," while libel suits were adjudicated before a jury of local peers.[18] What information was appropriate to share (or not) was shaped by local customs. Market supply and demand reflected these norms: if one walked into a bookstore in West Hollywood, one would find a very different selection of books compared with, say, Great Bend, Kansas.

If a complicated patchwork of local norms and rules were to govern the Internet, it could greatly hinder the flow of information, constricting its economic and societal potential. Businesses and perhaps users would have to comply with rules that are complex and unpredictable as to which apply where and when. The resulting uncertainty would make it harder for businesses to attract investment and less appealing for consumers to interact and transact. So, irrespective of the values a society wants to advance, the Internet age seems to call for governance mechanisms that are more general and enduring.

To an extent, this resembles the desire of states and large businesses in the West during the eighteenth and nineteenth centuries to push for nationwide governance in the form of formal laws. They saw the potential to reap economies of scale and scope and project power more efficiently. It resulted in what legal academics call "monist law"—rules and norms formally enacted and enforced throughout an entire nation.[19] The concept of monist law was seen as an antidote to scattered community norms that frequently weren't formal laws at all, but social rules often unevenly enforced. It also moved away from the idea that rules are linked to persons, instead being applied to everyone within a particular territory. Monist law coincided with the West's industrial and colonial push, suggesting perhaps that empires are more about space and territory than peoples. Still, monist law never fully replaced multiple sets of communal norms or the idea of personal law. For instance, professions continue to adjudicate their members, and religions retain some governing power over their believers.[20]

As the Internet rose to prominence, more and more areas of cyberspace became governed. Online communities established their own "netiquette," or norms constraining behavior.[21] Engineers embedded rules governing the flow of data packets into the technical infrastructure—rules that had been "enacted" by technical working groups such as the Internet Engineering Task Force (IETF), which worked on the principle of "rough consensus and running code" (when assessing whether a technical proposal should be adopted, members were literally asked to hum to gauge a proposal's support qualitatively; the louder the hum, the greater the support).[22] Ecommerce providers, such as eBay, set up and enforced their own sets of rules. The result was a cacophony of governance, covering a broad spectrum from novel and original normative setups all the way to nation-states sometimes awkwardly extending their physical world rules to virtual spaces.

While specific governance regimes persisted in many pockets of life online, larger players and nation-states—much like in the eighteenth and nineteenth centuries—pressed for norms with broader territorial scope. An increasing number of digerati and Internet users pushed for a governance regime that was not only more universal and durable, but also custom-made for digital information flows. But who would put such a governance regime in place? Internet law specialists David

Johnson and David Post argued that the Internet community should govern itself—discuss, enact, and enforce its own rules.[23] Others, such as Jack Goldsmith and Tim Wu, countered that applying formal national laws offered conceptual and practical advantages.[24] National laws were well-established, so it would not require building governance structures from scratch, and national policymakers—alerted by the public hype over the Internet—were ready to engage.

In the end, pragmatism won out: What resulted was an information governance bonanza built on (mostly) national laws. In the United States, for example, the much-debated section 230 of the Telecommunications Act of 1996 protected Internet companies from being held liable for the information flowing through the network.[25] No longer could an Internet provider residing in Los Angeles be held in violation of a community standard in Tennessee for transmitting information—or at least not as easily as before.[26] And beyond purely national laws, the European Union enacted rules in the same time frame, with the explicit goal of enabling ecommerce and bringing more consumers and businesses online.[27] It is little-known today that even the EU's pathbreaking information privacy directive aimed at harmonizing national privacy rules to facilitate transborder data flows within the continent—more universal norms to evolve cyberspace.[28]

The choice of more general and durable governance mechanisms made sense in the late 1990s. In these crazy and chaotic years of the first Internet wave and the ensuing dot-com bubble, when start-ups rose like rockets only to crash a few months later, stability was in short supply. The existing governance patchwork was confusing and complicated. Implementing more monist law-based governance mechanisms would lower uncertainty, thereby reducing cost. This would reassure businesses, investors, and consumers that information flows could endure because the governance regime was stable. It represented a shift away from community standards and local norms that could easily bend to changing preferences. The highly formalized governance regimes that we call law had seemingly conquered yet another territory, beating back idealistic dreams of a community in cyberspace fashioning its own formal rules.

But this legal turn did not fulfill its promise—at least in the eyes of those in the vanguard of the information age. They accused the law of being slow, off-the-mark, unclear, unfocused, and in the end simply ineffective as a mechanism of information governance in cyberspace.[29]

Context Matters

Law's failure was thought to be exemplified by its inability to produce the desired certainty and stability. In part, this was the consequence of a somewhat unforced error by lawmakers. Numerous laws in the late 1990s and beyond aimed to govern information in the abstract, disregarding the importance of context.[30] Prescribing governance of information at an abstract level is much more challenging because information is so versatile. A simple governance template that works across diverse situations is likely elusive.

Effective governance of information requires that we think about information *in context*. It necessitates that we look at information's role. Information is consequential when it is used to make decisions. Information matters when it becomes a means to an end—to facilitate human activity.

Lessig was quite aware of the importance of context and highlighted it frequently. Take for example his later work on the power of lobbying.[31] Following only lobbyists' financial contributions, Lessig argued, fails to fully reflect their influence and importance. It is *decisional information* provided by lobbyists that matters as well: Policymakers need to make decisions, for which they require information. Lobbyists provide them with information through position papers and talking points. That informational resource has significant impact because it ultimately shapes decisions more effectively and lastingly than pure financial contributions. It's why, for Lessig, lobbying reform must look beyond the money trail and govern the information flows to policy decision-makers as well.

Disregarding context reduces the effectiveness of whatever governance mechanism one employs. Where policymakers focused on information governance in decision contexts—think only of the increasing cases of "nudging" we mentioned in the previous chapter—the results were more encouraging. And yet, the contextual problem cannot fully explain the perceived failure of information governance through law. Something else played a key role in making law so unattractive to those increasingly moving their lives and interactions online.

The Death of Distance

Space and time are well-established categories of human experience in the physical world. But these boundaries hardly exist for bits. They travel across borders and cover thousands of miles, then get reassembled into the order they were in when they were sent off: a kind of informational version of *Star Trek* "beaming." Neither sender nor recipient decide upon or even know the path these bits take through the network to reach their destinations. Francis Cairncross, in one of the early leading works on cyberspace, called it "the death of distance."[32] Time, too, seems like a rather artificial dimension for bits. As digital networks increase in capacity, bits reach their destinations and get processed almost instantaneously—at least using human perception as scale.

In contrast, laws are creatures of human time and space. They are created and enforced incrementally, neither instantaneously nor with equal intensity. Their territorial scope is limited by jurisdictional boundaries. Even supranational laws apply to just a subset of global information flows. When the European Union, for example, enacted information privacy rules that seemed to require notice and consent for an individual's personal information to be processed, many regional US newspapers did not want to comply—and avoided the need to do so by blocking European users from accessing their websites.[33]

Laws may at first have appeared to be superior to local customs and community norms as a governance mechanism for information, but they aren't substantially so. Laws are local and temporal. For those surfing cyberspace, this makes them misaligned with seemingly instantaneous and distance-defying global information streams.

The digerati discovered another weakness of laws. They are nonbinary. Laws are artifacts of social processes, from enactment to enforcement. Because humans created them and other humans apply them, because they are written in human language, they are imprecise. They leave room for interpretation. This makes it challenging to predict outcomes of governance action—what will happen and when. In times of chaos, such as the frontier phase of cyberspace, governance with such substantial wiggle room is perceived as ineffectual and costly. With so much risk in the system already, the thinking went, at least governance should be straightforward. To the extent information needs guardrails, these guardrails need to be clear, concise, and effective. Law wasn't. But something else could be.

Code as Law

Bits flow across the Internet because they can be easily processed by digital computers. This processing happens through a step-by-step execution of instructions, as laid out by Alan Turing in his pathbreaking work.[34] Instructions are themselves bits, and we encode in them whatever processing we desire. Code can amplify and multiply bits, it can sort them, filter them out, or create new bits to add. It can direct bits and manipulate them. Through code we decide what information flows when, where, and to whom.

Considered from this vantage point, the instruction code in computers—what we today call software—*governs* bits. In fact, the digital computer as a combination of code and execution system is an extremely powerful and versatile mechanism to govern information. Because it can be programmed at will, such governance can reflect whatever values and goals one wishes (albeit with varying degrees of efficiency).

For a global digital network to function, appropriate standards of handling information flows must be established and adhered to. Such standards must ensure that all elements of the network know how to transmit bits so that they can communicate with each other, or, to use the technical term, interoperate.[35] But they do not necessarily delimit how these bits are manipulated, including whether the bits are transported at all. It is as if all elements of the system have implemented the same governance mechanism, even though each one of them can reflect different values and goals.

Another feature of the Internet is crucial in this regard: the "end-to-end" principle.[36] It is a technical principle devised in the early days of the Internet to solve the problem that each network element had only limited processing power. The principle is that information processing happens at the endpoints of a bit's path; network nodes en route are simply tasked with passing on the bits that arrive. That reduces the processing load for the in-between nodes and thus the overall processing needs of the network.

While its origins were pragmatic, some have suggested that the end-to-end principle is also political.[37] By decentralizing the task of processing bits, it limits power over information along the way and thus can be interpreted as deeply anti-censorship. The end-to-end principle certainly facilitated the development of early, decentralized communication applications, such as email, IRC for chat, FTP for file transfer, and Usenet as an early form of social media. But the durability of any such broader macro-level effects is unclear. Just consider that the principle did not prevent the later emergence of online platforms that greatly centralized information exchange and identity control.

There is, however, a consequence of the end-to-end principle that even more directly bears on information governance. By facilitating the processing of bits at the endpoints—sender and recipient—the principle enables these endpoints to effectively exercise information governance. When a consumer visits Amazon's website, what information is provided is decided by Amazon and, to a lesser degree, the consumer. How this information is presented depends on how Amazon processes the bits it sends and how the consumer's device processes the bits it receives.

Of course, in principle nodes in between can manipulate the bits they pass on. Some nations have policies that mandate information flows to be routed through specialized firewalls that identify and filter out certain types of information. The Great Firewall of China is a prime example.[38] The Internet's standards and protocols do not mean information governance happens only at the endpoints. The idea is that because the Internet is a network of linked digital computers, it can be used to exercise information governance very directly through software at its endpoints.

Taking these elements together, software becomes the new law. It can be an effective mechanism for information governance because it sits where information originates and lands. Software instructions are executed mechanistically, so unlike with laws there is no interpretative wiggle room, no unwanted leakage. It is binary—bits either pass through or not. Software is easier and faster to create, execute, and amend than law. It impartially enforces the rules embedded in it, without any ifs or buts.

Software is also built by programmers, not enacted by legislators. Governance through code does not require the participation of societal structures. It lacks the complex baggage of a deeply social system like the law. There is no need for cumbersome democratic vote-seeking in legislatures or time-consuming and unpredictable judicial processes. It can be done by private organizations and businesses, which are thus empowered as institutions of governance. Seen from the vantage point of effectiveness, software code embodies pretty much everything one would like in a governance mechanism. Seen from the vantage point of power, it enables the private sector to govern—and reduces society's capabilities to do so.

Little wonder businesses quickly embraced their empowerment. From the first dot-com bubble onward, information governance effectively shifted away from conventional laws and became increasingly embedded in software code created by corporate actors. MySpace decided what one could put on a web page with them. eBay developed a rating system for transaction partners. On its online store, Apple for years prevented users from rating its own products but permitted reviews of third-party products. YouTube instituted a largely automatized system to deal with copyright issues in uploaded videos. Platforms such as Google automatically scan images stored in their cloud for pedophilia. Microsoft tweaked its popular web browser to display its own content more quickly. These are just the tip of the iceberg.

Lessig foresaw this development in his book *Code*.[39] He characterized law as "East Coast code," produced by legislatures and enforced through courts, juxtaposing it with "West Coast Code"—software written by private entities. Lessig was wary of this change because of the lack of societal participation and procedural fairness.[40]

But there's an even deeper worry. Governance in physical space is based on norms that humans ought to follow but can choose to disregard. In contrast, computer code demarcates what is and what isn't possible in virtual space. This changes the nature of information governance. It no longer rests on deeply human foundations such as individual choice and responsibility; instead, the system ensures that only approved decisions can be taken, because it won't execute others. In terms of the metaphor with physical structures, it is like replacing flexible guardrails with insurmountable prison walls.

This suggests the dawn of a dystopian world resembling Orwell's *1984*, in which individuals are not only pawns of the powerful but have surrendered what makes them human; they began to love Big Brother. For such a dystopia to happen, software code's governance would have to be comprehensive and complete, devoid of alternatives, and without any unintended leakages. Fortunately, this has not taken place so far. But the shift in information governance has happened. Software code did turn into a nonperfect but surprisingly effective mechanism of information governance. Governance power did shift from society to private enterprises. We have been grappling with the resulting concentration of informational power ever since.

Information Capitalism

Almost two decades after Lessig started his work, the debate over information governance with a focus on informational power picked up again. From their own daily experiences, many Internet users developed a visceral understanding of the power of platform companies. Media investigations exposed a shocking plethora of problems with these digital behemoths, from flagging innovation, anti-competitive behavior, and illicit use of personal data to inhuman working conditions and, at times, a blatant disregard for the law. In many ways, these platform companies looked and behaved like the enemy of society.

Shoshana Zuboff, a retired professor at Harvard Business School, coined the term "surveillance capitalism" to capture the phenomenon.[41] In her analysis the culprit is not technology but the capitalist system, with its inherent dynamic of concentrating power without accountability. The qualities of digital tools and infrastructure made them an almost perfect accomplice.

Casting doubt on the very nature of our economic system isn't exactly new. Karl Marx is usually credited as the first powerful critic of capitalism. But Zuboff's characterization of the supporting role of information created an important new flavor of the age-old critique. Her thesis came soon after the global financial crisis of the late 2000s had prompted many in advanced market economies to question capitalism, and refocused popular skepticism onto the information economy.

Still, Zuboff's analysis was incomplete. If Lessig was all about the mechanisms of information governance—how code is law—Zuboff said little if anything about it, or about the role of governance in general. By identifying capitalism as the villain, she narrowed her view for remedies: Only by abandoning or drastically changing the nature of capitalism can society redeem itself.

This shortcoming was addressed by Julie Cohen, a law professor at Georgetown University. Building on critical economist Karl Polanyi's work, Cohen's book *Between Truth and Power* argues that capitalism is fundamentally unbalanced and unstable—a verdict not dissimilar to Zuboff's.[42] Cohen then looks at the existing elements of information governance and concludes that they have been configured to exacerbate and deepen capitalism's instability rather than addressing and mitigating it. For Cohen, governance regimes that could reduce the negative consequences of capitalism in fact do the opposite.

Her conclusion is sobering and important: Information governance is currently not a mechanism to improve human empowerment, through, for instance, facilitating the flow of information. Rather, it has been turned into a tool of the already powerful to further their goals and protect their position. This leaves our society disarmed and vulnerable at exactly the moment we most need the benefits that information governance could bring.

Cohen's argument links the realities of information governance with an analysis of the information economy that incorporates both technical qualities and economic dynamics. Her argument is thicker, deeper, and ultimately more persuasive than Zuboff's. She has reconnected the information capitalism debate with Lessig's governance discourse. Perhaps most important, her argument beats back the latent technological determinism that has been persistent and pervasive in scholarly discussions about information and its flows.[43]

Is Cohen a new Lessig for our times, offering us a succinct analysis of the information age and its governance, and deriving a normative blueprint for regulatory action? Possibly. There is an important difference, though, between Cohen and Lessig. Lessig looked at information governance as facilitating human action (via what we call the "decisional" context). Cohen sees information governance through the conceptual lens of economic and ideological systems. This difference in focus leads to differing normative values. Where Lessig feared that individual freedom to choose and to behave as one sees fit might vanish, Cohen highlights the societal need to control macroeconomic mechanisms that are creating crass social inequalities and appalling economic imbalances. Risking caricature, Lessig's unit is the individual, Cohen's the collective.

Despite such conceptual thoughtfulness and sharp clairvoyance by these renowned academics, experts and users alike continued to hold out for a technical fix to the challenge of information governance, and thus to believe that technology is what effectively governs information. It's this perception that has shaped information governance now for more than a quarter century. And however much thoughtful and eloquent commentators have opined against this simplistic view—dystopian or optimistic, historically grounded or rooted in admirable theory—it unfortunately still commands much of public debate.[44]

Toading Is Coding

To sum up the argument of this chapter, the 1990s debates over how to govern cyberspace offer several insights that endure. After initial confusion about what exactly constitutes cyberspace, the focus shifted to information and its flows. Discussions over the aim of governance broadened to include more abstract features. But governing information flows turned out to be too abstract; it needed context—whether macro-level economic dynamics, or more individual, human decisions. Even in this early wave of the Internet, we understood the need for information governance, carefully contextualized but sufficiently open to reflect both societal values and more abstract qualities.

At first, conventional law appeared to be an appropriate governance mechanism. It transcends the here and now and seems to offer consistency across space and time. But its advantages turned out to be limited in a context of near-seamless and instantaneous global information flows. The locus of governance shifted to an alternative mechanism: Technology began to regulate information flows, complementing and increasingly replacing the law, because of its unprecedented combination of being effective and empowering its agents. Lessig saw this turn coming and worried about it, encapsulating it in his phrase "code is law."

In the coming chapters, we look at three current governance challenges in the decision space that technological change has exacerbated. We describe the conventional guardrails used to respond to these challenges, why their effectiveness is lacking, and how this in turn has ironically facilitated the rise of technical solutions. We examine these new technical guardrails and look at what qualities—such as effectiveness, focus, or durability—the turn to technology has led society to emphasize. We contrast these qualities with those of alternative governance mechanisms we may find equally attractive. This forms the basis for a more normative discussion about appropriate qualities of decisional guardrails.

First, though, we need to conclude the story of the rape in cyberspace in 1993. It led the LambdaMOO community to initiate discussions over governance—but before these discussions could get under way, one of Lambda's programmers edited the user database to restrict the perpetrator from accessing the system. The offender was banished—"toaded," in the language of the community—not as the result of a judicial process based on societal rules, but by the hand of a master coder, who believed he had heard enough to take justice into his own hands. West Coast Code at work.

3

FALSITIES

For much of his life Joe Cassidy was a spy. A very special spy. To the world, he was a non-commissioned officer for the US Army, and after retirement a civilian employee. But from 1959 to 1980 he was a double agent hired by the FBI to feed his Soviet handlers tens of thousands of pages of carefully vetted US military documents, including highly classified ones. Interspersed in this stream of genuine documents, the FBI had him pass to the Soviets carefully forged information. Resembling a plot from a Cold War spy novel, the FBI—with Cassidy's help—fed disinformation to the Soviets. The term "disinformation" was coined by the Soviets themselves under Stalin, describing the task of providing the other side with "fake news." Joe Cassidy was a hugely successful disinformant.[1]

In the 1960s, the Soviets were deeply interested in the US chemical weapons programs. After World War II, both the Soviets and the United States had improved the production of deadly nerve gases such as Tabun, Sarin, and Soman. Insiders called them "G agents," labeling them alphabetically (GA to GF). US chemical weapons labs had tried to devise additional G agents but failed. One candidate had shown huge promise initially, with very high toxicity; but no effective treatment could be found for it, making it practically useless in combat. Chemical weapons experts also looked for nerve agents that were binary—created by mixing two relatively benign components. The United States concluded that research into additional binary G agents was a dead end, but suspected that the Soviets were looking into it. So, the FBI forged documents indicating a US breakthrough in chemical weapons research, with a highly toxic, binary agent: "GJ."

Of course, GJ did not exist. The idea was to put the Soviets on the wrong trail and cause them to invest time and energy chasing a nerve gas candidate the United States had already failed to make work. This would tie up Soviet research resources and delay work on their other nerve agents for years. It could decelerate the chemical weapons arms race. Disinformation to save the world—how much better to win a war with false information than with deadly arms!

The Soviets trusted the documents they received. Their chemical weapons labs began focusing on the elusive GJ agent. When they crashed against the same practical walls their US peers had earlier, they kept on researching, tweaking, and testing. The ploy seemed to be working. But then the Soviets actually did achieve a breakthrough. They developed a nerve agent deadlier and more effective than any other. The Soviets kept it a secret for decades. In the early 1990s, they did not disclose its existence when they had to declare their stockpile for the international treaty on chemical weapons. Only after the end of the Soviet Union, when one of the lead researchers became a whistleblower, did Russia concede its existence. It was called Novichok—and used, most spectacularly, in the 2020 poisoning of Russian opposition leader Alexei Navalny.

Although much of the material is still classified in both the United States and Russia, David Wise, a leading US writer on intelligence and espionage, argues that the FBI's own half-faked documents may have led the Soviets to Novichok.[2] If so, this disinformation project backfired badly, leaving the world with lasting collateral damage.

Joe Cassidy spread false information deliberately. But even unintentional misinformation is perilous because it has the potential to distort our decisions. In this chapter, we investigate the challenge this poses. We look at the ways in which we have historically dealt with false information, and why they have become less effective in the Internet age. Because these conventional responses seem to fail, we have begun to turn to technical solutions that seem to offer advantages. As we will explain, they also have serious drawbacks—though some could perhaps be mitigated. But we identify a further and potentially bigger long-term problem that may develop if the technical solutions work effectively—a problem we suggest is both structural and ultimately fatal.

Misinformation

We are all in this business of altering information flows. The FBI manipulated the flow of information available to Soviet spies. Marketeers amplify the positive qualities of their wares. Dictatorships prohibit a free, independent press. Privacy laws limit information to protect individuals. Official propaganda shapes what information is available. By selecting what information is available to others, we affect the decisions and actions people take. And so do selection algorithms of social media.

As we have become acutely aware in recent years, incorrect information is surging through social media, manipulating individuals' decisions. Take the case of Rudy Giuliani, the former mayor of New York City and personal lawyer of then US president Donald Trump. In March 2020, amid the first pandemic wave, Giuliani tweeted that the malaria drug hydroxychloroquine was "100% effective" against COVID-19. This information was factually wrong—hydroxychloroquine is useless against the virus, and has significant side effects. Barely a month later, the president himself dangerously suggested drinking strong detergents to kill the virus, prompting numerous people to ingest bleach.[3]

These instances highlight the challenge of misinformation—the first of the recent information governance challenges in the decision context that we examine. Misinformation is consequential when it leads to erroneous decisions. It becomes particularly problematic when it does not simply influence one person's decision but shapes the views of many—or when the ensuing decision is especially fateful (think of the decision to wage war based on a ruse).

Misinformation on social media platforms poses an unprecedented challenge for society, given their popularity and role as amplifiers of information. Researchers at MIT showed that misinformation on Twitter is shared 70 percent more often than accurate information, disseminates six times as quickly, and is more likely to spread widely.[4] In 2020, between about a quarter and a third of all user engagements on Facebook and Twitter contained misinformation, according to another study.[5] In the United States, more than half of social media users sharing information online say that they have accidentally shared misinformation.[6] But misinformation is also spread deliberately—and often not by humans, but by algorithms. In the third quarter of 2021, Facebook alone eliminated 1.7 billion fake accounts, many of them run by bots to disseminate misinformation.[7]

About a third of young Americans get their news and information predominantly through social media.[8] If that information is false and they trust it, they make decisions based on a substantially distorted version of reality.

To make matters worse, utilizing online platforms to spread deliberate misinformation is far easier and cheaper than doing so through conventional media or old-fashioned word of mouth. Creating accounts on platforms is practically costless; fake accounts have almost the same capabilities to spread information as real accounts. By the same token, as research has amply demonstrated, identifying such misinformants isn't trivial, even for experts.[9] Propaganda is not obvious from its content and origin. It blends into the maelstrom of information we are exposed to on these platforms every day. And it infiltrates our minds.[10]

We have seen it for years. Attempts by Cambridge Analytica and the Russian government to influence the 2016 US presidential elections through floods of Facebook posts are well documented.[11] So are similar attempts before the Brexit referendum in the UK as well as national elections on the European continent.[12] Russia's aggressive war against Ukraine in 2022 coincided with another misinformation push by the Russians, flooding online platforms.[13] Other governments are involved as well. China, Iran, and North Korea are all said to operate large armies of hackers to inject huge streams of misinformation into Western social media.[14]

Perhaps in our multipolar world, it is inevitable that nations will aim to influence the decisions of others. But the impacts are far-reaching. During the pandemic, when billions of people had to make urgent decisions affecting their health, disinformants from Russia and elsewhere spread rumors on Western social media to disrupt the effectiveness of the public health response.[15] Some policymakers, such as Donald Trump, willingly (if perhaps not knowingly) passed on carefully planted false information to their supporters, further increasing its negative impact. This was no longer about who wins an election; it was about who dies because they take an unproven drug or refuse an effective vaccine. False information was shaping decisions about human survival.

With social media platforms as its accelerant, misinformation is a substantial challenge for society today. But as the case of Joe Cassidy highlights, false information predates the digital age. It's been with us since the early days of human communication—and we have always struggled to deal with it.

Free Speech

We really don't like to be lied to, even though most of us fudge the truth sometimes. We feel deceived when lied to by our spouse, or a friend or colleague at work. If it's a big lie, we feel violated. We can understand why through the prism of decision-making. False information is bad input. It directly bears on the quality of our decisions. Lies aren't just a betrayal of trust, they make us make the wrong choices.[16]

Unsurprisingly, humans have put in place guardrails at multiple levels to induce us to communicate honestly. Lying is frowned upon in most societies and proscribed in many religions. In the Bible, the Eighth Commandment prohibits perjury; the Catholic Church has interpreted this to proscribe all forms of lying. In Islam, lying is seen as a "sin of the tongue." In Hinduism, lying is permissible only in a small number of circumstances. This is remarkable, because religions are founded on belief, not objective truth. By insisting on truthful communication, religions do not directly further a human belief in God, but a better life on Earth. It's yet another indicator of the utilitarian value societies associate with being honest. In the sixteenth century, Christian reformer Martin Luther took a further step. He encouraged individuals to read the Bible themselves, to find their own path to salvation. The faithful should believe because they saw it as true, not the other way around. After Luther asked Christians to find truth in scripture, lying took on an even more sinister meaning. It would keep others from discovering their paths to God, preventing their souls from going to Heaven.

The social and spiritual aversion to lying seeped into public practices and state actions. Not much later, European nations began to judge those accused of crimes by seeking the truth, rather than trying them through ordeal. The centuries of enlightenment can be seen as a quest for truth, for using our minds to accurately capture and understand the world around us even if we did not like what we discovered. The sciences, too, aimed at exposing the truth through the "scientific method," as political philosopher Hannah Arendt explained (even though philosopher of science Karl Popper suggested that at best we can uncover falsities).[17]

The intellectual roots of freedom of speech are intertwined with this desire for honesty and truthfulness. If our quest is truth, people must be at liberty to say true things, even if it causes inconvenience or awkward moments. Free speech has value far beyond the immediate effect of instilling trust and strengthening social bonds. It fuels improved decisions through better input. Some guardrails may constrain information that isn't true; but the unrestrained flow of true information ought to be protected.

This principle, however, is less clear cut and simple than it may look. In early democracies, enthusiasts for free speech such as Thomas Jefferson and Benjamin Franklin (a publisher by profession) envisioned public debates revealing information to enable voters to decide well.[18] But debates often turned out to be more an exchange of opinions than a sharing of accurate factual information. What do such exchanges of opinions offer to better decision-making?

Opinions are neither true nor false, so the principle of protecting truthful information does not tell us what to do with them. Statements like "I hate him" or "I think she's smart" may be honest (and in that sense true), but they represent views, not hard facts. Shall subjective opinions be allowed? What if they exaggerate? Is everything that cannot be indisputably proven to be true axiomatically an opinion, and hence with less merit and value for human decision-making? Differentiating between fact and opinion may make conceptual sense, but is hard in practice. In our daily exchanges, we mix information and opinion, color facts with judgment. Neatly disentangling the two is incredibly hard—even trained scientists' reports on their research are often clouded by their views.[19]

Debates have raged around this issue for centuries, in the courts of law as well as public opinion. There is no uniform solution, but guardrails in many nations and international treaties now protect the free flow of information largely irrespective of whether or not what is being communicated is purely factual. As long as opinions contain some element of information, they can be useful from a utilitarian perspective even if critical and hurtful.[20] As a consequence, only information that is obviously incorrect (and perhaps deliberately or at least recklessly put forward), or opinion that is without any basis, can be constrained. This guardrail affords a broad and powerful protection of the free flow of information.

Difficulties arise not within the core areas of factful information or fact-based opinion. They surface when, shocked by posts on digital social media and their potential consequences, we look for guardrails to "clean" all public discourse. To understand the subtle but important differences between diagnosis and treatment of this societal ill, we follow accomplished Viennese media lawyer and free speech proponent Maria Windhager.[21]

A Vexing Problem

In 2014, Windhager was approached by Austrian politician Eva Glawischnig, who had been the victim of crude and hateful verbal attacks on Facebook. Glawischnig wanted Facebook to have these baseless, factless posts deleted.[22] Windhager took the case and ended up arguing it before the European Court of Justice.

Austrian law was on Glawischnig's side. Like laws in other European nations, it required social media platforms to take egregious cases of hateful postings offline when notified of them. Facebook balked at these requests, fearing that taking posts offline might turn it into an auxiliary information police for national authorities, and pointed to EU-wide rules limiting platform liability. But the court detected no violation of EU law and let the national rules stand. Facebook lost, Glawischnig won, and her case set a benchmark for hate speech regulation for the continent.[23]

For some, the verdict restricts free speech, shifting societal guardrails—carefully calibrated over decades—away from the free flow of information. But cabining true hate speech may have little negative impact on the flow of information that is the basis for human decisions. Cyberlaw scholars such as Danielle Keats Citron have impressively shown that much hate speech contains no factual information, and inflicts real harm.[24] And Windhager isn't a free speech skeptic—quite the contrary.

The youngest of four girls, Windhager grew up in a household filled with debate. Her father, a lawyer for the social security agency, was a political moderate, voting for center-right Christian democrats most of the time. He despised Nazism and fascism and cherished pluralism and democracy—and inculcated his views in his children. From an early age, Maria Windhager loved a good argument. After initially wanting to become an architect, she changed her focus to journalism and thought that studying law might prepare her well for that career.

Easily recognizable by her fiery red hair, quick witted and argumentative, Windhager became a gifted writer and outstanding debater. While still in law school, she started a student-run law journal with friends. Through it she got involved in a fateful free speech case. It involved Gerhard Oberschlick, who published and edited the FORVM, a monthly journal well respected among liberal intellectuals. In one of his editorials, Oberschlick attacked a right-wing politician who had defended Nazis. The politician sued for libel. Oberschlick lost in national courts, then appealed the case to the European Court of Human Rights.

The Court decided in Oberschlick's favor, significantly expanding the boundaries of free speech in Europe and resetting informational guardrails. It made clear that opinions, even when polemical, are not necessarily libelous when they are built on an element of fact. The Court's decision was remarkable because of how it linked opinion and facts—it explained that protection is strongest for expression of views based on an analysis of evidence.[25]

It was a sweet victory, and it got Windhager hooked. When she saw the verdict in print, giving authority and power to the protection of speech, Windhager gave up on the idea of journalism and devoted herself to the law. "My entire professional career has revolved around the question of what one must be permitted to say," she muses. And, she concedes, she loves to win.

For Windhager, there is no real tension between the decisions in Oberschlick—protecting even insulting opinions linked to facts—and in Glawischnig, prohibiting hate speech. Insults that are clearly baseless have long been considered subject to regulation, while insults based on at least some facts have not. But while enjoying her successes, Windhager is also pensive. She sees hate speech—utterly baseless insults—skyrocketing on social media and wants platforms to accept their responsibility. She also worries that as platforms show reluctance to act on hate speech, it leads voices to grow louder in support of politicians requiring platforms to play a more direct role in eliminating all kinds of misinformation. Windhager worries that pushing platforms to shift from reactive to far broader proactive moderation may do fundamental damage to free speech—and society.

The Threat of Fragmentation

Reacting to the problem of misinformation, societies have long imposed formal punishments for sharing some types of utterly untruthful information or unprotected opinions. This has typically been financial compensation through civil litigation—think of libel, for instance, and criminal prosecution in extreme cases. But such processes take time, and in that time the claims can continue to be made. Society did not leave those harmed by speech defenseless, but its formal guardrails surely erred in favor of information flows.

Many of the new national hate speech laws cropping up around the world are based on a very different process. With information spreading at light speed, the assumption is that a quick reaction is necessary to stop a hateful tsunami or counter a dangerous piece of misinformation. Instead of having to sue and win in a court of law and take the court's decision to social media platforms for implementation—which could take months, if not years—these hate speech laws oblige the platforms to handle the process. They require that platforms set up a complaint process which individuals affected by a post can initiate. The platform then must assess the post in question, decide on its legality, and either leave it in place or take it down. The platform needs to react within days if not hours, so there is little time available for evaluation. There are stiff penalties for noncompliance.[26]

Setting up structures to manage these processes turned out to be a significant challenge for platforms. But it wasn't a completely novel responsibility. Because of copyright laws, many of the large platforms already had procedures in place for copyright holders to lodge requests to take down copyrighted content. These processes proved able to function rapidly at scale, as rights holders lodged huge waves of take-down requests. Google, for instance, received 757 million take-down requests in the first half of 2022 for its YouTube subsidiary alone.[27] Overall, by early 2023 Google had received more than 6.4 billion requests, and it aims to respond to most of these requests within hours.[28] Other platforms have similar organizational infrastructures in place, so they are able to repurpose these structures and processes to moderate content.

But there is a further complication. As we learned in the previous chapter, in the early years of the Internet, some pundits argued that the Internet should remain a place without rules—or at least a place with its own, universal rules. They worried about a fragmentation (or sometimes even called "Balkanization") of the Internet, with countless jurisdictions pushing to have their rules enforced.[29] Whether we like it or not, this fragmentation has arrived. When we google something, the results depend on where we physically reside. They are carefully crafted not only to meet our preferences and expectations, but also to comply with local norms and regulations.

All large online platforms operate in numerous jurisdictions. The same content may be subject to a take-down request in one place but represent protected speech in another. It is often not possible to make a binary choice of either taking down everywhere or leaving in place for all. Instead, a more gradual approach is needed in which information is made selectively available or taken down, depending on the local jurisdictional rules. This means, at least potentially, that for every piece of content, online platforms must manage and follow rules for every jurisdiction.

Technically this is complex, but it's the human element that makes this situation close to untenable. Hundreds of thousands of humans currently work for platforms around the world, assessing the validity of take-down requests, as social media scholar Sarah T. Roberts has impressively chronicled.[30] In 2009, when it had 120 million monthly active users, Facebook reportedly employed only twelve people to moderate the content those users flagged.[31] Fast forward a decade and the company employed more than 15,000 workers to view and eliminate violent, sexually explicit, and offensive content. Facebook describes it as "the most comprehensive effort to remove hate speech of any major consumer technology company," but it may still not be enough. According to news reports, for example, the 15,000 people cover more than 70 languages—yet Facebook offers services in more than 110 languages.[32] On average, 350 million photos are uploaded to Facebook per day, in addition to all other content that's posted 24/7 by nearly 3 billion Facebook users.[33]

Assessing take-down requests is costly, but cost is only one challenge; quality of assessment is another. Assessors need to be sufficiently trained in the rules of various jurisdictions, including complex details, to evaluate whether a request should be granted. But how do online platforms ensure that human assessors evaluate information correctly? What if one is more lenient than another? Does the exercise of free speech on digital platforms depend on the chance of which assessor one gets? Or even the mood a particular assessor is in? Who trains these assessors, and how often are they retrained? What's the quality of their judgments—and are they treating apples and apples alike?

Facebook has developed internal guidelines for the 15,000 human content moderators tasked with applying legal guardrails across so many different contexts, languages, and geographies. While a version of the guidelines was made public, many details remain confidential. We know from former content moderators, though, that even with guidance it's very hard to make case-by-case decisions. As one describes it: "It's really hard to make a policy that actually captures what you want it to. You have to get into this really technical, specific, and often arbitrary detail. You spend a lot of time talking about nipples."[34]

In part, this is because—as we mentioned in chapter 2—context matters. Take what became Canada's news story of 2021, when the Tk'emlúps te Secwépemc First Nation reported that it uncovered unmarked graves of 215 missing children buried at the site of the former Kamloops Indian Residential School in British Columbia.[35] Moved by this shocking discovery, an artist crafted a wampum belt—a North American Indigenous art form often used in rituals or as a gift, in which shells are woven together to record stories, messages, or events. The person posted a picture of the belt on Facebook with the title "Kill the Indian / Save the Man." In the post, the artist described how the Kamloops discovery inspired the images on the belt, the meaning of the artwork, and the history and educational purpose of wampum belts. The user also apologized to the survivors for any pain the art might cause, noting that the "sole purpose is to bring awareness to this horrific story."[36] One day after the artwork was posted, it attracted more than 4,000 views and 50 shares—and was taken down by Facebook.

Here's what happened behind the scenes: An algorithm flagged the post for a possible violation, a human reviewer agreed and removed the content. Upon appeal by the artist, a second reviewer confirmed the first finding. The Facebook Oversight Board then assessed the case and concluded that the removal decision was an error. It violated Facebook's own guardrails, which permits so-called counter speech where the user's intent is clearly indicated. While the phrase "Kill the Indian" read in isolation could constitute hate speech, it was permitted under the policy *in the context* of this post. After all, its sole purpose was to draw attention to and condemn the actions at the core of the Kamloops discovery.

The challenge of applying guidelines to make subtle contextual decisions is complicated by both the contexts and the guidelines changing frequently over time. Larger changes in guidelines are often driven by local incidents, such as the 2016 US presidential election, the campaign of misinformation that spurred ethnic violence in Myanmar against the Rohingya minority, or the Christchurch terrorist attack.

The struggle of dealing with the inherent contextuality of information and an avalanche of removal requests is, of course, not unique to Facebook. In May 2014, the European Court of Justice ruled that individuals can ask Google to take down certain search results related to their name, and Google must make case-by-case determinations.[37] To comply with the ruling, Google had to build up a dedicated infrastructure and hire a team of lawyers, engineers, and paralegals. Reportedly, Google assigns every single such right-to-be-forgotten request to at least one staffer for manual review, without any automation in the decision-making process.[38] By the end of April 2023, Google had received more than 1.4 million requests to de-list 5.5 million URLs, granting about 49 percent of them—and the numbers are growing each day.[39]

And yet, all of this is only the beginning. Consider hate speech again: Despite all the nuances in play, it is relatively easy to identify. One must mainly look for certain hateful words and phrases and be careful about the context, to avoid constraining parody, sarcasm, accurate reports, and appropriate debate about hate speech incidents. Things will get far more complicated should the focus of assessment shift to false information.

Sharing Fake News

Attempts to protect the free flow of information generally do not include the intentional sharing of misinformation. Indeed, formal guardrails tend to reflect the importance of accuracy. For instance, by allowing proof of factual correctness as a defense in libel cases, society made clear that the opposite—deliberately seeding misinformation—can and ought to have consequences. But how do we know what information is true and what isn't?

In the age before mass media, the reach of misinformed rumors was often constrained. Children learn by playing telephone that word of mouth travels fast, but quickly becomes comically unreliable and should not be trusted. Misinformation in mass media—newspapers, radio, television—has far greater spatial and temporal scope to influence people in their decision-making. That's why our expectations for mass media are different than for information shared through word of mouth. Even there, though, we have learned to differentiate and sense trustworthiness. We are fine reading about flying saucers and aliens in the *National Enquirer,* for instance, mainly because of the entertainment value and because most people know they ought not to base their decisions on what they read in the *Enquirer.*

Social media has blurred most of the established social boundaries that helped us interpret information and practically differentiate between accurate and erroneous news. Posts on these platforms have global reach and remain accessible for a long time. They, at least seemingly, come from a myriad of different sources, providing us with little clue as to what information to believe. So, we look for possible proxies. For instance, when information is posted or forwarded by somebody we know, we transfer some of the trust we have in that person to the information that's shared.

In doing so, we may overestimate the likelihood of it being accurate. Because sharing and forwarding information we receive is so simple and swift, we are enticed to do so without exercising editorial control—especially when the information seems to confirm what we already believe to be true. Social norms, too, play into our information-sharing behavior. If somebody shares information we posted, we perceive it as a social gift, and are inclined to reciprocate. The situation is exacerbated by online platforms' algorithms selecting content for each user with the goal of maximizing engagement and time spent on the platform. Unfortunately, this leads to amplification of radical and extreme posts as they prompt more reaction and greater engagement by others.

Misinformation is so widespread and insidious—and our guardrails, designed for a different world of local word-of-mouth and conventional mass media, so seemingly ineffective—that many have called for a technical solution to the problem of "fake news": to delete misinformation swiftly wherever it surfaces. But for such an approach to work, reaction time is key. If misinformation is erased weeks after it has spread, much of its damage may already have been done. So could social media platforms be officially tasked by society with proactively seeking and interdicting misinformation?

Information Filters

At least in principle, the idea is straightforward. As we explained, digital platforms have in place structures and processes of content moderation. Evaluators on platforms already make complex judgments about what should and shouldn't be taken down—and in what jurisdiction. This existing content moderation infrastructure could conceivably be reused to filter misinformation.

In some ways, misinformation may seem easier to evaluate than hate speech. Drinking detergents either is safe and kills the virus or it isn't and doesn't. Less flexibility for interpretation could mean faster, cheaper evaluations. Filtering misinformation may arguably also be more important, warranting a redirection of moderation resources. Hate speech may wound the mind of its victims, but swallowing bleach kills.

Proactive content filtering run by digital platforms would represent two key shifts in our approach to misinformation. First, the process would resemble the systems for hate speech moderation in being entirely in corporate hands—set up and controlled by the platform operators—rather than a societal process. Second, to minimize the negative impact of misinformation the moment of intervention would be pushed forward, closer to when the content in question is posted. To achieve this feat at scale, digital platform operators are already developing and deploying a range of technologies to automatize the process as much as possible, while keeping overall costs in check. The idea is that over time, more and more filtering decisions can and will be made by AI and algorithms rather than through human evaluation.

The result is going to be a public sphere that's run and managed by private actors. Largely social institutions of information regulation, including courts, would be replaced by a socio-technical setup in which the technological part is dominant and social elements are in retreat. It is guardrails through technology—or, as Lessig might say, law through code. If everything works according to plan, people may still disagree with each other but misinformation will be filtered out quickly before it spreads widely. Public discourse will be constantly and largely invisibly cleansed of fake news.

To many, this may seem a genuine advance—a "good thing." Aren't technologies devised precisely to spare humans repetitive and tedious work? Isn't automatic filtering of misinformation, like dishwashers and TV dinners, saving us precious time so that we can focus on what truly matters to us? Large players are actively developing the necessary capabilities. Meta for instance, has invested heavily in AI technology to review millions of pieces of posts across the world every day for harmful content such as hate speech, bullying, harassment, violence, and incitement—"all of which require understanding of language, nuance and cultural norms."[40] Technology like this has clear potential to be applied to misinformation, too.

However, detractors argue that we may be headed in the wrong direction.

Technology Critique

Critics of the use of technology to filter misinformation offer three main arguments. They are concerned about the shift from public to private enforcement, the swiftness of filtering, and the idea that assessing the factual validity of information is simple enough to be automated. Let's look at each of these critiques in greater detail.

First, the agent of enforcement. Having a private actor make decisions about what information can and cannot flow seems a quite dramatic deviation from the established regime governing free speech. Are we privatizing a core task of society? It's not that simple. Commercial online platforms are private entities; they have always had the right to choose what information to transmit and what to filter out, much as they choose what information to amplify by inclusion in users' timelines. In this sense, they are not different from a shopping mall where speech can also be regulated by its owner (although there are limits, albeit not clearly defined).[41] The situation is, however, a bit different for dominant online platforms. If they interdict the flow of certain kinds of information, it does have consequences for public debate. And if this happens without sufficient quality control, driven by the desire to make a profit, it may present even more reason for concern.

The second critique focuses on the swiftness of proactive filtering. Even societies with guardrails to stop the spread of false information, such as libel laws, tend to be extremely wary of content control before publication—what we call censorship. While ex post guardrails create incentives for civilized discussion, ex ante content control stops information exchange in its tracks. One impoverishes public debate; the other enhances it. Of course, direct and unfettered censorship would take place only if all posts were scrutinized before being shown to others. But even comprehensive and swift filtering after a post has been made could still be perceived by the public to be similar to censorship, as it eliminates information before it can reach the broad audience it was intended for. That would indeed give us cause to be worried, because censorship is the bluntest of governance measures regulating information flows.

The issue comes down to whether or not information is being meaningfully shared before it is assessed. If filtering takes place after information has reached many but perhaps not all of its intended recipients, it may be closer to ex post controls. If filtering is so quick and comprehensive that it stops information before it can reach most or perhaps even any others, it would be more akin to censorship. Paradoxically, therefore, the more effective the socio-technical system proves to be, the more worrying we might find it.

The third line of criticism harks back to the challenge of interpreting information. Algorithmically identifying hate speech turns out to be hard.[42] Leaked internal documents—known as the Facebook Papers—show for instance Facebook's difficulties when dealing with Arabic languages: The algorithms used to filter out terrorist content wrongly flagged posts an estimated 77 percent of the time due to a lack of contextual understanding.[43] While superficially one may think that linguistic nuances matter less in evaluating factual information than hate speech, interpretation and opinion as well as context are, as we have suggested, subtly woven into facts.

Much of the information we share every day is an interpretation of the data we possess based on our perspectives and views. For example, in the early weeks of the pandemic some US public health authorities advised against the widespread use of masks. Was this a fact or an opinion? Of course, factually, masks constrain the spread of aerosols contaminated with viruses and thus reduce infections. But at that time, the main pathway for infections was still unclear—was it shaking hands or sneezing at each other? And there was a dearth of masks and healthcare workers needed them more than the public. So was it right to suggest that the costs of widespread mask use would exceed their benefits because healthcare workers would no longer have sufficient supplies? The need for interpretation that may change over time makes it substantially more difficult for machines to algorithmically separate accurate facts from potentially dangerous misinformation.

These three arguments show that proactive filtering by technology is no simple solution. Perhaps a limited scope of filtering could be made palatable, leading to guardrails that eliminate some misinformation without causing too much collateral damage. This would require fine-tuning various levers of the machinery of content control, from picking the right moment of filtering to ensuring transparency of underlying rules to combining machines with humans, albeit at significant cost. The prospect of even just a partial success might be enticing enough for societies to bet on filtering, even if at best it will tackle only a portion of the problem.

However, proactive and algorithm-supported filtering by online platforms may lead to an even bigger problem at the nexus between flows of information (accurate or not), societal opinion forming, and individual decision-making.

Social Myth-Busting

The socio-technical elimination of misinformation implies a very deterministic process, in which clear rules are applied to decide whether or not information is permitted to flow. The very term "filtering" suggests a mechanistic task of sorting information into well-defined categories. However, many of the boundaries involved are fluid: How do we interpret information when we lack sufficient context? What is fact and what opinion, what is true and what is false?

There are no easy answers to these questions. There simply is no universal canon of how to interpret and identify misinformation that we can code into algorithms. Societies have traditionally addressed this challenge through social processes: We determine what we perceive as factual and trustworthy and what is not through debate—a social give and take. Debating and thinking about the validity and value of information has numerous benefits for us individually and for society.

First, it lets us change our assessment. As we exercise our cognitive muscles, we develop templates about certain types of information, depending on its content, its source, and other qualities. These templates help us to select efficiently what information to rely on, and we can share them with each other, leading to cultural learning. The templates may be durable, so we can reuse them with ease, but they are not immutable: Information that seemed true to us yesterday we may question tomorrow.

Changing our mind includes being open to revising our views of what is fact.[44] The sciences teem with examples of how we had to revise seemingly well-established facts—that time is not absolute, but relative; that germs rather than miasma lead to illnesses; that average temperatures on Earth are not stable, but rising. We witness the same in the social sciences and the humanities. Sometimes it takes decades if not centuries for a change to take hold, at other times it happens quickly. But it does happen. These course corrections are crucial moments of cultural learning that advance us individually and as a species.

The correctness of information also depends on cognition and context—on how precise, for example, we want to be. For instance, would we accept as true and accurate that the world is a globe, even though it is more precisely an ellipsoid, wider at the equator and flatter at the poles? Different people have different views of what information to trust and use. Superficially, this may look like a flaw. How can information be true for some, but false for others? Isn't factual truth universal? Perhaps in mathematics, but elsewhere we may accept something as true in one context that we wouldn't in another. The determination of what is true is a cognitive and social process linked to context.

Evaluating information, individually and socially, also helps us adjust our assessment when external circumstances change. Take average temperatures: They were relatively stable for centuries. But as more greenhouse gases entered the atmosphere, average temperatures jumped upward. The world changed; we must adapt our view of which facts are still current and which are outdated.

Questioning our assessments of information isn't costless. It takes time and effort. Sometimes, we must bust myths repeatedly. We are pushed to come up with better facts and more persuasive arguments. It's not like the trials of Sisyphus, but at times it might feel like it. We do it because the world we live in is constantly evolving—and so is our knowledge of it. If everything that was true yesterday would be true tomorrow, frequently reevaluating information would be a shocking cognitive and cultural luxury. But the more changes happen, the greater the benefits we derive from our ability to adjust our assessment of what information is worth basing our decision on. Taken together, this affords resilience as it provides us with the ability to adjust.

Checking facts and debunking myths also produces a macro benefit: It strengthens our social fabric. Superficially, one may think that questioning information could sow the seeds of mistrust in each other. But cooperating with others to assess information—gaining from their insights and using their guidance to avoid mistakes—is far superior to having to struggle through alone. As our social ties help us survive, we are grateful to our peers. It is why cooperation made us advance as a species.

Cooperating to "bust myths"—to debate as we assess what information to rely on—obviously works best in societies that encourage robust and open debate. Perhaps one reason why liberal democracies emerged and flourished is that the common assessment of information tends to produce more reliable results, providing members of society with a democratic dividend that bolsters individual decision-making.

The cognitive and cultural process of evaluating information, then, keeps our judgments of what's true adjusted to what we know and need; makes our societies more resilient; and helped the evolution of liberal democracies. Contrast this deeply human and social mechanism with automated information filtering. Such a system would likely be uniform, leading to an informational monoculture. It would be stuck in time and context, unable to adapt and evolve. It would rob our society of resilience, weakening social ties and diminishing the benefits of social cooperation. And it would undermine liberal democracy. These are heavy prices to pay for gains in speed, cost, and efficiency.

To address some of these concerns, we could, of course, imagine automated filters being adjusted regularly by humans. But who would select what should be filtered? Would a group of elite censors be tasked with that role? Would that not also undermine social cooperation, limit cognitive diversity, and thus reduce resilience and adaptability? In theory, societies could institute broad, open, and continuous debates about what to filter—but what would then be the advantage of technology? Such a social and cultural process is precisely what we already have in place today.

Examining which facts we can rely on is a function so crucial to an open society and so critical to it deciding well that we may not want to delegate it to technology and commercial platforms. So, notwithstanding the possible efficiency of technical filtering of misinformation, we may conclude that a rather more social process of evaluating information, however onerous and costly at first, may be beneficial in the long run, even if we have to engage in such evaluations again and again; in fact, that may strengthen our ability to assess facts—much like a muscle is trained through frequent use.

No Silver Bullet

In this chapter we have seen how certain guardrails at multiple levels— from constitutional guarantees of free speech to libel laws and hate speech prohibitions, from religious edicts to social norms proscribing deliberate misinformation—help ensure that accurate and useful information can flow freely while lies are discouraged. This matters because misinformation clouds our decision-making.

But as our societies are battered by misinformation on social media, our existing guardrails no longer seem sufficient. An increasing number of policymakers and citizens want platforms to filter "fake news" and suggest that it could be done effectively with technical measures building on infrastructure deployed by commercial platforms to battle hate speech and related informational ills. Critics are less certain that this would work on a technological level.

But the real issue about algorithmic filtering by online platforms is more fundamental. Pushing for a seemingly effective technical fix to a social problem may be valuable at first but risks unintended consequences by changing our society's continuing ability to assess the truthfulness of information. Letting technology do the work may diminish that ability, leading us to shed resilience and the capacity to adapt. Technology may at first look like the "silver bullet" mechanism we need to counter misinformation, but it isn't necessarily so. And, as we'll see in the next chapter, it's not the only proposed technical fix for guardrails in the decision context that turns out to be questionable.

4

BIAS

It was supposed to be the high point of an amazing sports career. In August 2016, twenty-four-year-old US athlete Abbey D'Agostino was at the Olympics in Rio de Janeiro to compete in the 5,000-meter race. The most successful track athlete from an Ivy League university, D'Agostino had trained hard for this; it was her chance to show what she was capable of.

In the qualifying round, with four laps to go, D'Agostino was running just behind New Zealander Nikki Hamblin. It was a splendid day, sunny and warm. Suddenly the contender just in front of Hamblin slowed. Hamblin tripped and fell, bringing down D'Agostino as well. Within a moment, D'Agostino jumped back on her feet. She might still have had time to make a dash to catch up with the pack in front. But instead D'Agostino reached out to Hamblin, still on the ground, and aided her back to her feet. It was a powerful gesture. By deciding to help her competitor, who she had never met before, D'Agostino was giving up her chance of reaching the final.

Hamblin and D'Agostino began to run again. Within a few meters, D'Agostino buckled, her injuries too painful to sustain the pace. This time Hamblin stopped and helped D'Agostino. She, too, chose to do what ran against her competitive spirit. Together they limped on, finishing far behind the rest, but supporting each other.

Hamblin and D'Agostino each made a decision in that moment—to give up their Olympic dream and help a fellow contender. It wasn't something for which they had practiced or prepared themselves. They did not have a mental blueprint ready on what to do if tripping and falling over another athlete. As they got up, they did not know whether they were injured and how badly. Their adrenaline must have been pumping. Everything in them—instincts, training, experience—must have told them to charge forward, to try to make up lost ground. And yet, they chose differently.

How do humans make decisions? Was the decision D'Agostino and Hamblin made the right one? How can we judge? What circumstances make it more likely for humans to pick the best choices? Do we need guardrails to help individuals not only to gather information to improve their decisions, but also to decide well? And if so, what are such appropriate guardrails?

In this chapter, we focus on the act of deciding. We look at its elements and the process that combines them and highlight human shortcomings. We show how humanity has evolved a rich toolkit of decision guardrails, yet we continue to make mistakes. Given recent advances in AI, some have suggested a technical fix—by replacing human-made decisions with algorithmic ones. We look at the likely consequences of such a fundamental shift, expose a vulnerability it could lead to, and point at a possible alternative.

But first, we need to take a closer look at what it means when we decide.

The Right Choice

What marks a "good" decision? And what differentiates it from a bad one? It is tempting to think that decision-making is about turning relevant information (input) into deliberate action (output). As we have seen, information is the basis for our conclusions and good information can improve our choices. If input into our decisions were the only thing that mattered, guardrails for the decision context could be narrowed to the informational issues we analyzed in the previous chapter.

But the process of translating information into decisions isn't mechanistic. The same input doesn't always trigger the same action. Sometimes, two people facing identical challenges with the same information arrive at very different solutions. There must be more to decision-making than squeezing informational input into a mental formula that solves to an optimal choice.

Looking at outcomes rather than input, one could say that a good decision is one that furthers our aims given the circumstances that we are in. That draws attention to two ingredients of good decisions—alignment with our goals and appropriateness in the situation—that take us away from a mechanistic, input-oriented conception of decision-making. The same input can lead to different decisions when people have different goals and values—or when people pursue the same goals but find themselves in a different situation. Much hinges on the internal process of deciding, and this is non-deterministic. It can produce results that are surprising—not only to the outside world, but also, as Abbey D'Agostino discovered, to ourselves.

Researchers have found that the internal process of deciding involves two components: generating multiple options and picking one to turn into action.[1] It's as if we first open a funnel to obtain a variety of possible choices, then narrow it again as we zero in on the option we select. Both components are important. Without collecting alternatives, we would not know what is possible and artificially reduce our option space. And without the process of comparing and evaluating the choices we have identified, we would not be able to arrive at a decision and translate our intentions into actions.

Our mind has some awesome mental tools at its disposal to facilitate this process. If decisions need to be made extremely fast, we have a quick-reaction system that zooms in on a small set of default choices. It's a remnant of our ancestors surviving in the savanna. For instance, when we are surprised by a strange and threatening sound, we duck or run. Nobel laureate psychologist Daniel Kahneman refers to it as system 1.[2] However, for most of the important and consequential decisions we face in our modern lives, we have time to ponder. Our choices are less instinctive and our choosing more deliberate. Kahneman calls it system 2.

As we carefully contemplate our alternatives and choose from them, we think in mental models—representations of reality. Mental models help us focus on the features of reality that matter most in a particular situation. A mental model is a bit like a magnifying glass that narrows our field of sight but enlarges details in front of us. Within the mental model, we generate suitable alternatives to choose from. We reduce a vast option space to choices that are more likely to be appropriate and implementable. It's a beautiful mechanism to help us see multiple paths without getting lost following dead ends.[3]

If this description seems to suggest a cleanly linear two-stage process of generating choices from which we then select, don't be fooled. The actual process is often far messier and iterative. We may generate a few choices, only to realize once we evaluate them that they are unsatisfactory, and so we generate additional options. The cognitive engine of decision-making helps us turn our aspirations into reality, to the extent circumstances permit—but understanding it involves art as well as science.

Cognitive Deformations

Implicit in this understanding of decision-making as a deliberate cognitive process of conjuring and selecting choices is that some options are better than others. Good decision-making is about picking these favorable options. Unfortunately, humans are often poor at choosing well. Psychologists and behavioral economists have shown that we suffer from a plethora of cognitive biases as we evaluate reality and ponder our choices.[4]

For instance, recency bias causes us to highlight what we experienced lately and disregard what happened earlier but may still be relevant. Confirmation bias amplifies everything that confirms our views—for example, if we believe we only ever encounter red lights while driving, we will notice every time we are stopped by a red light but fail to notice when we sail past a green one. Loss aversion bias inclines us to avoid risking the loss of something we have, while taking more risks to regain something that's already gone; it's a particular trap for gamblers and simpleton investors, who often double down rather than cut their losses. And there are many more of these cognitive deformations.

These biases aren't cognitive accidents, the result of some bad wiring in our brains. All of them evolved because they provided advantages in certain situations in the past. Much like the human instinct of "fight or flight" when facing danger, some biases are less useful today; other biases continue to offer value. Take recency bias: When circumstances change, it helps to depreciate memories of experiences when things were different. Or consider confirmation bias: By reassuring us that our views are correct, even if they aren't, it fans our confidence that we can navigate our complex world. We may not actually do as well as we expect, but having the confidence to try may work out better than becoming too insecure to have a go. Despite the value some biases offer, however, taken together they put us at risk of making inferior choices. That in turn reduces the effectiveness of our actions.

The discovery of these biases over the last decades shattered the idealistic view from the Age of Enlightenment of perfectly rational human beings. Psychological studies have poured cold water on the hope that the human mind could rise above instincts and ill-founded beliefs. Research has shown that even if we are aware of our biases, we cannot easily switch them off. Of course, we can be cognizant of them and careful in our decision-making, but we can't simply train our biases away. They are a structural feature in human decision-making. And because our cognitive biases evolved for a simpler world, the more complex our world gets, the larger a problem they become. As we have to digest and make sense of more pieces of conflicting information, our biases become more distorting.

We may not benefit from our biases, but others do. The more researchers discover about our cognitive deformations, the more vulnerable we become to others employing them strategically to influence our decisions. Advertising exploits our biases to make us want things we do not need. Salespeople use our biases to make us pay more than we should. Bookshops are full of guides to shaping the decisions of others—and use biases themselves to make us purchase them. We are often oblivious to others exploiting our biases, and we are even easier prey when an opaque algorithm does it. Machines can get us to fall for scams, or become addicted: research, for instance, has shown that the recommendation algorithms of social video sharing platform TikTok are designed deliberately to induce users to choose to watch far more of its short videos than they had planned.[5]

This is the human predicament. So much depends on good decisions, yet we are victims of cognitive deformations that impinge on our ability to choose well. Long before cognitive biases were formally researched, however, humans realized that they often made faulty decisions and thought about societal guardrails that could improve the decision-making process. Today, if we look closely, we see these guardrails everywhere.

Decisional Guardrails

Individuals do not have to start from scratch when honing their decision skills. We can draw on insights beyond our own personal experiences. This became far easier when we developed language that let us express ourselves comprehensively, rather than having to rely on limited signals indicating the presence of danger or food. Such learning can take place informally, when we tell others about our experiences and the consequences of our decisions. That way "good" decisions are replicated and spread while "bad" decisions are eliminated and avoided.

The ancient idea of apprenticeship is learning over time by watching others, then doing it ourselves. That way artisans and other experts have been able to convey not just knowledge and information—such as how to smelt ore into iron, or navigate with the stars—but also decision guardrails, such as whether or not to pursue a deer in a particular situation. By helping others to see which choices to pursue and which to avoid, we reduce the complexity of decision-making for them.

Formal schooling can similarly be seen as more than an institution to convey knowledge. It exposes the next generation to sets of choices that have been shown to produce favorable outcomes. This not only guides our children to select options that will lead to what we believe are better lives, it speeds up the decision process and makes it more efficient, too.

Beyond formal schooling and apprenticeships, many professional workshops, retreats, and seminars aim to develop and spread a culture of good decision-making. Management tomes suggest the most appropriate choices in situations such as motivating a sales team or running a factory—we call them "best practices" or "standard operating procedures" and give them memorable acronyms—while self-help books guide us on ways to break up a relationship. They may appear very different in form and content, but they have in common that they encapsulate decision choices in ways we can use. Similarly, nudging aims to repurpose our cognitive biases to coax us toward what society feels is the right choice.

All these guardrails are not so much about the choices themselves but how to choose; their aim is to facilitate the process of deciding. They may exist as rules in organizations, such as constraining how an employee at McDonald's can respond to a customer complaint, or placing limits on when members of an organization can enter into a romantic relationship, especially across hierarchies. Sometimes these rules are literally lifesaving, as when airlines clarified how pilots should respond when an automated collision warning contradicts human air traffic control.

Organizational guardrails have drastically improved the quality of human decisions in many domains, from engineering to social science research. In the medical field, doctor and writer Atul Gawande chronicles the development of simple yet extremely effective guidelines for emergency situations in his book *The Checklist Manifesto*.[6] One such checklist initiative in Michigan led to a 66 percent drop in infection rates among patients in ICUs, an amazing success that saved lives and money.[7]

Decisional guardrails also exist as broader social norms, clearly indicating to everyone what one ought not to do. In the cult TV series *Big Bang Theory*, Sheldon Cooper's behavior is so awkward because he fails to follow social norms, making decisions that annoy his friends or put him in hot water. Religions often suggest or even order us to choose a particular way in certain situations. Devout Christians must follow the Ten Commandments. Orthodox Jews have little choice about working on Sabbath, pious Hindus aren't permitted to eat beef, while virtuous Muslims ought not to charge interest.

Laws are essentially formalized social norms linked to special institutions and enforcement procedures. In many ways, laws reduce the variety of decisions individuals can make. As we mentioned in chapter 1, at times laws force us to disclose something to others; they may prohibit us from adding certain clauses to contracts, or contracting at all. Laws may be in place for a wide variety of reasons, but often they work by constraining human decision-making in ways that aim to help the less powerful, limit potential conflict, or maintain order in society.

Humans can still choose to disregard laws—or schooling, religions, checklists, or nudges—although the consequences of such a choice may limit their ability to reach their goals. To prevent people from making decisional errors despite the existence of guardrails, sometimes constraints are embedded into the physical world so we no longer have a choice—the decision is made for us. Initially, these constraints may be perceived as a loss of human volition. When Airbus presented the first A320 aircraft, it featured sophisticated computers that limited the maneuvers pilots could fly. Pundits suggested that pilots would hate such nannying of their decisions. But in many cases, we have come to accept decision constraints being designed into potentially dangerous equipment: Just think how the safety features in machinery on factory floors have saved countless lives. They can come with side effects, though. If the airplane automatically lands most of the time, pilots no longer practice their skills and when they must land by themselves are more prone to mistakes.

Perhaps the most extreme example of an external constraint on human decision-making is the Soviet-era "Perimetr" system, which remains in place today. The system can autonomously launch nuclear missiles if it judges that a nuclear attack is under way and formal human command has been incapacitated. It might be shocking to think of the survival of humanity being delegated to a machine, but the intentions of its creators were comparatively rational and benign. Soviet war planners were worried about trigger-happy military commanders and political hotheads ordering a premature nuclear assault. It was thought that if politicians and generals knew that Perimetr could launch a revenge attack even after human decision-makers had been killed, they would be less likely to order a counterstrike when an incoming attack was suspected but not confirmed. Perimetr would nudge them to act more rationally. It was an astonishing acknowledgment that human decision-makers were perceived to be the weakest link.

We may applaud such attempts to prevent humans from choosing doomsday. But Perimetr also signifies a deeply problematic tendency: Benign decision guidance winnows human decision options.

Projecting the Past

We have increasingly moved to curb human volition, by embedding rules in the objects we interact with so they cannot be disobeyed. It may save humans from making stupid decisions, but limiting human volition has a fundamental weakness: It ossifies the decision space. As more and more decisions are constrained, we lose the ability to react to change.

Our decision guardrails are based on what we know about previous decisions. This works for similar situations, or if the past was more knowledgeable than the present: Reviving Greek and Roman traditions lifted Europe out of the intellectual slump that characterized much of the millennium we call the Middle Ages. But if circumstances change or if we adjust our goals, existing decisional guardrails will push us to adopt outdated choices. To work again, they need to be updated.

Not all rules have proper update procedures in place, and even where such mechanisms exist there's a time lag before rules are properly over-hauled. During that time lag we may end up thinking we decided well when we did not, because we acted in accordance with an outdated decisional guardrail. Adapting laws, for example, involves a time-consuming formal process even if all stakeholders agree—and if consensus needs to be built, it takes far longer. During this period, outdated legal rules remain in force and shape a society's trajectory, as if the past continues its lock on the future.

Social norms can be altered without formal processes. But that does not make them necessarily easier to adapt to changed situations. In fact, social norms turn out to be incredibly persistent. Even in modern Western nations with a strong belief in the rule of law, ancient communal and local norms persist in shaping behavior, sometimes contrary to legal rules.

Embedding norms and rules in machines is making it even harder to prevent the past being projected into a changing future. But one new technology promises to help us make decisions while remaining inherently adaptive and flexible. Ossification would no longer be a concern because decisional guardrails evolve automatically. This is the lure of what the popular media refers to as AI, but experts prefer to call "machine learning."

The Soul of the Machine

Machine-based decision-making is an interesting vision for the future: Humanity, crippled by its own cognitive deformations, tries to improve its lot by opting to outsource its decisions to adaptive machines—a kind of mental prosthetic.

For most of the twentieth century, AI was based on representing explicit sets of rules in software and having the computer "reason" based on these rules—the machine's "intelligence" involved applying the rules to a particular situation. Because the rules were explicit, the machine could also "explain" its reasoning by listing the rules that prompted its decision.[8] Even if AI had the ring of going beyond the obvious in reasoning and decision-making, traditional AI depended on our ability to make explicit all relevant rules and to translate them into some machine-digestible representation. It was transparent and explainable, but it was also static—in this way, it did not differ fundamentally from other forms of decisional guardrails such as standard operating procedures (SOPs) or checklists. The progress of this kind of AI stalled because in many everyday areas of human activity and decision-making, it is exceptionally hard to make rules explicit.

In recent decades, however, AI has been used as a label for something quite different.[9] The new kind of AI analyzes training data in sophisticated ways to uncover patterns that represent knowledge implicit in the data. The AI does not turn this hidden knowledge into explicit and comprehensible rules, but instead represents it as a huge and complex set of abstract links and dependencies within a network of nodes, a bit like neurons in a brain. It then "decides" how to respond to new data by applying the patterns from the training data. For example, the training data may consist of medical images of suspected tumors, and information about whether or not they in fact proved to be cancerous. When shown a new image, the AI estimates how likely it is to be cancer. Because the system is learning from training data, the process is referred to as "machine learning."

Such data-driven AI offers two important advantages over conventional AI. First, humans no longer have to make rules explicit to feed into the system. Instead, rules emerge from the training data. Alex Davies, author of the book *Driven* on machine learning and self-driving cars, puts it succinctly: in this new paradigm "the computer gets lessons, not laws."[10] That means we can use such AI for the kind of everyday knowledge that's so difficult to capture with explicit rules. We may laugh at the mistakes modern AI systems still make when trying to understand spoken language or identify cats in images, but the progress that has been made on such tasks is staggering.

In 2016, Google's AI subsidiary DeepMind had its AlphaGo system play Go against a human champion. Go is a board game with simple rules but very complex gameplay. Because so many options are possible for each move, evaluating every potential move and countermove quickly exhausts even the most powerful supercomputers. That's why experts had long assumed that Go would remain human-dominated. But DeepMind had different ideas. Instead of a brute force approach, they had AlphaGo play against itself hundreds of thousands of times. Every game generated training data for AlphaGo to learn from. When it then played a five-game match against a human champion, it won by four games to one.[11]

More important than its victory is how AlphaGo achieved this feat. It succeeded by playing "exquisite," "beautiful," and "unconventional" moves, according to experts commenting on the games. Apparently when sifting through its massive mountain of training data, AlphaGo deduced unknown patterns that led to winning moves.

Human expertise is often built on a complex web of implicit knowledge that we acquire with practice over time—what we call "experience" in our job resumes. That's true of every profession from architects and hairdressers to musicians, leadership coaches, sales staff, and law enforcement personnel. Data-driven machine learning offers a tantalizing opportunity to capture this kind of implicit knowledge and operationalize it for better decision-making. GPT and similar generative AI models are an excellent case in point. By being trained on half a trillion words of training text, including everything from books and manuals to Wikipedia, it ingested a wealth of knowledge about the world without such knowledge being expressed in obvious rules. As an analogy, think of cooking: Recipes may offer a step-by-step way to prepare a meal, but almost all of them leave out certain steps that its authors deemed obvious, trivial, or perhaps too subtle to mention. But when one carefully reads between the lines of many of them, the implicit knowledge can be accessed. That's how generative AI works as well, and why it is a step change from what came before it.

The second advantage—which is even bigger, in our context—is that because rules are derived from training data, they don't have to be fixed. Instead, they can be adapted as more (and newer) training data is used. This should prevent the stiffening that lessens the effectiveness of many decisional guardrails as times change. It enables looking at patterns not only from the past but also from the present to deduce rules that can be applied to decisions in the future. It has, in other words, a built-in mechanism of updating rules.

Such data-driven AI promises better decisions in a wide variety of fields, from medicine to climate change, from agriculture to manufacturing. Advocates suggest that we should incentivize the use of machine learning in an ever-increasing number of contexts, and even mandate it—much like collision warning systems have become obligatory in commercial aviation.

While this might sound dramatic, the change may actually be more gradual. In many instances in our daily lives, we already have machines making decisions for us, from the relatively simple—such as an airbag deploying in a car crash—to the more sophisticated, such as Siri selecting music on our smartphone. And we profit from it: Machines aren't as easily derailed by human biases; they perform consistently, irrespective of their emotional state. They also act efficiently—capable of doing so within a split second and at relatively low cost.

However, critics of the use of machine learning in decision contexts point out that these significant advantages seem to be balanced by similarly important drawbacks.

A Black Box?

Machines that have digested reams of training data remain black boxes to their users—that is, we can't look inside to see what "rules" they identified and how they apply them to new data. This, some experts like Frank Pasquale argue, makes them profoundly different from more conventional machine decision-making, in which humans remain in control of which explicit rules are coded into the system.[12] If we let systems make decisions but have no idea on what exact basis these decisions rest, they say, we expose ourselves to machine fiat. Without sufficient evidence that machine learning systems work as we want and expect, users cannot and should not entrust them to make their decisions. The argument rings true. Who wants humanity to pass control to something that is unknown?

A closer look, however, reveals a more complicated picture. In our everyday lives we all rely on many kinds of machines we don't understand. As drivers and passengers, for example, we may have a faint idea of what the ABS systems in our cars are for, but most of us have no clue about their exact inner workings. Of course, people who design and build these systems understand perfectly well how they work. But is the reason we trust ABS brakes because we find it reassuring to think that some other human understands them—or because experience tells us that we can rely on them?

In a recent study, Derek Bambauer and Michael Risch showed that many who are initially uncomfortable about the lack of transparency in data-driven AI will change their minds when the decision outcomes are generally positive.[13] Their research is so illuminating because it highlights what users seem to care about: improved outcomes rather than procedural translucency. The siren song of transparency may sound appealing (and one of us fell for it[14]), but it turns out that people care more about results than process, more about the destination rather than the journey.[15]

In this context, it's important to note that critics of AI often commingle two issues that are actually distinct: how transparent the decision process is and how well machines decide. As the successes of machine learning make evident, lack of transparency is no hindrance to a machine's decision-making being of high quality. Conversely, not every theoretically transparent decision is necessarily a good one. Imagine having to choose between taking advice from someone who always fully explains their rationale but is frequently wrong, and someone who is inscrutable but usually right. Who would pick transparency?

Fortunately, we don't have to choose. Recently, methods have been developed to test the decision quality of machine learning black boxes without requiring full transparency. For instance, one can have the machine assess a carefully crafted edge case that we would want it to decide in a particular way. If the machine decided incorrectly, something is off and needs to be adjusted.[16]

In addition to the lack of transparency, a further weakness of machine decision-making that is often mentioned is that it may be biased, with its decisions discriminating against certain groups or individuals.[17] One critical reason for this is easy to pinpoint. Data-driven AI are trained with actual data, including previous decisions. If the training data are themselves incomplete or biased, they will lead the AI astray, as human biases are captured in decision data and when used for training an AI become embedded in the knowledge representation the machine constructs.[18] Or, to adapt a phrase from computer science: bias in, bias out.

The cause of bias isn't necessarily just bad training data. The problem can also be the result of an inappropriate machine learning algorithm, or its misconfiguration, or a bad overall setup.[19] Much can and needs to be done to ensure all elements of data-driven AI systems—from training data and their treatment to the choice of machine learning algorithms—are fit for the intended purpose and employed properly.

By the same token, we also need to be careful what benchmark we are evaluating AI systems against. If it is perfection, we'll likely be disappointed, because of flaws in data and their use, but also because not all biases can always be fully eliminated. Even sophisticated measures to eliminate one kind of bias can solidify another bias, not just because these measures are insufficient, but because social realities are messy. If, on the other hand, our benchmarks are decisions made by humans, AI systems may not perform worse than human decision-makers.

That does not, however, give machine decision-making the "all clear." Here, too, looms a further and more devastating structural weakness.

The Right Stuff

As we have seen, the central idea of decisional guardrails is that past experiences can be employed to decide well in the present. That works when the world doesn't change—not the circumstances in which we must decide, nor the goals we want to attain through our decisions. Hard-coded rules are a poor fit for times of change; in theory, this is where data-driven AI should be able to shine. If a situation changes, we should be able to add more training data that reflect the new situation. However, there is a flaw in this line of reasoning.

Autonomous driving company Waymo illustrates the argument— and the flaw. For years, Waymo has had hundreds of cars roam the roads in the United States, collecting enormous heaps of data on roads, signage, conditions, weather, and the behavior of drivers. The data were used to train Waymo's AI system, which then could drive autonomously. These cars were the guinea pigs for the Waymo system. Mistakes observed (including by their own drivers) in turn help the Waymo system to learn to avoid them. To identify the best driving behavior for any given cir-cumstance, such a system needs not only data about a wide variety of situations, but also data about the outcomes of many different decisions made by drivers in each situation. Learning is richest when there is suf-ficient variability in the training data, so the system can deduce what works best in what conditions. To get diverse training data, Waymo needs to capture drivers making a variety of choices.

Because Waymo never stopped collecting training data, even small changes in circumstances—such as in driving laws and resulting driving behavior—were reflected in the data collected and eventually embedded in the Waymo system. It was a machine that not only learned once, but never stopped learning.

However, let's imagine a world in which we increasingly rely on machines when making decisions. The more machines shape our choices, the more these decisions will become the only source of training data for ongoing machine learning. The problem is that data-driven machine learning does not experiment; it acts based on the best practice it has deduced from data about previous decisions. If machines begin to learn more from choices we made based on their recommendations, they will amplify their own, conservative solutions.

Over time, this will narrow and drown out behavioral diversity in the training data. There will not be enough experimentation represented in it to enable the machines to adjust to new situations. This means data-driven machine learning will lose its single most important advantage over explicit rule-based systems. We will end up with a decisional monoculture that's unable to evolve; we are back to fixed decisional rules.

The flaw is even bigger and more consequential than not being able to adjust to changed circumstances. Even if reality doesn't change, we may miss opportunities to improve our decision-making in the future. Many innovations that end up becoming successful are less useful than existing choices in their initial form. But any new decision options emerging from the training data will likely only be adopted if they yield better results than existing choices straight away. This closes off any opportunity to experiment with promising new ideas.

For instance, the first steam engines used far more energy than they could translate into motion and power.[20] If a machine had compared them to the existing solution of using horses for power, it would have discarded the idea of steam power right away. The only reason the steam engine succeeded is because stubborn humans thought that they could improve the invention in the long run and stuck with it. These tinkerers had no data to support their confidence. They just imagined—and kept tinkering.

Of course, most such would-be innovators fail over time. The path of progress is paved with epitaphs to dogged tinkerers following crazy ideas. Occasionally, though, small changes accumulate and lead to a breakthrough—a far more optimal decision option. Modern societies have permitted tinkering to persist, though it is almost always unproductive, even destructive, in the short term—because of the slight chance of a big payoff sometime in the future.

Data-driven machine learning, if widely utilized, would discard initially suboptimal inventions. But in doing so, it would forego the possibility of long-term breakthroughs. Machines can learn only from what already exists. Humans can imagine what does not yet exist but could. Where humans invented steam power, data-driven machine learning would instead have found more and more efficient ways to use horse power.

Human dreaming can go far beyond technical novelties. Our ancestors once dreamed of a world in which slavery is abolished; women can vote; and people can choose for themselves whom to marry and whether to have children. They imagined a world in which smallpox is extinct and we vaccinate against polio. And they worked to make these dreams happen. If they had looked only at data from their past and present, none of these dreams would have been realized.

Decisional guidelines, from SOPs to nudges, emphasize constancy. Traditional education, too, often aims to perpetuate—suggesting there is a right answer for decisions much like for math problems. But decisional guidelines are just that—suggestions that can be disobeyed if one is willing to take the risk (and shoulder the responsibility). For eons, some members of the younger generation have been willing to take the risk. Young people have frequently revolted against their parents and teachers, pushed back against the old, the conventional and predictable, and embraced instead not just the original and novel, but the still only imagined. Humans continue to dream—of a world, for example, that will warm by less than two degrees, or in which people have enough to eat without depleting the planet.

In contrast to humans, machine decision-making is optimized toward consistency across time. Even if data-driven machine learning has access to the very latest data, it will still limit our option space. It will always choose a more efficient way to travel along our current path, rather than try to forge a new one. The more we use it to make decisions, the more it will take the variability of decisions out of the data and shed its ability to progress. It will lead us into vulnerability, rigidity, and an inability to adapt and evolve. In this sense, data-driven machine learning is an adulation of immutability, the anathema of imagination.

With a machine making the decision, Abbey D'Agostino would have charged on rather than help Nikki Hamblin get back on her feet. With a machine making the decision, Nikki Hamblin would have taken D'Agostino's hand to get up, but dashed off as D'Agostino fell again. All the machine's training data would have told it that this is the way to optimize for the desired result of doing as well as possible in the race. D'Agostino and Hamblin chose differently, because we humans can.

No technological adjustment can remedy this easily. If we want to increase diversity in the data, we will need variability in machine decisions. By definition, this means machines that make suboptimal choices. But the entire argument for using more AI in our decision-making is premised on AI's ability to suggest better choices consistently across space and time. In many instances, it would not be societally palatable to deliberately introduce variation into what options a machine picks, thereby increasing the near-term risk of bad decisions in the hope of long-term benefits. And even if it were, it would not necessarily produce the experimentation we hope for. Very often, the theoretical decision space is immense. Randomly iterating through decision options to generate the diverse data necessary would take a very long time—far too long in most instances to help in timely decision-making. Even when iterations are non-random and can be done purely digitally, such as when AlphaGo learned by playing against itself, it would require massive computing resources.

In contrast, when humans experiment, they rarely decide randomly; instead, they use mental models to imagine outcomes. Done right, this can dramatically narrow the decision space. It's that filtering based on cognitive modeling that differentiates human experimentation in decision contexts from the random walk that the machine, in the absence of a mental model, has to employ. And if machines were to use a particular mental model, the resulting data would be constrained again by the limitations of that model. A diverse set of humans experimenting using diverse mental models is simply very hard to beat.

We began with an analysis of the shortcomings of human decision-making, which left us with what looked like an opening for a technical solution—a hugely capable, ostensibly adaptive and learning system of machine decision-making, or at the very least machine decision-assistance. A technical fix for an acute challenge to established guardrails. A closer look, however, revealed that this seemingly impressive technical solution may have unintended consequences, limiting the very agility and adaptability its advocates so championed. If our goal is to enable and facilitate choices like Abbey D'Agostino's and Nikki Hamblin's, perhaps we don't need machines to tell us how to decide as we have always done. Instead, we could need quite a different kind of decisional guardrails.

Decision Variability

The starting point for such guardrails is questioning the belief that decisions have a correct choice. The axiom of correct choices holds only if there is complete knowledge and absolute stasis—if all is known and nothing changes. Quite obviously, this is rarely the case. And yet, we fall for the lure of the single solution all the time. Individuals and teams are asked to "solve the problem," as if solutions are available for all problems. Schools expose students to problems with predetermined solutions, pretending that life is little else than a string of puzzles that can be cracked.

If we want decision variability, we first need to challenge this axiom and not institute societal structures and processes that push us to converge on single solutions. Making better decisions depends on being willing to keep trying new and diverse choices. A decision is considered optimal only based on what we know. Through careful trial and error, we may discover an alternative decision that's better and adopt it. But we can only do so if decisions can vary.

We don't need to mandate experimenting, but we should encourage and facilitate it. Humans imagine all the time, they see things differently and arrive at different decisions. Humans instinctively train from an early age to generate decision options—it's a key benefit of the pretend play that children engage in regularly from the age of just over a year.[21] Adolescents and even adults continue to hone such skills, for instance when we read a novel, watch a play or movie, or engage in a suitable video game. And yet, experts in cognitive science suggest that we still aren't fully utilizing our imagining of decision options.[22]

Guardrails for decision variability ought to address such institutional limitations. For instance, instead of mostly emphasizing the acquisition of knowledge in formal education, we could also aim to train our skills to imagine better (or at least additional) decision options. More generally, we could avoid talking about solving problems as if there is only one valid solution—and rather underline that a variety of decision options exist, each with its own pros and cons.

Our society is often in awe of those daring enough to break away from traditions and forge their own path, especially when they then turn out to be successful. We idolize entrepreneurs like Steve Jobs and Elon Musk, who we believe have been breaking the mold. We applaud trailblazers like Mary Johnson and the other female computers at NASA, portrayed in the movie *Hidden Figures*, who deliberately chose non-traditional careers.[23] President Kennedy even wrote his doctoral thesis profiling politicians of courage who had made important decisions against the conventional wisdom, knowing fully well that it would be unpopular, hard, and challenging.[24]

But for all that we cheer on those with alternative views, innumerable mechanisms in our society privilege obvious choices. It's what we are mostly taught in schools and what seems to get us a large stable of friends. Those who pick the accepted route hardly ever have to defend their judgments. It's the new ideas, the unusual options that are put under a microscope and face intense societal scrutiny.

If we want to increase decisional variability, we may want to change some of these mechanisms of decisional conformity. In situations where we otherwise might tend to mock rather than celebrate alternative perspectives, we should recognize them as fertile ground for potentially improving our decisions. SOPs and the like are fine if we understand that they are decision crutches, workable only when context and goals are stable and decision efficiency is crucial—and if we give ourselves room to doubt them, test them, disregard them at times, and be ready to put forward alternatives and replacements.

Societal guardrails that enable decision variability are valuable for the same reason that markets have been so successful as mechanisms of coordination. With markets we were able to advance individually, one transaction at a time, without everyone having to march in the same direction. But for this to happen, people had to have the freedom to choose as they saw fit—to make promises to each other and to be held accountable for them.[25] The rise of what became known as private or civil law—formalizing the freedom to transact based on individual volition—was one of the main factors that contributed to the steep acceleration of economic then societal progress in Europe that began about three hundred years ago.

Of course, in practice this progress was muddled. Laws also perpetuated existing roles and hierarchies. Power differentials led to agreements that were grossly unbalanced. Deeply embedded social values held back possible change. Many of these deficiencies required other kinds of societal guardrails to shape the decisions individuals can take. Yet giving individuals a legal mechanism to turn their decisions into transactional agreements remains a foundation for decision variability, which in turn leads to human experimentation—and better decision-making.

Volition Unbound

Human progress has always required a balancing act between constancy and change, between decisional lock-in and actual choice. Finding this balance is a costly and tiring process, with frequent dangerous tilts one way or the other. But humans are also amazingly robust in protecting our freedom to dream and to transform those dreams into actions.

In this chapter we have seen that data-driven AI promises to replicate this flexibility, offering us a type of guardrail that is effective yet agile—but a closer look reveals that AI's elasticity depends on a constant stream of data capturing diversity and change. The more we let AI decide for us, the more homogenous these data will get. Over time data-driven AI may lose its agility precisely because it trains on short-term decisional success.

This is the trap of technical solutionism, of believing that technology opens a shortcut to a decisional nirvana, which we already encountered in the previous chapter. AI may seem like an impressive answer, but only if our goal for decisional guardrails is limited to perpetuating the past. If we want to make our decision-making more flexible and adaptable, we do not need a narrowing of the choices people can take, but a broadening of it; guardrails would then be tasked with facilitating decision variability. Rather than have technical guardrails advance an obvious solution, we see two alternative approaches for guardrails—information diversity and decision variability—emerge. Is this a pattern? Let's see whether it holds, as we take a look at a third crucial governance challenge in the decisional space.

5

DOUBT

For all the hype about autonomous vehicles, the general public remains deeply skeptical about them. Only one in ten American drivers would be comfortable riding in a fully self-driving car, according to an industry survey.[1] Partly this reflects a phenomenon known as robophobia, which makes us less willing to forgive errors made by automated systems than errors made by humans, even if the automated systems make fewer errors overall.[2] Societies tolerate a level of mistakes by human drivers that lead to 1.25 million people dying in road crashes annually. Yet—as the CEO of Toyota put it—we "show nearly zero tolerance for injuries or deaths caused by flaws in a machine."[3]

But the survey also points to a specific kind of decision that worries people most about autonomous vehicles: life-and-death situations in which swift decisions are required, but the available information is insufficient. It's a structural problem inherent to any decision-making. We may not be able to access all relevant information, or information that would be relevant may not even exist yet.

Digital technologies profoundly shape how decision-making under conditions of uncertainty plays out across a variety of areas of life. As with the topics covered in the two previous chapters, the challenge of deciding with incomplete information is not new, but thanks to recent technological advances it has gained urgency. In response and because of limitations of existing guardrails, societies have opted for technical fixes that seem to offer stability. But, as we'll see in this chapter, these solutions can undermine their own efficacy. In contrast, societal guardrails have greater capacity than technology to deal with uncertainty in ways that allow humans and society to meet the challenge of decisional doubt.

Information Gaps

When highlighting the difficulty of self-driving cars making human-like choices in life-or-death situations, critics often refer to versions of the "trolley problem," a genre of decision-making scenarios involving ethical dilemmas. The original trolley problem imagines a runaway trolley coming down a railway track on which five people are trapped. A bystander can flip a switch that would divert the runaway trolley onto a side track on which one person is trapped. Should the bystander do nothing and allow the trolley to kill the five people on the main track, or pull the lever to save those five people but cause the trolley to kill the one person on the side track? People's instincts differ.[4]

While this scenario is hypothetical, human drivers may face split-second decisions that are similar. For example, imagine a pedestrian steps onto the road in front of a car you are driving. It is too late to stop in time: If you slam on the brakes, the pedestrian will likely be killed. You could, instead, swerve off the road and into a ditch. This would save the pedestrian, but put you at greater risk of being seriously injured yourself. Or a human driver may slam on the brakes, not swerve into the ditch, to protect herself. But what is right? Should the software that controls self-driving cars be programmed so that it values the safety of the car's passengers more than that of potential victims outside the car if some kind of collision becomes unavoidable?

Granted, not all ethical dilemmas are equally realistic. A project developed at the MIT Media Lab offers people a tool to express their opinions on what decisions should be programmed into a self-driving car when confronted with variants on the trolley problem. Some of the dilemmas are clearly far-fetched: "What should a self-driving car with sudden brake failure do when the options are (1) to swerve and crash into a concrete barrier, resulting in the death of 1 female executive, or (2) to continue ahead and drive through a pedestrian crossing, leading to the deaths of 1 large man, 1 female athlete, 1 criminal, 1 dog, and 1 boy?"[5]

Some scientists have argued that such scenarios are too extreme and disconnected from any real-life situation to be useful in informing the design of autonomous vehicles. More fundamentally, others have challenged the assumption that the design of algorithmic systems should be informed by utilitarian ethics. And a third group has highlighted that trolley cases ask for a moral answer when instead a policy response is needed: we might, for example, think differently about the case morally depending on who is in the car, but not want self-driving software to consider the identity of the passengers when deciding how to act. It is indeed doubtful that trolley scenarios are useful thought experiments to capture the ethics of autonomous vehicles.[6]

Perhaps, though, the crucial insight is different: that the trolley problem isn't just an ethical dilemma, it highlights a decisional challenge—that improving a system's decision-making architecture by adding more information can only go so far. Consider what information would be required to decide in the MIT scenario above if we assume, for argument's sake, that such a decision would be based on classic utilitarianism—that is, without going into theoretical complexities, the basic idea that the most appropriate action is one that achieves the greatest good for the greatest number of people. We might want to know, for example, in what industry the executive works; how likely the criminal is to reoffend; and so on. An insurmountable information problem becomes immediately evident. There's simply no reasonable way to calculate the total sum of good and bad produced by actions according to either option 1 or option 2 given that it's virtually impossible to know anything about the people who might be involved in a potential future accident.

Recasting the trolley problem as a decision challenge helps us see the information gap at its heart. Like some of the other challenges we described, such gaps aren't novel; they have been with us forever. That's why, as we explained in chapter 3, enabling robust information flows is so important for good decision-making. But the trolley problem emphasizes something beyond the need to gain access to as much pertinent information as possible. It highlights not a practical, but a conceptual limitation. Even if we have access to all the information that's available to anyone, some things are still not known, and perhaps cannot be known—at least not at the time we need to decide.

In the trolley context, for example, we may know the gender, age, profession, and family background of each of the individuals involved. But we do not know how much weight to give each of these pieces of information—and this is not just a decisional problem but an informational one as well, because we cannot know what the individuals might achieve in their lives if they live. What if one of them is going to discover a cure for Alzheimer's disease? What if another turns into a famous author, an acclaimed painter, an amazing athlete, or a successful entrepreneur? What if one will be raising a large and happy family?

Even if we could somehow travel into potential future timelines to investigate life trajectories before returning to the present to make our decision, we would run into another problem. Our own decision-making process may change over time, leading us to different choices even with the exact same facts. Today, we might, for example, choose to save the future famous artist over the future happy parent—but in a few years, if asked to make the same choice again, we may value and prioritize things differently and save the future parent instead. Falling in love or starting a family often prompts such readjustments (as the two authors of this book can certainly attest to), as do education and job changes. These adjustments of our values and preferences happen all the time, unexpected and unforeseeable.

There's no escaping this basic predicament: No matter how much information is thrown at a decision-making problem, we are cursed to make decisions with insufficient insight—and we will inevitably come to regret some of our decisions in the future.

Mitigating Ignorance

Societies have responded to this quandary by devising a variety of social guardrails that all share a common thread: They help pool information from multiple, but similar, contexts. The idea is quite simple. If we cannot know everything of a specific case, perhaps by aggregating information from many similar cases, we can plug some of the information gaps—if not in concrete detail, then at least directionally.

This way of dealing with information gaps is intertwined with our ability to rationally estimate and manage risk. Take insurance. One foundation of insurance is to pool unconnected risks, so that one event does not trigger a chain reaction. That's why it is bad for an insurance company to cover all houses in a neighborhood against fire but have no insured houses elsewhere. If there is a devastating fire in that locality, the insurance company might be bankrupt. This is one reason why insurance companies want to scale up and diversify their customer base. Another is that it creates a more robust pool of data for estimating the average likelihood of an insured event. By collecting and combining information from lots of customers—especially after an incident occurred—insurers hope to minimize the impact of information gaps in relation to new customers.

Insurance companies are not the only ones doing this. Everyone involved in managing risk uses similar strategies: banks assessing creditworthiness, regulators evaluating drug effects, space agencies calculating launch hazards, even intelligence communities estimating geopolitical threats. Societal guardrails provide valuable support in such contexts, for instance by requiring that individuals be accurate and truthful when providing information that will be used for calculating risks. Other guardrails seek to ensure that algorithms to calculate risks are robust and accessible, and use diverse information inputs. Still, it has always been difficult, practically speaking, to collect and analyze massive amounts of data and identify similar cases swiftly and efficiently. Consequently, risk models have tended to be relatively simple and coarse, and the scale of information pooled has been limited.

Much like with the other two challenges we have examined in the preceding chapters, here, too, conventional societal guardrails have been pushed aside by digital technology and modern data analytics, and their promise to overcome some of these limitations. With the rise of ecommerce, a transactional space evolved in which similar data can be pooled at comparatively low cost. What has emerged is a technical strategy to address the information gap, reduce uncertainty, and improve decision-making. It's a new kind of guardrail that taps into information streams to make society more calculable.

Data Aggregation

This brings us right back to the early days of the Internet and the story of eBay. Launched in 1995 by tech entrepreneur Pierre Omidyar, eBay set out to "bring together buyers and sellers in an honest and open marketplace."[7] It would use the new possibilities offered by personal computers and the World Wide Web to create a digital version of private auctions, garage sales, flea markets, and classified ads.

As intriguing as eBay's vision was at the time, a fundamental implementation problem arose rather quickly: Separated by time and space, the participants in eBay's novel marketplace had little to no information about each other. Often, they were in fact perfect strangers. After all, back in the day it was thought that the Internet allowed users to maintain high levels of privacy, affording them a mask of anonymity.[8] This lack of knowledge about transaction partners became a significant barrier when people had to decide whether to take the risk of shipping an item and hoping for the money to arrive in return—or, from the perspective of buyers, to pay ahead of delivery. In abstract informational terms, the core issue resembles the one encountered earlier: how to make decisions in the present without having the benefit of fully grasping the future.

Omidyar realized that eBay could flourish only if buyers and sellers had at least *some* information about each other. The hard question was *what* pieces of information would give users enough confidence to feel comfortable about doing business with someone who otherwise was a stranger. Omidyar's solution to the problem was both simple and brilliant. He realized that if eBay could come up with a system that keeps track of user A's past behavior, it might give user B enough information to make a judgment call about A's likely behavior in the future.

The system eBay developed was called the feedback forum. It provided registered participants the possibility to "[g]ive praise where it is due [and] make complaints where appropriate" after a completed transaction.[9] In addition to written comments, customers were encouraged to give each other standardized numeric ratings, which were then used by eBay to calculate a score for each user, displayed next to their name. By design, the system reinforced good behavior by flagging troublesome users and rewarding trustworthy ones.

With the launch of the feedback forum, a powerful reputation system was born. The underlying idea represented a scalable solution to the decision-making problem: By standardizing and aggregating information about a user's past behavior, others could make informed guesses about the future. Similarly, by pooling information from numerous transactions, product rating systems helped people to overcome the information gap by better predicting the suitability of a product for a particular task.[10] Since then reputation systems have joined brands and influencers as key enablers when people need to make otherwise risky decisions. Not just ecommerce platforms but service platforms such as Uber or Airbnb rely on similar systems to facilitate transactions among users.

Yet, for all their ubiquity and success, reputation systems harbor structural weaknesses. They are only as good as the information they pool and make easily accessible. If users do not tell the truth about their experiences and transactions, the predictions built on these erroneous data will be wrong. It happens frequently. For instance, as we mentioned in chapter 1, sellers found they could improve the grades they got by rating buyers very positively even before the completion of the transaction, irrespective of the actual experience. Buyers perceived this as a reputational gift, and often felt socially obliged to reciprocate.[11] Other sellers on eBay would deliberately wait to rate buyers until buyers had submitted their feedback, frequently to retaliate against negative ratings. This dynamic got so out of hand that eBay had to curtail how sellers could rate, essentially cutting off its scope (and thus utility) just to ensure that the rest of the system would not be too skewed.

A related problem, rampant on many platforms, is ratings bought wholesale to boost one's reputation. A cottage industry for "fake" ratings has developed. All large ecommerce platforms struggle with this issue, regularly deleting millions of ratings they perceive to be phony. But research has shown that identifying "fake" ratings is not trivial.[12] Even well-meant purges are likely over- and under-inclusive, eliminating some legitimate rating information while leaving some fraudulent scores in the system. The platforms and the fake rating providers are engaged in an escalating game of cat-and-mouse. Resulting media reports about the size of the fake rating industry and its consequences have dented consumer trust in at least some reputation systems, evaporating some of the informational value generated.

Even if ratings are perfectly accurate and truthful, they can be gamed to be misleading. This is because all reputation systems expose past information to enable the prediction of future events. But just as the person at the switch in the trolley problem cannot know the life trajectories of the people she can choose to save, we cannot know with certainty how a potential transaction partner will behave, regardless of how much information we may have about her. This was shown by a publicized case at eBay a few years ago.[13] Over years, a merchant of porcelain figurines had accumulated a near-perfect reputation score. Then, within a few days, he sold figurines he did not have for hundreds of thousands of dollars. When the figurines did not arrive, buyers eventually discovered he had disappeared with their money. He was essentially cashing in on his past reputation. All information in eBay's reputation system was accurate, but it was no longer predictive.

Similar cases have taken place on many platforms with rating mechanisms. The fundamental problem is that reputation systems are built on extrapolating information from the past into the future. As prospectuses from investment firms state, past performance is no guarantee of future results. This is the Achilles' heel of pooling known information to address the decision challenge posed by the information gap. Even the best technology to collect, collate, and make such information easily accessible through sophisticated reputation systems will suffer from it. The technological solution is just a Band-Aid—vulnerable to all kinds of exploits.

As eBay and other platforms realized the limitations of reputation systems, they also began to understand another problem: Even at their best, reputation systems can perhaps partially prevent transactional trouble, but not solve it when it happens, especially when both sides are innocent.

Dealing with the Unexpected

In some instances, decisions go wrong in ways that could not have been predicted based on information about past behavior. For example, what if the goods arrived damaged? What if the seller did not get the goods from the manufacturer as promised? What if the purchased item was shipped to the wrong address? In the pre-Internet age, the possible answers to such commercial disputes between transaction partners were relatively simple: Accept the loss, negotiate a solution, or involve the court system as society's formal dispute resolution mechanism.

In the case of eBay (and similar ecommerce platforms), however, relying on courts often didn't make sense. It was unrealistic to expect consumers to litigate about purchases of second-hand items which were frequently inexpensive, especially when the parties lived in different jurisdictions. And even if consumers had litigated, courts would soon have struggled to keep up as the platform handled more and more transactions.

A new approach was needed, and researchers at the University of Massachusetts had begun working on one; they called it ODR, or "online dispute resolution." Ethan Katsh, a pioneer of the work, recalls that by around 1994 "it began to be clear that cyberspace, in the future, would not be a harmonious place and that there would be a need for tools, resources and expertise in responding to the disputes that would occur."[14] Katsh and his collaborators at UMass Amherst studied the characteristics of disputes that emerged in the online environment, and developed a sense of how to address them.

In 1999, eBay asked the team to conduct a pilot project. The platform started to link from its website to a complaint form, informing its customers that they could get assistance in transaction-related disputes by filling out the form. The forms went to Katsh and his team, who assigned them to an experienced human mediator. Using email to communicate with both parties, the mediator engaged in shuttle diplomacy—hearing them out, framing or re-framing the dispute, organizing information, and facilitating the will to settle. The pilot was a success. In two weeks the UMass team worked through a few hundred complaints, and almost half were mediated successfully.[15] Based on this early success, eBay then contracted with start-up SquareTrade to provide a service similar to the one Katsh and his team had initiated, successfully resolving millions of disputes.[16]

Emboldened by the early successes, in time eBay built its own in-house ODR team and framework. The most common reasons for activating the dispute resolution process were not receiving an item or receiving an item that was not as described in the original listing. As eBay gained experience with common issues, it developed software that could assist the parties to resolve relatively straightforward disputes, with human mediators getting involved only in the more complicated cases.[17] This may seem like a novel technical solution to disputes caused by the unavoidable information gap, but the reality, again, is more nuanced. ODR establishes channels that help the parties to communicate and offers them possible solutions, but it is humans who do the actual lifting. In the end, the disagreements are resolved through social engagement, not technical enforcement.

Some in eBay even saw their ODR as functionally equivalent to a court of law. As one insider put it: "Many times at eBay we observed that we were essentially building a civil justice system for an online country."[18] However, ODR is unlike courts in two important ways. Courts engage in a formal process aimed at uncovering the truth, and they make decisions that can be enforced. ODR does neither. Indeed, any party who is unhappy with an ODR outcome can always bring the case to a court of law—and this is a powerful incentive for both sides to find mutually acceptable grounds on which to settle. Without the existence of formal courts, ODR would likely be less successful. Nor does ODR solve the more fundamental problem: information gaps at the time of a transaction. However successfully it facilitates dispute resolution, it cannot ensure that disputes don't happen. But recently technologists have touted a very different solution to exactly this decisional challenge: smart contracts.

Smart Contracts (Dry Code)

Smart contracts are a much-hyped combination of computer code with blockchain, the technology that enables records of transactions to be distributed across computers participating in a decentralized network rather than held in a traditional, centralized database. Smart contracts promise to overcome the limitation of the "add-more-information" solution by changing the paradigm and going in the opposite direction. Instead of facilitating more information, smart contracts are designed to *limit* the richness of the information available to parties at the time of a decision. By doing so they aim to shield against surprises in the future.

Consider a traditional vending machine as an analogy. It is designed to accept solely coins and dispense in return a specific product. It is a self-contained and secure system that leaves virtually no room for ambiguity. It predetermines every step of the transaction and requires no human intervention. (At least unless the can of Coke gets stuck in the machine, at which point kicking it often turns out to be an effective and truly human response.)

Smart contracts take the vending machine model and generalize it for a variety of digital applications. A smart contract involves the terms of a transactional agreement between contracting parties being directly written into lines of code. The code and the agreement are then placed on a blockchain—a tamper-proof digital ledger. The code will automatically execute the agreement, without any party being able to interfere. Smart contract transactions are trackable and irreversible.

Smart contracts aim to strip away the human element in transactions to the greatest extent possible. They require human-readable language to be reduced to machine-readable code. A smart contract relies exclusively on what its inventor Nick Szabo called "dry code"—a set of "if-then" statements that can be executed by a machine.[19] Traditional contracts, by contrast, involve "wet code"—that is, language that needs to be interpreted by human brains and comes with all sorts of ambiguities.

Smart contracts are not only designed to eliminate informational ambiguity about the definition of contractual terms, such as might occur on eBay if a seller and a buyer turn out to have understood different things from the words the seller used to describe the product. Like vending machines, they are also designed in a manner that the agreement can be *executed* by and through code, leaving no room for human interruptions or breaches. Certain types of smart contract transactions depend on future variables such as benchmark prices or weather conditions, in which case the parties agree in advance on a third-party "oracle" that will provide this information. But as long as the code controls the delivery of goods or services as well as payments, smart contracts remove the need and possibility of any human—including lawyerly—intervention throughout the entire transaction.

Evangelists for smart contracts have written extensively about how they promise to revolutionize business in every corner of the digital economy, from finance and global trade to real estate and waste management.[20] They believe that smart contracts are more *efficient* than traditional wet code contracts governed by law. The arguments in favor of smart contracts fall into roughly three categories. One, by eliminating the messiness of human semantics and reducing language to what is machine-readable, they are said to be transparent and unambiguous. Two, they are secure: Agreements written into the distributed ledger are protected by complex cryptography and difficult to hack—at least without being noticed. And three, they are self-executing. Like in the case of the vending machine, no time-consuming and error-prone human intervention is needed to execute the terms of the agreement.

Smart contracts promise to solve another, more fundamental problem that eBay hasn't been able to resolve: Parties can trust that their counterparts will stick to the terms of the agreement without needing to trust each other, or a third party—such as the platform, or its ODR mechanism. Tech entrepreneur and investor Reid Hoffman calls it "trustless trust."[21] Blockchain tech expert and scholar Kevin Werbach puts it succinctly: "In any transaction, there are three elements that may be trusted: the counterparty, the intermediary, and the dispute resolution. The blockchain tries to replace all three with software code."[22]

The jury is still out on whether smart contracts really trump conventional "wet code" agreements, although it does raise serious doubts. Smart contracts can be used only for transactions that can be precisely specified at the moment of decision-making. Even if the blockchain it-self might be bulletproof, smart contracts are software applications that run on top of it and come with bugs and vulnerabilities. Where code fails, human intervention is still needed. And it's questionable whether shifting trust from humans to machine code in the context of a specific transaction contributes anything to the trust challenge that matters most: to create trust in commercial transactions in general.

It *is* clear, however, that smart contracts are not the solution to the information gap at the core of this chapter. Smart contracts presume that transaction partners at the moment of contracting have agreed to a complete set of terms and conditions that govern the transaction throughout its life cycle. This may be conceivable for short and simple transactions like exchanging coins for a can of Coke, but in many cases it is a mission impossible. Experts have pointed out for a long time that contracts are necessarily incomplete and parties often must renegotiate them when dealing with changed circumstances. No one has compre-hensive foresight and can anticipate all possible changes in circum-stances. Even if they could, negotiating what would happen in all these eventualities would add prohibitively to the transaction costs of making an agreement.[23]

Deterministic code can fall apart quickly when circumstances change unexpectedly. A case in point is the story of The DAO, the first digital finance firm built entirely out of code. The DAO was envisioned as a digital firm of the future, without traditional owners, boards, or human officers. Instead, it was an encoded network of contractors, curators, and token holders. Its launch attracted widespread attention and serious fi-nancial capital.[24] But the theory was too good to work out in practice.

Soon after the launch, The DAO crashed due to a bug in the code that was exploited by a hacker, draining about a third of the firm's capital contribution to a separate and inaccessible account.[25] After intense de-bates within the community over whether to accept the code as origi-nally written as binding, or to give up the "code is law" mantra and just change it, the majority decided that human intervention was warranted to recover the initial investment (a minority held on to the original code and launched a separate digital asset). Controlling code alone could neither prevent a radical turn in the trajectory of The DAO nor offer a way to deal with the crisis that emerged from these unforeseen events. Humans trump code, and all code is inherently malleable.

It is an intriguing idea to solve the problem of not having access to information about changing future circumstances at the time of decision-making by limiting what information matters. But it doesn't seem to survive the test of reality. On closer examination, smart contracts and other manifestations of immutable code don't address but *ignore* the hard information problem that is inherent to human decision-making. Even if we accept that smart contracts might be more efficient than traditional agreements in a narrow set of circumstances, it seems that "wet code" is a much more *effective* approach to dealing with information problems involving transactions that extend from the present into the future.

Traditional Contracts (Wet Code)

To illustrate the striking differences between the supposedly clean future of smart contracts governed by "dry code" and the blockchain, and the messy realities of good old "wet code" contracts, consider a case that fittingly involves a transaction about . . . fish. *Haakjöringsköd* is a classic case in contract law involving a dispute over shark meat.

At first glance, the facts seem unexciting. Two merchants, the buyer Gustav and the seller Matthias, entered into a cross-border business deal over a large quantity of a fish with the exotic-sounding name "Haakjöringsköd." The contract nailed down all the essential points. It stated the exact amount of fish meat, defined the purchase price "per kilogram/net cash against bill of lading and policy," and even clarified how the goods had to be shipped from Norway to Germany (via a boat named *Jessica*).

Soon after the contract was signed, Gustav paid the purchase price. However, when the fish meat arrived on *Jessica* in Hamburg, it was confiscated by customs authorities based on import regulations applicable to certain types of fish. In return for the confiscated fish meat, Gustav received some compensation from the authorities—but it was a much lower amount than he had already paid to Matthias. As a result of these events, Gustav not only did not get the fish he purchased, but also suffered a significant financial loss.

What was the reason that a standard commercial transaction between two merchants took such a turn? Here's where the case gets more interesting. When Gustav and Matthias agreed on Haakjöringsköd, they both believed that this Norwegian word means whale meat. Yet, the goods sold to Gustav were in fact shark meat—as it turns out, the true meaning of the term Haakjöringsköd. While whale meat wouldn't have fallen under the import regulations and been subject to the seizure, the shark meat did.

Disappointed with the outcome, Gustav decided to take Matthias to court. He claimed that Matthias had to reimburse him for the financial loss because the goods supplied (shark meat) were contrary to the terms of the contract (whale meat). The court ruled in Gustav's favor. It held that both parties wanted to conclude a contract about whale meat, and it didn't matter that they used the wrong term to describe their shared intention. Accordingly, the court stated that whale meat should have been delivered. Since shark meat "lacks the characteristic of being whale meat," as the judges put it, it needed to be treated as a "defect in the things" under German law. As a result, Gustav had a right to ask Matthias for money to compensate for the loss he suffered.

On the surface, the Haakjöringsköd saga seems to highlight the shortcomings of wet code. All the trouble started with a human-language misunderstanding of the meaning of the word Haakjöringsköd. But under the hood, this unusual case points toward some virtues of traditional forms of contracting. First, contract law honors the actual human intention. As long as both parties wanted the same thing, the use of a word that objectively suggests a different thing doesn't count. This makes sense from a human and economic perspective: Both parties wanted to buy and sell whale meat, and the law was there to facilitate this transaction. The logic of a dry code approach would force them to complete the transaction in shark meat, which neither had originally contemplated.

At a more abstract level, the case also illustrates that contract law offers a set of background principles that lay out how to deal with instances in which a transaction doesn't pan out according to plan. These guardrails see contracts not as "fixed" containers for a given transaction, but as expressions of dynamic relationships that are shaped by the passage of time and the parties' interactions with each other and the world around them. Not only smart contracts, but also current trends toward detailed written contracts, spelling out as many details as possible, ignore this core role of contract law and might put at risk our ability to bargain in light of uncertainty.[26]

In contrast, the *elasticity* offered by guardrails in contract law helps to deal with the information problem at the core of this chapter. But it also goes further, as the following excerpt points out: "Contract law is fundamentally a remedial institution. It is concerned less with changing how parties act when entering into an agreement than with achieving the right result after the fact. It incorporates a variety of doctrines— unconscionability, mutual mistake, illegality, capacity, consideration, fraud, duress—that allow a party to escape from even clearly specified obligations."[27] In other words, contract law does not prescribe the continuation of an "unhappy marriage"; instead it offers a "managed divorce."

Views on exactly how elastic contract law is or should be, and whether elasticity is more of a bug or feature, vary across different schools of thought and are subject to intense scholarly debate. In the United States and Europe, these debates take place under banners such as "theory of incomplete contracts" and "relational contracts theory."[28] The extent of elasticity in contract law is heavily shaped by culture: The traditional Asian conception of a contract, for instance, stretches the Western understanding of elasticity still further. From this perspective, a contract about a transaction traditionally "anticipates rather than defines the ensuing relationship. The contract memorializes not the 'conclusion' of a business deal [. . .], but the business relationship's beginning."[29]

Despite these differences in detail, the key insight here is that guardrails governing wet code contracts specialize in substantive and procedural norms that guide human behavior when circumstances and relationships change over time. Dry code, in contrast, seeks to lock things down to determine the future course of a transaction based on what's known at the time of decision-making. Elasticity makes law—and not code— able to take a broader societal perspective on the problem of incomplete information at the time of decision-making. This has taken on new importance as we reimagine the guardrails that govern decision-making in the digital age.

Law's Elasticity

Law is often perceived as a bundle of guardrails that confine people to a limited set of choices and roles. But as we have just seen, that's not necessarily true. In fact, contract law is not the only area of law with guardrails designed to guide human decision-making in light of changing circumstances. Specific elasticity norms are written all over the legal system that help people navigate the need to revise their decisions if circumstances change. Examples include rules regarding legal separation or divorce in family law; norms in corporate law that enable changes in ownership and organization to meet the changing needs at a given moment in the life cycle of the organization; insolvency laws that regulate situations where debtors can no longer pay their debts; a right to erasure or correction of personal data, and so forth.

In addition to these substantive norms, a wealth of procedural rules exists within and across different domains of law to determine under what conditions, when, and how information about such changes can or should be introduced to the legal system. They include rules of evidence in criminal or civil law, and reconsideration rights in administrative law. These procedural norms give the law elasticity when shaping behavior *within* a particular relationship, whether it's among family members, business partners, or citizens and government.

While each area offers different degrees of elasticity in specific circumstances, law as a formal system of societal guardrails also affords *general* elasticity that derives from the fact that it is, itself, information. As all legal norms are in one form or another expressed in language, law can achieve its effects only by "speaking" to people, usually through written text. It can't influence the physicality of things directly—even the threat of sanctions or force is nothing more than information.

One implication is that laws have a certain degree of *ambiguity*, which fields of study such as semiotics and the philosophy of language have shown to be an integral feature of human language.[30] Indeed, legal scholar Mireille Hildebrandt argues that ambiguity is at the core of what she calls law's adaptive nature.[31] This general elasticity allows us to absorb changes over time and contexts that inform our understanding of what the law is or ought to be. Elasticity is both a reflection and enabler of law's evolutionary nature.

Again, opinions differ on whether and to what extent elasticity is a good or bad thing. Much depends on how much decision-making power one believes should rest with those who interpret the law. In the US context, for instance, there's strong disagreement on how to interpret the language of the Constitution. Should it be read as a "living document," where the Constitution's text is interpreted in the light of current times, culture, and society? This approach emphasizes law's elasticity. The opposite view promotes a judicial approach known as "textualism" or "originalism," which says the Constitution means no more or less today than it meant to those who originally wrote and ratified it. The outcome of many hot button cases—from abortion to climate change legislation—often depends heavily on the degree of elasticity that the Court considers to be appropriate. In the current configuration of the US Supreme Court, "textualism" is the prevailing approach; but that, too, can change, as justices are replaced over time. It's this openness to change, this structural elasticity that has made law into a successful regime of social guardrails.

To some extent, the elasticity of law depends on how laws are written. In the field of finance, for instance, legal scholar Katharina Pistor shows that the extent to which laws use open language or introduce elasticity-enhancing norms shapes how much discretion decision-makers have when dealing with a crisis in a system.[32] At some point, of course, even laws that are written without much elasticity can be suspended or rewritten—but this is a political, at times brute force, process that goes beyond the concept of elasticity of law highlighted in this chapter.

Law is not the only flexible set of guardrails, of course. Elasticity is inherent in many other kinds of social guardrails as well, in part because their social nature makes them more amenable to change. But law's flexibility is particularly intriguing given that it tends to be perceived as rigid.

Building on the Unexpected

This chapter examined a structural decision problem that even the smartest technology can't solve: that the future is uncertain and inherently uncontrollable. Time and again, changing circumstances challenge the soundness of decisions made in the past. To some extent technologies can help us mitigate this problem by making better predictions about what will happen in the future—for example, through data aggregation and machine learning, or feedback systems on platforms. But it's impossible to anticipate all possible future changes in circumstances, given the complexity and uncertainty of the world we live in.

Because of this, we may need guardrails that are flexible enough to handle disputes between transaction parties when circumstances change. We looked at one purportedly technical solution—eBay's ODR—that on closer inspection facilitates the role of humans rather than replacing them. Another hyped solution, smart contracts, promises to eliminate the human element but has severe limitations. Neither can replace conventional law's functional ability to achieve dynamic stability through elasticity by offering a wealth of norms, substantive and procedural, that can help individuals and society at large deal with the unexpected.

Viewed from that perspective, law can be understood as a sophisticated social and cultural bundle of guardrails that—in contrast to technological solutions, but very much like other types of social guardrails—has evolved over centuries to allow humans today to *embrace* an increasingly uncontrollable, unpredictable, and uncertain future deeply shaped by digital technologies.

6

PRINCIPLES

March 23 came and went like the day before. Snow was falling. It and the wind made it impossible to see anything. So, the three of them stayed put—cold, exhausted, weakened, depressed, and eleven miles away from the next depot with food and fuel. They would not leave their tent again, dying one after the other over the course of the week.

The Terra Nova Expedition, as it was officially known, failed miserably. Its leader, the ambitious British naval officer Robert Falcon Scott, and his party reached the South Pole on January 17, 1912. They'd hoped to be the first—but Norwegian Roald Amundsen had beat them by a month. While Amundsen returned without incident, Scott and his fellow explorers lost their lives. Much has been written about the reasons for it.[1] Almost at every turn, it seemed, things went wrong; wrong decisions were made, with catastrophic consequences.

Often noted as one key element was Scott's choice to use motor sledges for a significant part of the journey across Antarctica. Internal combustion engines were relatively new at the time. They turned out to be not robust enough for the extreme conditions Scott's expedition encountered, breaking down easily. Consequently, Scott had to abandon them far earlier than planned, slowing him down. In contrast, Amundsen relied on dog sledges—well-understood, workable, and trusted even in exceptional circumstances. The dogs served him well; Amundsen's party returned from the pole so well fed and healthy that they weighed more than when they departed. Did Scott's infatuation with a new and untested technology to solve his transportation needs doom the expedition? Would sticking to a different technology have turned the expedition into a success?

Scott had, in fact, trialed the motor sledges in Norway's winter. He had iterated their design, and the sledges had shown their prowess. Dog sledges aren't without challenges either—sled dogs need lots of food and some will tire over time. When they work, motor sledges may be as reliable and even more efficient.

The problem with motor sledges is deeper. It requires expertise to operate and keep them maintained throughout the journey, even repair them if necessary. Scott had worked with an engineer, Reginald Skelton, to design, trial, and improve the motor sledges. Skelton knew everything about the sledges that there was to know, and then some. He would have been the perfect companion to take along. But Scott did not ask Skelton to join, because of a guardrail he felt bound by. Earlier, Scott had chosen Teddy Evans to be second in command of the expedition. Both Evans and Skelton were military officers, and Skelton was higher in rank than Evans. With Evans and Skelton on the team, somebody lower in rank would have to command somebody higher, a violation of social norms within the military and unacceptable to Evans. Having to decide between Evans and Skelton, Scott picked Evans. Without Skelton, however, the motor sledges failed badly, ultimately dooming the expedition.

It wasn't the only bad choice Scott made, but it illustrates sharply how decisions are shaped by social guardrails, even terribly unhelpful ones. Understanding how such guardrail structures emerge, how they are operationalized, and how they shape our decisions can inform our efforts to identify—and ultimately work toward—guardrail principles in support of sound human decision-making.

Technology's Decision Trap

In the previous three chapters, we looked at recent digital challenges that influence what information is available and how decisions are made. We saw how they render some existing guardrails largely ineffective. As a result, social guardrails partially give way to technical ones, ostensibly to further the goal of improving decision-making. Information filters are established to narrow the scope of information available and prevent "fake" information from distracting decision-makers. Artificial intelligence takes over from humans in some areas to ensure the "right" decisions are being made. Smart contracts are introduced in an attempt to guarantee that new information does not undo decisions that have been taken and promises that have been made.

It is all done in good faith, and yet it risks serious long-term consequences. Filters eliminate unconventional and unorthodox information—including early warning signs of changing circumstances, as well as novel insights that aren't yet part of the accepted decisional canon. AI decides based on extrapolations from the past and the present; it can't come up with decision options beyond what's already known, because it can't imagine. Smart contracts keep humans wedded to decisions even if switching to an alternative option would be advantageous not only for them, but overall.

In each case, those advocating for technical guardrails—let's call them technological solutionists—took a careful look at existing social guardrails, extracted what seemed to them to be the essential aim of each, and developed technical tools to further these aims. They thought that decisional guardrails exist to shrink informational noise, to reduce bias in human decision-making, and to eliminate mutability once a decision has been made. After all, don't our social guardrails try to sharpen decisional focus so we make the "right" choices? Isn't sticking by our choices the building block of trust, the glue that links individuals into communities?

As we examined the technical tools that reflected these goals more closely, we found them wanting. We discovered that diversity of information broadens our view and readies us for new insights. We realized that occasionally making the wrong decision is the price of dreaming and experimenting, which leads to progress. We understood that sometimes we need to revise decisions when new information becomes available or our preferences change.

Of course, technical tools can be useful, including those that reflect aims such as rigidity and immutability. When the best possible solution is already known for a specific challenge, it would be foolish to opt for a different course of action—and embedding the solution in technical artifacts is an efficient way to have us stick to it. The best way to avoid an imminent midair collision, as the tragic crash above Überlingen exemplifies, is to have pilots strictly follow the instructions of the automated collision avoidance system. But all this breaks down when circumstances change—conditions evolve or goals shift. Then conventional solutions may no longer work and continuing to apply them is simply reckless.

Whether we like it or not, we will increasingly face situations that are fundamentally different than before, from changing climate and rising conflict in a multipolar world to social inequalities caused by the technological transformation of economies. But as the world changes, so does our understanding of it. Knowledge in medicine, for example, is said to double every decade.[2] This means some frameworks for diagnosis and treatment may become outdated quickly. As the ground shifts below our feet while we comprehend more and more about what's happening, we can rely less and less on existing answers.

Our analysis of the three emergent governance challenges seems to leave us with two sets of very different kinds of guardrails: one set aims to narrow the focus of information and decision, the other aims to encourage decisional diversity and experimentation. They represent very different strategies for improving decision-making: replicating decisions that worked, or trialing. They seem black and white, forcing us to make a binary choice. But simply replacing one set of guardrails with another is not an option.

Solution Spaces

It may be tempting to think of guardrails as pieces of a coherent and consistent governance framework that is universally valid. If that were true, all we would have to do is to choose and implement the right framework: If the one we have been using turns out to be suboptimal, let's switch to an alternative one. But individual guardrails aren't always right in all cases: What guardrails are appropriate depends on concrete circumstances. Nor are they part of a single framework—a single set of universally valid rules. The diversity of guardrails that we encounter in society reflects this.

Sometimes guardrails urge us to decide as we have done before; in other situations, different guardrails help us appreciate the variety of alternative options, even if some of them have never been tested before. Sometimes our decisions should stand, at other times we are better advised to amend them in light of new information. When circumstances are constant, we may want to follow successful decision precedents of the past; when the situation changes, however, we may be better off imagining additional options and experimenting with them.

Guardrails are specific normative responses to particular governance challenges. They exist in a space of possible governance solutions. For instance, guardrails that enable reversibility are at one end of a continuum representing a particular dimension of decisional governance, and guardrails that ensure immutability are at the other end. Together, more continua like these form a multidimensional solution space in which guardrails can be located. This isn't a binary, black-or-white choice between distinct sets of guardrails, but a complex, multifaceted, mix-and-match choice of different shades and colors. Governing decision-making is about understanding context, identifying appropriate guardrails, and putting them in place. The solution space is wide and varied.

In the abstract, it may sound simple: Make transparent and ponder our governance goals, debate their appropriateness, especially considering the concrete circumstances, then design (or select) the guardrails accordingly. But in practice these tasks are daunting. Effectiveness of the guardrails we institute will depend on the meaning of vague and abstract assessment criteria, such as "appropriateness." We risk getting lost in a sea of possibilities with no practical guidance how to choose. If we shrink the solution space in which to look for guardrails, selecting them gets easier; but reduce it too much and useful guardrails may get eliminated.

The key is to devise qualities and use them as principles to map out concrete solution spaces and identify specific guardrails within them. If these principles are good, a resulting solution space will retain a variety of guardrails that are valuable without drowning us in opportunities.

There is precedent for how this can be achieved, but perhaps not in the most obvious way.

The Myth of Consistency

When we ponder the qualities of solution spaces for governing, we may first think of the importance of coherence and consistency: Guardrails should reinforce rather than undermine each other. Human decision-makers should be able to easily understand what decision society would like them to make. Often it isn't that simple, as social norms may contradict each other. But a subset of guardrails—law, as formalized norms that we must obey or face consequences—ought to provide a logically consistent framework. At least, this is what lay people assume: a neat and concise system offering above all coherence, so that when you follow it, you know you are doing the right thing.

There is factual evidence that supports this view. Law in many societies incorporates a variety of mechanisms that aim at overall consistency and coherence. The making public of laws and judgments in numerous nations suggests that scrutinizing legal norms for contradictions is welcome, as it helps internal stability to evolve. Appeals processes point at the goal of avoiding judicial errors, including dangerous incoherencies. The possibility to have a constitutional court review laws for being sufficiently aligned with other and higher legal rules facilitates overall consistency. When different laws are found to clash, long-standing rules of legal interpretation offer a set of seemingly logical heuristics to resolve these clashes: from privileging the more recent norm over older ones, to accepting the more specific over the more general. Consistency, aspiring lawyers are told, is necessary to avoid confusing humans in their decision-making, but also to maintain the view of the law as a coherent logical system.

Such a stylized understanding of law is perhaps useful in the very early stages of a student's legal education, but it fails to capture the essence of social reality. Experts have long pointed out that as various overlapping rule regimes evolve, individuals find themselves having to obey multiple rules that are sometimes quite contradictory.[3] This doesn't just happen in rare cases in which jurisdictions of national laws overlap, but more frequently with clashes of national law and community norms—think for instance of religious regimes such as Jewish *halakhah* or Islamic *sharia*, or coexisting local rules only partially superseded by colonial laws. Many individuals and communities around the world are quite familiar with such situations and how to deal with them. In theory there may be a complicated "right" way to solve their normative dilemmas—but rather than being overwhelmed by trying to find it, in practice many opt for pragmatic solutions.

Incoherence, as economists point out, leads to additional transaction costs: We have, for example, to deal with more time-consuming procedures, or factor in the extra risk of unexpected enforcement. But intuitively at least, most of us understand our varied lives lead to unforeseen situations reflected in legal inconsistencies. It's an unavoidable grist of societal governance. Think of the alternatives: Either we would have to govern at an increasingly micro level to adequately capture eventualities, constraining individual volition far more than today; or we would have to govern dramatically less, limiting the reach of societal guardrails to the most common and obvious decision situations. That may sound appealing to some libertarians but isn't compatible with governing a complex and varied modern society.

Comprehensive consistency of rules is elusive not only because often situations develop that are unforeseen, but also because different bodies put norms in place that come into conflict. The fundamental underlying challenge is thus not only our limited ability to foresee what situations will develop, but also the increasing complexity of how humanity organizes itself.

Students of legal pluralism, the phenomenon of competing legal norms, point out that history teems with examples. Brian Tamanaha explains that the very Western idea of a comprehensive and consistent singular legal regime came about relatively recently, even in the West.[4] Before the eighteenth century, people were beholden to norms and rules that connected them to some group or community. As many belonged to multiple groups—think of professions, religious beliefs, and ethnicity—it meant obeying multiple rule sets. The rise of the nation-state greatly fueled the concept of a unitary set of rules for all people within a nation's territory. Benedict Anderson argues that the reverse is also true: Having a common law, like a common language, helps nation states to rise and endure.[5] Intriguingly, though, legal pluralism persisted in the age of the nation-state—advocated at times by representatives of the very states intent on broadening their nation's power as part of Western colonialism. For example, they wanted their traders residing in other states to be exempt from local laws; they also devised hugely complex overlapping and competing legal setups to further their influence.[6]

Today we see competing and conflicting norms in many localities, partially as a result of internationalization of law and partially driven by globalization of the flow of goods, people, and information. We see it in the European Union when the European Court of Justice and national high courts openly differ in their views. We see it in the differing interpretations of how the Brexit agreement pertains to Northern Ireland by the British, the European Union, Ireland, and the authorities in Northern Ireland. We see it in the United States when local, state, tribal, and national rules contain subtle but important differences and an internally split Supreme Court refuses to offer guidance.[7] And we see it in complex tussles in international arbitration cases about what rules apply when and where.

Legal pluralism is a fact. Neat consistency and coherence of social guardrails do not exist, not even in the formalized world of law. As we have learned to negotiate these inconsistencies and incoherencies, we have developed a rich and pragmatic mental and institutional toolkit to deal with such situations, so that problems can be resolved without forcing us to question or break the entire system.[8]

This, though, begs the question: If consistency and coherence aren't key design principles of social guardrails, what are? In the rest of this chapter we put forward three such principles: to empower the individual to make good decisions, to be socially anchored, and to encourage learning.

Decisional Empowerment

Some may think that guardrails are intended to force humans to behave as desired—that humans are mere agents of the regulatory regimes within which they live, the objects of decision-shaping mechanisms. That is a fundamental mistake. On the contrary, social guardrails acknowledge human volition at every step.

Society aims to influence human decisions through guardrails, because humans interact with the world through the decisions they make—so if we want to improve human actions, we need humans to make better decisions. But in doing so we presuppose the existence of human volition. Yes, humans may face consequences if they decide to act contrary to what guardrails mandate, but it is up to them to choose. The notion that humans *can choose* how they act is foundational to the existence of modern guardrails. The notion of freedom of contract that permeates much of private law in many jurisdictions around the world is about empowering individuals to make decisions rather than taking decision power away from them. If humans have no agency and bear no responsibilities, guardrails would make no sense.

Imagine for a moment a world in which machines decide for humans. To shape decisions, societal guardrails would then no longer be addressed to humans, but to machines. That would require different substance, processes, and institutions—in short, a different system from what we have today. All current guardrails would become useless, whether informal social norms, formal laws, or physical nudges (think speed bumps on residential streets). They would be addressed to the wrong agent. Instead, decision rules would have to be communicated to machines and in unambiguous form. Without human volition, machine-readable decision rules could, at least in principle, result in perfect compliance. There would be little need for adjudication, appeal, or enforcement. And there would be no room for deviation.

Almost a quarter century ago, the introduction of the funny-looking two-seater SMART car provided a hint of how such a shift might occur. To avoid being toppled over in high-speed turns and by gusty winds, its computer would not let drivers go beyond 130 km/h (about 80 mph).

Some drivers were incensed: What if in a dangerous situation they needed their car to speed, but the car's computer would not permit it? Critics even suggested that the SMART was a car for those that did not know how to drive well and needed being nannied by a machine. Others argued that with human volition curtailed, human responsibility would be limited as well: "The machine did it, not I." The core of the critique wasn't the existence of a speed limit, but that it was built-in, overriding human decisions.[9]

In contrast to this fundamental undermining of human volition, many existing social guardrails not only accept and presuppose human agency, but actively enable an environment in which human decision-makers feel empowered. Take for instance the idea of "cap and trade" in environmental regulations. It gives companies the right to emit a certain amount of pollutants each year. That amount is reduced year by year, increasing pressure to pollute less. Companies that have put pollution-avoidance measures in place and no longer need some or all of their emission allotments can trade them with others, leading to a market of pollution certificates that benefits those investing in clean technology. The setup does not tell companies how to decide and act. The economic incentives may shape individual decisions, but overall decisional freedom is enhanced, not diminished. There are multiple strategies and decisional paths for each company to proceed.

The transparency rules for listed companies that the US Securities and Exchange Commission (SEC) imposes are another example. Corporations must tell their investors what they are doing so that investors can make informed decisions. But executives are largely unconstrained in their decisions to shift strategies or change their business. As long as they are sufficiently transparent, they retain the privilege of action. We see similar approaches (albeit with varying degrees of success) in health care, social security, and even education. There is no guarantee that well-intended measures to enable decisions will lead to successful outcomes. Some implementations may be wanting. Guardrails may offer ineffective incentives or the wrong ones, leading to unexpected and even perverse results. Informational empowerments may not be sufficient to overcome real-world power differentials.

But there is no denying that a fundamental quality of the governance spaces that most societies have put in place is to empower humans in their decision-making, to help them evolve and become better at deciding rather than directly supplanting their volition with the second-guessing of either the collective or the machine. This design principle endows the individual; but it is also linked to society.

Socially Anchored

Guardrails may be addressed to individual decision-makers, but they are deeply social in nature. They are born out of societal discussions, particularly in democracies. This includes formal law. Most legislative processes are the consequence of debates about specific governance needs and with what concrete legal guardrails to address them—from a local petition for a new pedestrian crossing to a continent-wide tightening of competition laws for online platforms as a result of public debate about crass corporate abuses of informational power.

Once such guardrails have been put in place, their implementation and enforcement, too, take place in a social context. This involves relevant institutions and relies on established processes that are all deeply social in nature—from decisions of human judges to public involvement in environmental impact assessments. Historically speaking, the establishment of this social connection was a substantial achievement. Being adjudicated by one's own peers—whether judges from the community or laypersons acting as jurors—led to judgments that were not only less capricious than the previous method of trial by ordeal but that also were deeply rooted in one's community. It acknowledged and embraced the idea that humans aren't objects to be ruled over, but subjects of their own destiny—individually and societally.[10]

In doing this, it also made obvious toward whom human responsibility is directed. When a human decision hurts another human, that human isn't the only victim. Society itself, the peaceful cohabitation of individuals, has also been hurt. Remedying this situation requires more than just a settlement between the parties. The very idea of public trials by one's peers is that because society has been offended, a societal process may be necessary. By the same token, once that societal process has run its course, the injury caused by individual action has been addressed and there is, at least in principle, no room left for further revenge or retribution. With each execution of its regulatory regime of guardrails, society reiterates its engagement in the process of communal adjudication as well as healing.

The social dimension of guardrails does not end with their operationalization. As all guardrails are products of social processes, they need to be open to criticism and modification—even abolishment—as society changes. Debates over the guardrails that are currently in place are not just reflexive exercises in democratic participation, but societal deliberations about whether the contours of governance need to change. Lawrence Lessig, who we mentioned in chapter 2, once said in response to the argument that the protection of intellectual property is immutable, that copyright—a legal guardrail limiting the use of intellectual creations—is in fact a creation of society and can be modified if society so desires. We may be tempted to think that this is the consequence of democracy, but it is more than that. It is a consequence of law as a *social system* that can be analyzed, critiqued, altered, and changed. All such guardrails, including legal ones, are but transient outcomes of a societal consensus; they can and will change as society evolves.

In 2022, the US Supreme Court ruled that abortion is not a constitutional right, reversing a long line of precedents dating back half a century.[11] We disagree with the decision, but we also want to highlight that the Supreme Court did not prohibit abortions. It simply said that society, through laws, can do so. Many US states had already put such laws in place, with a provision that they would come into effect if abortion were no longer to be afforded constitutional protection.[12] If society disagrees, these laws can be changed. Perhaps the conceptual upside of the court's hugely controversial decision is that we realize guardrails are plastic. They reflect ongoing processes in our society. We are never "done" making or amending guardrails. Those who believe guardrails themselves are or should be immutable, including some of the Justices sitting on the Supreme Court, are proved wrong by the very decision they joined.

More than a century ago, US Supreme Court Justice Oliver Wendell Holmes reminded us eloquently of the transient and contingent nature of law in his dissent in the case of *Gitlow v. New York*.[13] At issue was whether handing out leaflets that advocated for socialism could be prohibited. Holmes emphasized not only the process of democracy, but the plasticity of law as a deeply social construct: "If in the long run the beliefs expressed in proletarian dictatorship are destined to be accepted by the dominant forces of the community, [...] they should be given their chance and have their way."

The creation, execution, critique, and modification of guardrails is anchored in society, its mechanisms, institutions, and processes. The fact that legal guardrails were established in a particular, formal way makes them different from other, perhaps more informal guardrails. It means legal guardrails may persist longer than other social norms—but, perhaps surprisingly, they also may turn out to be far more fleeting than some social rules that reflect deep-seated beliefs. Despite their distinct mode of creation, laws are social products as much as any other guardrails, and fundamentally plastic to emerging societal needs and changing preferences.

Social guardrails are thus linked to society in a bidirectional fashion. They are what sociologist Anthony Giddens called "structures": they bind agents—individuals and groups—and shape their behavior; but they themselves are populated by agents, and are creations of their actions.[14]

Information technologies are plastic, too—that's a consequence of the very idea of a computer being a Turing machine[15]—but guardrails embedded in information technologies aren't socially anchored. They lack comprehensive connection to the social at every level, from creation and implementation to critique and modification. They may be effective, but they aren't social artifacts the way, for instance, legal guardrails are. It's a flaw that technical guardrails cannot overcome. Of course, information technologies are themselves the product of social processes, and persist because of human support—they, too, are socially contingent.[16] But they result from processes that are often oblique, with limited involvement of those who are to be bound by them, and they lack robust processes and institutions to guarantee their social embeddedness. Their social anchorage is as shallow as the anchorage of social guardrails is deep.

Taken together, the two design principles—individual empowerment and social anchorage—afford guardrails with a mechanism that guides rather than supplants individual decision-making by embedding it into a larger social context. They also facilitate a third design principle.

Encouraging Learning

Good guardrails encourage learning, individually and collectively, to improve decision-making. This benefits individual decision-making, but also furthers learning more generally.

Humans are impressive learning systems. At a very basic level, we learn as we respond to repeat stimuli, a bit like Pavlov's dog salivating once it heard the ring of the bell that indicated the arrival of food. But, importantly and unlike most animals, we can also generalize from what we experience in the here and now, so that we can create abstract learnings and apply them to novel decision situations. Because we can devise mental templates of how the world works, we don't have to experience every situation ourselves to learn from it. It enables us to learn from the experiences and insights of others—a shortcut facilitated by incentives to share experiences among us. This kind of learning is hugely versatile—it allows us to transcend the boundaries of specific situations and circumstances.[17] But there is more: Such learning also entails actively reflecting on decisions we have made, being open to critique, and being ready for adjustments to reap the benefits of cultural learning that we mentioned earlier.

Learning is deeply rooted in our perception of individual human volition. Our mental templates are fundamentally causal. We "see" cause and effect everywhere, even if we are wrong. Our bias toward causality has been explored and rightly critiqued.[18] But it offers a significant advantage for survival, which is why evolutionarily humans developed and held onto it. Understanding the world through causal templates underscores that humans have agency—that their actions, and thus the decisions that precede them, matter. Our causal bias may make us think our actions are more important than they are. But that also makes us attach significance and weight to the decisions we make, which in turn may increase the impact we have.

With our causal mental templates, we can imagine next steps and predict possible outcomes. In our minds, we can play the game of life a few steps ahead. That lets us see beyond the present and peek into a future that we tend to believe we can actively shape. Research has shown that humans believing they have agency are more involved, more assertive in their decisions, and more focused on their actions. And they tend to be more satisfied with their lives (our cognitive bias to forget failures and remember successes surely helps here, too).[19]

Because agency is a crucial element of how we learn, guardrails enabling learning require, build on, and reinforce human volition and decisional empowerment. This third design principle is directly linked with the first.

As we described in chapter 3, human progress would not have been possible if everyone had to learn for themselves, even with our cognitive ace of generalizing to build causal templates that enable us to imagine and predict. Nor would biological evolution have been as capable or fast. The key ingredient to fast learning across groups and time lies in our social nature. Recent research points to more specific enablers of humanity's amazing path of learning. Psychologist Michael Tomasello's studies of primates suggest one such enabler is that humans developed the preference to live in well-coordinated social groups with distinct identities.[20] For anthropologist Joseph Henrich, competition between social groups facilitates group cohesion.[21] Cognitive psychologist Steven Pinker adds the development of a complex language.[22] It offers ways to convey differences between past, present, and future, while the use of metaphors enables the expression and absorption of general mental templates and concepts.

Researchers debate the exact configuration and interplay of these enablers. But what is obvious for our purposes is the foundational link between social groups and learning—as individuals, communities, and a species. It is no accident that all our learning institutions involve learning from and with others, whether it is in schools and universities, as apprentices, or in seminars and workshops; it reflects the connection between learning and society, linking the third design principle to the second.[23]

In a decision-making context, learning entails far more than the concept that individuals facing similar decisions can improve over time. Every decision offers a learning opportunity for all of us—and we have evolved the biological, cognitive, and cultural tools to do so. Humanity as a whole can make progress if we use these tools.

Technologists sometimes speak about "generativity," a design principle to support the creation of new technical products and services. Jonathan Zittrain, one of its proponents, explains that generativity aims to keep many doors of possible innovation open.[24] Generativity enables progress and learning, but it is narrower than the more general design principle of learning that we are interested in here. Learning with the help of guardrails encompasses all decision-making situations, not just technological change; and while generativity is about keeping many doors open, learning is more an iterative process of opening the right doors.

Even seemingly rigid and formal guardrails, such as laws, emphasize learning in the decision context in a myriad of ways. They put the focus on individuals, giving them the opportunity to decide for themselves— even if taking the decision away from them might improve outcomes or be more economical in the short run. Their procedural transparency enables us to mentally retrace guardrail processes and evolve our individual and collective decision-making. By letting us revisit most decisions, from formal appeals and recurring elections to the concept of reversibility we mentioned in chapter 5, the law acknowledges not only that circumstances can change but also that learning can prompt us to want to revise some of our previous choices. Even when individuals are sent to prison, the stated aim is not revenge but learning and betterment. Quite deliberately, law affords us with second chances through learning, at least in many societies and for most cases.[25]

Beyond the law, innumerable other social guardrails incorporate learning as one of their design principles. But the principle of enabling learning goes further: As societies pick specific guardrails from their solution space, they are also deciding—and like any other decision, whether a guardrail works is something that can be observed and assessed. Learning can take place at the level of guardrails as well.

I CAN(N)

A quarter century ago, just as the Internet was turning into a mass phenomenon, legal scholar Tamar Frankel became the surprising hero of choosing guardrails to enable learning. Arguably, without her the Internet would not be what it is today—a global resource of information and communication.

Frankel was born in British Palestine. She studied law. Later her government sent her to Europe to negotiate financial aid for the fledging Israeli state. She did so with aplomb. In her forties she switched from practicing law to thinking about it, became a legal academic, and joined Boston University's law school as a professor. Her specialty was the rather arcane field of fiduciary law; Frankel was keenly interested in when, why, and how people trusted each other. She was accomplished in her field but had little to do with this new hyped thing called the Internet—until a former student of hers, now working with the US government, called and asked for help.[26]

For the Internet to run smoothly, all computers connected to it must be able to understand each other. This means they must communicate according to the same rules. These rules are enumerated in technical protocols devised by a group we met earlier: the IETF, or Internet Engineering Task Force. But each computer also needs to have a unique identifier so that a data packet can find its way to the intended recipient. In the early years of the Internet, all its available addresses were managed by Jon Postel, a knowledgeable but opinionated nerd under contract to the US National Science Foundation. Because numerical identifiers are hard for humans to remember, the Internet also has a system of so-called domain names, such as "amazon .com" and "nih.gov." All this needed to be managed, and a company called NSI had contracted with the US government to administer a substantial part of it.

All involved knew that this arrangement would not be sustainable as the Internet grew into a global infrastructure. Other governments and Internet companies were pressuring the United States to transition the governance of the Internet's name and address space to some form of international or global oversight. Postel and his mates resisted, because they wanted to ensure that Internet governance would remain with the engineers. The White House proposed to solve the problem by creating a new institution, the Internet Corporation for Assigned Names and Numbers (ICANN). How ICANN should operate, and who should govern and oversee it, was up for grabs. Stakeholders floated the idea of meetings around the world to discuss and hash out details.

Tamar Frankel was called to manage that process, as much as that was possible. She may have had little understanding initially of the technical details of the Internet address and name space (although she learned quickly), but she did know a lot about setting up governance institutions people can rely on. During 1997, she deftly ran a stakeholder consultation process, pushing the parties to coalesce around a consensus. Postel—and, after his sudden death, his colleagues—wanted ICANN to have bylaws that would give all power and oversight to a small board of hand-picked engineers. Frankel knew that this idea fell shockingly short of what was needed. But by the end of 1998, the nerds seemed to have won. ICANN was founded as a California nonprofit, with the CEO and chairperson of the board that Postel and colleagues had wanted. But the nerds had counted their chickens before they hatched.

For ICANN to function, it needed the US government to delegate powers that had rested with the Department of Commerce. The government sided with Frankel and required ICANN to negotiate with its critics. The result was an amendment to ICANN's bylaws, so that nine board members would be chosen through a global election process open to all Internet users, which would guarantee broader international and stakeholder representation. Over the next two decades, ICANN went through multiple iterations of governance structures, abandoning direct elections for board membership in favor of creating two global advisory bodies—one for governments and one for various other stake-holders. These kept the pressure on ICANN to continue the path toward more transparency and inclusive oversight. The process was often messy and fraught with setbacks, but through many adjustments ICANN matured and grew into something functional *and* inclusive.

This was made possible in significant part by guardrails that enabled learning by the relevant decision-makers. In later interviews, Frankel was quite clear about what, to her, were the right ingredients for such learning—not just for ICANN, but for any such institution: clear aspirations and goals, with a structure and guardrails that permit "muddling through"—the phrase she used for the iterative process of learning step by step. The nerds had focused strongly on the initial institutional structure and somewhat less on aspirations. Frankel understood the importance of informal as well as formal guardrails. Informal guardrails ensured outside pressure could be maintained for further inclusion, transparency, and oversight. Formal guardrails ensured bylaws could be amended so that critics could become board members. Together they shaped ICANN's decisions in the direction Frankel wanted—not toward a particular ideology or political bent, but toward recognizing the importance of iterative improvement, of trial and error, of facilitating course corrections.

Importantly, this learning wasn't limited to the operational decisions ICANN executives took. It also extended to the guardrails themselves; over time ICANN changed its bylaws and how it was institutionally set up and structured, responding to deficiencies and addressing concerns. The engineering community initially had strongly resisted the calls for broader participation. But they eventually realized that Frankel's "muddling through"—guardrails-enabled iterative learning—wasn't fundamentally different from their own pragmatic ethos, which we met in an earlier chapter, of "rough consensus and running code."

ICANN's governance history highlights the importance of the linkage between formal and informal guardrails—between bylaws, which are close to laws, and relentless pressure from outside, for instance through constant media attention. The former is textual and concrete, the latter is more social and diffuse. But both are social guardrails, both shape decisions and constrain behaviors. In this case, both were squarely focused on learning and iterative change. And, as this case shows, they can reinforce each other to create a more comprehensive and durable fabric of guardrails.

What Learning Entails

As we consider applying this design principle, it is important to keep in mind what learning entails and what it does not. In the decision context, learning is about guardrails that help individuals improve their decision-making. That suggests change. But as we saw in earlier chapters, critics point out that regulatory regimes often stabilize the status quo, limiting change and protecting the existing distribution of power. For instance, social psychologist Shoshana Zuboff argued that a digital-age variation of capitalism is reflected in the rules and regulations that our society has put in place.[27] Legal scholar Katharina Pistor showed how law transforms assets, such as land and knowledge, into capital, thereby steadying a particular economic system.[28] This echoes earlier critical scholars who highlighted the role of law in preserving and perpetuating the might of elites in societies.[29] If law is so ossifying, how does that align with formal guardrails enabling change through learning?

It would be easy to cast aside this question by contending that design principles focus on guardrail mechanisms—how we govern—rather than the ultimate values and goals we aim to achieve with them. But that would be simplistic. At some level, there is significant alignment between the critics' views and ours. Both we and these critical observers understand law as a social construct with distinct qualities. Throughout this book we have talked about social guardrails and have recognized law as part of them. For us, law isn't some exogenous normative system, but the product of social dynamics that continue to shape it. We'll return to this line of thought in the final chapter.

Even as we see guardrails as social constructs, we also acknowledge that the three design principles are not value-neutral. When we say that good guardrails are anchored in the social, we imply more than that they are the product of social processes. We suggest normatively that linking guardrails to social processes and institutions is valuable for a species that has historically gained much through cooperation and collaboration. Similarly, the importance we assign to individual volition reflects a particular worldview that is likely at odds with more collectivist perspectives. And while learning implies change, such change takes place within the system—building on the past, rather than radically breaking with it.

Empowering individual decision-making, anchoring this process in the social, and enabling learning at all levels are key design principles for good regulatory solution spaces as well as the appropriate guardrails that stem from them. These principles aim to improve decision-making; but equally, they also reinforce humanity's focus on decisions as the means through which we interact with the world and make our own role in it matter.

To the extent that these principles are expressed in law, they arguably explain its success as a system shaping human decision-making. But law has no natural monopoly on them. Anthropological and historical research has discovered that social norms and informal community rules can similarly empower individuals' decisions, connect to society, and enable learning.[30] From the perspective of decision-making, the type of guardrails and solution spaces matter less than how well they reflect these three principles. This brings us back to the question of how to best govern in the decision context.

Cyberlaw Revisited

In chapter 2, we described how the meteoric early ascent of the Internet challenged the foundations of modern law—a governance system designed for an analog, but text-based, world. Modern law moved away from earlier concepts of law as a complex mosaic of personal guardrails and instituted a more coherent set of rules applying to most individuals within a defined geography. Being anchored in space and time gave law comprehensive reach and the impression of uniformity. But law failed to adapt swiftly enough to the needs created by the speed and breadth of the Internet's rise. Technical solutions—ostensibly incorporating law's aims—were put in place, but failed because they optimized on proxy goals. Put metaphorically, technological governance reached its target faster, but it turned out to be the wrong destination.

This doesn't mean that technology has no place in the governance of decision-making. Quite the contrary, as we shall see, especially in chapter 9. But it does suggest that technology is no *replacement* for the variety of social guardrails that shape the human decision space. The reason is linked to the need to imagine solution spaces, rather than rely on fixed sets of concrete guardrails—and the importance of the guidance provided by the three design principles we discussed in this chapter.

If technology isn't the answer, how should we approach the challenge to conventional guardrails posed by global digital networks? How can social guardrails, including law, evolve? To us, the answer is conceptual (and by now, we hope, clear). Earlier attempts to transition social guardrails into the digital age failed because, by privileging principles such as reach, effectiveness, and consistency, we disconnected the qualities we designed our guardrails for from what we ultimately hoped to achieve with them. The remedy is not to make guardrails behave more like a technological fix—fast, efficient, comprehensive—but to revert to the design principles that stem from what we want guardrails to achieve: individual empowerment, anchorage in the social, and the facilitation of learning.

In the following chapters, we explicate how this could work, how many of the necessary elements are already in use, and how guardrails, when taken together, can evolve into useful governance systems that are effective yet maintain the design principles we value. But before that, we need to appreciate a further, crucial design element.

7

SELF-RESTRAINT

Kaprun, access point to one of the Alps' most famous skiing regions, is a dream destination for sport fans. It is also remembered as a place of human tragedy. On November 11, 2000, 162 passengers boarded a funicular train for an early morning trip to the slopes through a tunnel in the mountain. An electric fan heater in the unattended cabin at the lower end of the train caught fire and caused an emergency stop about two thousand feet into the tunnel. The fire, fueled by leaking flammable hydraulic fluid from the brake system, spread so rapidly that it turned the tunnel into an inferno. Passengers caught in the train, with exit doors blocked, tried to escape by smashing the shatter-resistant windows. A group of twelve at the rear of the train successfully broke a window with a ski pole. Moments later, the conductor managed to unlock the doors manually, giving the 150 passengers who were still trapped a way to exit. Sadly, all 150 in this larger group lost their lives. Only the twelve passengers from the rear of the train survived.[1] What changed the fate of these twelve passengers?

One decision. Counterintuitively, the twelve who survived ran down the steep incline. In contrast, the far larger group ran upward to get away from the burning funicular—and perished. One person was decisive in the direction taken by the twelve survivors: a volunteer firefighter with twenty years of experience. Given his training and knowledge, he immediately realized what everyone else missed in this life-or-death situation: that the steep tunnel was acting like a mega chimney, sucking oxygen in from the bottom and pushing lethal smoke, heat, and the fire upward. If there was a way to survive, it was by running downward, even if that meant running the risk that the burning train might come crashing down the tracks.

The disaster has many more dimensions, and resulted in years of litigation. But for our purposes, we offer this short recount as a powerful demonstration of a fundamental point about human decision-making: Decisions are deeply shaped by the information that individuals have at their disposal. To the great fortune of the survivors, the volunteer firefighter had internalized *one* critical piece of contextual information and used it; that turned out to be lifesaving.

The decisions we make are the result not only of what is in front of us at a given moment in time. In ways often less visible, they are shaped by previous information that has accumulated. As with the hero in the Kaprun disaster, what we already know and have experienced so far permeates our understanding of our options right now and the actions we may take based on it. In a fundamental sense, human decision-making is inherently linked to where we came from and who we have become. It may be individual but is embedded in a broader social *context*.

Our life experience is full of examples that prove the point. The current weather and traffic conditions shape how fast or slow we drive the car. Whether I'm willing to accept an unfavorable fare for a transatlantic flight depends on the purpose of the trip. How much information I need before arriving at a decision depends on how much time I have available to do the research. And so on. Context also shapes how we think about our own and other people's decisions. When people disagree about a decision made in the past, the root cause might be less in the outcome of the decision than in a different understanding of what constitutes the relevant context in which the decision took place—or arguably should have taken place. Such disputes may get particularly thorny when folks lack the ability to at least recognize different contexts in which decisions have taken place, and that their own understanding might be different.

In short, context is challenging. Fortunately, guardrails can help us to deal with context—but that, too, is far more complex than one would think at first sight. The first set of complications arises when operating within guardrails tailored for a specific context.

In one recent case, a person exercising the right to be forgotten (RTBF) asked Google to remove links to an article that contained a satirical, photoshopped picture together with a local politician.[2] According to European law, the search engine must comply if the links in question are "inadequate, irrelevant or no longer relevant, or excessive."[3] What sounds straightforward on paper turns out to be tricky in practice. The question whether to remove the link hinges on a balance between the local politician's right to privacy and data protection, and the public's right to access information. In the landmark Google Spain judgment, the European Court of Justice provided some guidance on how to weigh these competing interests.[4] Contextual issues—such as the nature of the information in question, its sensitivity for the data subject's private life, and the data subject's role in public life—matter a great deal. Context can be assessed only on a case-by-case basis.

A similar pattern plays out where legal or ethical guardrails demand that customers, clients, patients, and so forth are properly informed to enable them to make good decisions. How much information and what kind of information needs to be shared are shaped both by the information needs of the individual and the context in which the interaction takes place. If an attorney seeks advice from another attorney to evaluate the prospects of litigation, the information they need will be different compared to that for a layperson. If a patient lands in the emergency room after a car accident and time is of the essence, it is okay for the physician not to go into the same level of detail about possible risks of treatment as they would with a scheduled medical procedure.

But the contextual challenge runs even deeper. Guardrails are not only inevitably confronted with contextual factors that may hamper their effectiveness in a given situation. Complicating matters even more, guardrails emerging in one specific context might shape decisions in entirely different contexts down the road. The Kaprun tragedy offers a glimpse at this phenomenon. The fact that the volunteer firefighter had a crucial piece of information available on a ski trip was interlinked across time and space by the tough training routines, protocols, and drills that together form the decision-making guardrails aimed at steering firefighters' decisions when they are on duty. Those passengers who were not privy to experiencing the same guardrails died.

This chapter offers a closer look at some of the main strategies available when guardrails cope with the multifaceted challenges emerging from the inherently contextual nature of information and decision-making—characteristics we encountered in previous chapters. This chapter examines in greater detail what we might do from a guardrails design perspective to address the context problem. Unfortunately, we can't offer an easy solution. To the contrary, the following sections will reveal that some of the most intuitive strategies we might deploy are destined to fail. What is needed is a more radical reframing of the problem. As an alternative future pathway, we propose *self-restraint* as a final design feature of future guardrail regimes, which refers to a guardrail's built-in capacity to tame its own power to enable better decisions.

Mixing Oil and Water

Whatever form guardrails take—from technical filters for hate speech (as we detailed in chapter 3) to legal norms such as the European RTBF—they inherently generalize across contexts and individuals to be able to steer. Human information processing and decision-making pose a unique challenge for guardrails compared to other subjects that need "steering" through some sort of mechanism—whether it's automobiles on the street, food in the stores, or something as complex as genome editing in the field of biomedical research. In some ways it's like *mixing oil and water*: All guardrails need to generalize, while information and decision-making are inherently contextual and individual. The tension becomes more acute when a lot of information needs to be governed on which decisions will be made.

One of today's most vexing problems in selecting effective guardrails for online platforms is that information that seems OK in the context where it's been published might not be OK in another context where it's received and processed. This problem has long been in the making. Since the early days of the World Wide Web, courts and lawmakers across the globe have struggled with it. As far back as 1996, in an article titled "Sex on the Internet," *The Economist* asked a quintessential question: "When Bavaria wrinkles its nose, must the whole world catch a cold?"[5] The author of the article wondered about the implications of a widely reported case in which Felix Somm, director of CompuServe Germany, was indicted (and later convicted), receiving two years' probation, because the German subsidiary helped the US mothership to disseminate newsgroup content to German users that was illegal under German law. (Mr. Somm was ultimately acquitted on appeal based on a change in German law that constrained legal liability.) Despite such early warnings that contextuality matters, large social media companies went ahead and built billion-dollar businesses that expanded the problem by orders of magnitude, with resulting social costs largely externalized.

To be sure, the "oil and water" problem of designing information and decision-making guardrails isn't limited to the digital world. The same pattern plays out on a much smaller scale in the domains where the contextual challenge doesn't involve big tech companies. In medical research and care, for instance, professional bodies have come up with increasingly detailed guidance on how to live up to legal requirements concerning risk disclosures, advocating for an increasingly patient-centered approach. In consumer protection, legal norms have become more granular in an attempt to "contextualize" requirements by listing in more detail the type and quality of data that need to be disclosed. Recent regulation in Germany concerning digital products, for instance, expanded the information that needs to be provided to include information about updates that affect the functionality of the goods or compatibility and interoperability.[6] According to general principles of consumer protection law, this information must be shared "in a clear and comprehensible manner." What that means, yet again, is left to the seller, who must take into account the characteristics of the context in which the negotiation with consumers takes place.

No matter the environment, governing information for decision-making faces the challenge of balancing between generalization and individualization, between abstraction and contextualization. Large online platforms such as Facebook and Google, however, have put the problem on steroids. By offering literally billions of people from diverse backgrounds access to information, disseminated over global networks, they have not only flattened the world, but also systematically decontextualized some of it. In pushing out information across borders and boundaries, social media can strip local context away from a particular news story, user-generated video, or other snippet of content. The promotion of "friendships" and "groups" on these platforms can be seen as attempts to recreate some connective tissue, to establish some shared context, but they are only crude fixes. After all, in the attention economy algorithms power news feeds or search results in ways that maximize profits, not preserve context.

The ensuing challenge is a daunting one: Online platforms are massive de-contextualization engines—yet the pressure is on to reestablish some context when it comes to the decision-making challenges at the core of this book. The problem has grown so big that humans alone are unable to cope with the flood of decision-relevant information circulating online: Managing these tensions in the data age increasingly requires the use of advanced machine learning and other AI techniques. But even the best AI, at least in its current state of development, isn't sophisticated enough to have a sufficient understanding of context in the large number of cases that aren't clear-cut. Despite all the progress made, and despite resource constraints, human assessments are needed to make sense of the contextual and individual dimensions of information and decision-making.

Failing Strategies—Part I

How to build context awareness at scale is arguably one of the biggest design challenges in the world of guardrails. Whether deploying technology, law, social norms, or any other instrument to shape human action, the permeation of human information flows and decision-making with contextual and individual elements ultimately determines how effectively guardrails can steer behavior. The two main strategies that can be used to push this barrier and tailor guardrails to context rely on "more": adding more and finer grained rules to capture more and more contexts; and adding more "smart" technology to try to triage between clear-cut and not clear-cut stuff.

Over the past few decades, we have witnessed an incredible growth in new regulations and laws. Whether taxation, compliance, environmental, or labor law, new rules seem to hit us at an accelerating pace. This increasingly finely woven web of norms seeks to address the ever-growing number of guardrail problems in more and more detailed ways, tailored to increasingly narrow and specific contexts.

Common sense tells us that highly interconnected societies go hand-in-hand with more and more complex legal rules, and science confirms it: Based on a network analysis of federal legislation of the United States and Germany, an interdisciplinary team of researchers was able to demonstrate an "extensive growth in legal complexity as a function of volume, interconnectivity, and hierarchical structure of the legislation . . . —evidence that the highly industrialised countries we study seek to manage behavior by building increasingly complex bodies of legal rules."[7]

The overall growth of the universe of legal guardrails is driven by a trend toward norms that are tailored to a particular kind of situation. We're witnessing a flood of new rules that seek to address in increasingly fine-grained resolution particular instances of human decision-making and govern the information involved in them. Food safety and food labels are a case in point. The current version of the FDA's Food Labeling Guide, which helps to concretize the FDA's laws and regulations, is 130 pages long, addressing an incredibly rich array of issues: "Would a strawberry daiquiri mix have to bear a percent juice declaration?"; "How do you declare the ingredients in a food when the food itself is made from other foods containing multiple ingredients?" The array of norms, level of detail, and range of specific situations addressed is astonishing.[8]

Alongside more tailored and granular substantive rules, it is becoming common to get more specific when regulating the process of decision-making. Consider norms that offer protection to consumers, for instance against unfair terms in consumer contracts. Designed for the analog world, these rules served well over decades—until doing business online created new dynamics. The European Union recently enacted a sweeping new consumer rights directive to enhance consumer trust, with procedural safeguards to regulate online contracts—ranging from managing the flow of information to governing the process of withdrawal from such contracts.[9] In similar ways, the past few decades have brought us more and more process rules governing decision-making in areas as diverse as drug development, civil litigation, or international business transactions. The aim is to nudge outcomes toward socially desirable results by making norms and regulations more contextual.

Some argue that we're only at the beginning of a norm explosion. Experts predict a "golden age of regulation," with further waves of regulation focused on information and decision-making in the digital realm, ranging from upgrades to consumer protection, data privacy, and competition law to entirely new AI legislation.[10] To quote Microsoft's president Brad Smith, "the 2020s will bring to tech what the 1930s brought to financial services."[11] In anticipation of more and more detailed regulatory requirements, many large companies already plan to make big investments in growing their regulatory teams (at the time of writing, the head count at Microsoft's legal and corporate affairs unit had just grown by 20 percent in the past fiscal year alone).

Enacting more and more granular norms is one approach to cope with the "oil and water" problem of information and decision-making guardrails. Another one is to deploy advanced technologies when applying general norms to specific cases.

As described in chapter 3, Meta is using machine learning techniques and other AI methods to make content moderation more context-sensitive. The same tools are used across industries by companies as diverse as the *New York Times*, Amazon, and Zurich Insurance to address a series of problems ranging from hate speech to resource optimization that pop up as contexts shift and at times collapse in the digitally connected age.[12] AI is increasingly deployed to apply general norms—such as laws, corporate policies, terms of services, or insurance terms—to individual cases on a large scale.

Not only companies, but lawmakers too have started discovering technology as a means to apply a growing number of legal requirements to specific contexts of information and decision-making. Three examples from Europe demonstrate the idea. The recently overhauled EU Copyright Directive imposes an obligation on large online platforms such as YouTube or Facebook to monitor content posted by users for copyright infringements.[13] In practice, such preventive monitoring relies on the use of software filtering tools, resulting in a de facto mandate to use such technologies. The new European regulation to combat the dissemination of terrorist online content requires platforms to remove terrorist content within one hour of having received a removal order from the authorities; many civil society organizations see this as incentivizing online platforms to use automated content moderation tools, including upload filters.[14] And the EU Code of Practice on Disinformation—which has been agreed to by platforms such as Google, Meta, Microsoft, and TikTok—includes a commitment by the companies to invest in technical tools "to prioritize relevant, authentic and authoritative information where appropriate in search, feeds, or other automatically ranked distribution channels" and to develop tools that make it easier for people to find diverse perspectives about topics of public interest.[15]

Unfortunately, such government-induced technical approaches share the same challenge as social media companies have already experienced in their own use of technologies for content moderation: Assessing the context in which information flows and decisions take place remains an area where humans have an advantage over machines. A case in point is the fight against online piracy, as a story from the other side of the Atlantic illustrates.

The Digital Millennium Copyright Act (DMCA) is an important piece of US legislation.[16] It was enacted in the late 1990s to "upgrade" copyright law from the analog to the digital world. Among the problems it addresses is users sharing music clips, movies, and other copyrighted content illegally over platforms such as YouTube. In what was at the time an innovative move to promote the growth of online businesses, it provides platforms with immunity from liability stemming from illegal acts by their users as long as they meet certain requirements, such as expeditiously removing copyrighted material once they receive a valid takedown notice from the copyright owner, and terminating the accounts of users who are repeatedly accused of infringement.

For large platforms, it's far from trivial to uphold this legal requirement—for example, YouTube has to deal with 500 hours of video being uploaded to the platform every *minute*.[17] YouTube developed a sophisticated system called Content ID to ensure compliance with the DMCA at scale.[18] If a video is uploaded to YouTube, it is scanned against a database of files that have been submitted by rightsholders. If there is a match, the whole video gets blocked from view. Or the rightsholder can decide to "monetize" the video by having ads placed on it or by claiming the revenue from the ads already on it. In some cases, they will share the revenue with either the video creator or other rightsholders who have matches. They may request that the video's viewership stats be shared with them. Rightsholders can choose any of these penalties to be automatically applied, requiring no further action, unless the video creator wants to challenge the match, in which case a rather complicated process kicks in.

According to YouTube, 98 percent of copyright claims are handled through Content ID, which is equivalent to more than 122 million claims per year.[19] Yet again, one of the limits of the system is to understand the context in which a piece of content is shared. "Fair Use" is a case in point; it is a legal doctrine in the United States that says that someone can re-use copyright-protected material without getting the rightsholder's permission under certain circumstances.[20] What these circumstances are is the tricky part. It requires analyzing and weighing four factors, including whether the use adds new meaning to the original or just copies from the original. For instance, it may be "fair use" to share a music clip in the context of a review, as an illustration in a historical piece, or as a demonstration in a lecture on copyright law and fair use. But Content ID can't determine whether this kind of context applies.

The takeaway so far: The contextual nature of human information exchange and decision-making creates a challenge to every system of guardrails. Attempts to "maximize" the reach of guardrails by getting more and more contextual and adding ever finer-grained rules or more sophisticated technologies when enforcing the general rules will only take us so far. Whether it's through the means of law or technology, there are limits to how context-sensitive attempts to shape human action can ultimately be. At the end of the day, steering collective matters through guardrails necessitates some degrees of abstraction and generalization.

Failing Strategies—Part II

Another approach to the challenge of context is to ignore it altogether. Instead of tailoring guardrail systems to an ever-increasing number of specific contexts, this approach superimposes very broad "catch-all rules" to regulate human behavior. This path is particularly troublesome if we care about human flourishing. The fate of Shi Tao Shi, a Chinese journalist and writer, clearly depicts this.[21]

When Shi Tao received a letter from the Communist Party in 2004, he was probably not aware that it would mark a life-changing event for him and his family, putting him in jail. And it's safe to assume that he couldn't have anticipated that the events that followed would later serve as a lesson in a book on decisional guardrails. The document sent to Shi Tao ordered journalists not to report on the upcoming fifteenth anniversary of the Tiananmen Square massacre of pro-democratic protesters in Beijing and other cities. While entirely in line with the Communist Party's approach to strict media regulation, the message was a major provocation in the eyes of pro-democracy activists in China and abroad. Shi Tao didn't want the order to go unnoticed. To raise awareness, he used his Yahoo! email account to post an anonymous message describing the order on a Chinese-language pro-democracy website based in New York.

The consequences were dramatic. One and a half years later, Shi Tao was arrested under Chinese state security laws on the charge of revealing state secrets and sentenced to ten years' imprisonment for leaking documents abroad. Shi Tao's defense that he was unaware that an official memo was considered a state secret didn't help. Much to his detriment, the Chinese Law on Guarding State Secrets contains extremely broad and widely ambiguous provisions that allow the government to classify state secrets—even retroactively and without any judicial oversight.

What happened to Shi Tao is first and foremost a tragedy on a human level. But it can also teach us something about the damage "catch-all" guardrails can do. Shi Tao's detainment is a prime example of a dangerously broad and vague guardrail that ignores all context. The risk that law as a particularly powerful instrument in the guardrail arsenal can turn against people is especially real in—but unfortunately no longer exclusive to—political environments where the government is understood to be above the law, with the ability to create and execute law to preserve its own power, when necessary, regardless of the effect it has on people's human rights.

An Alternative Path?

Human information and decision-making processes are difficult horses to catch. As we have seen, the dominant approaches to steer human action—more and more rules and more and more technology to implement them—can't really solve the contextual challenge. Instead, putting guardrails on speed begins to reduce rather than foster human flourishing the more contexts it seeks to enclose. The extreme alternative approach, a "catch-all" disregard for context, is even worse. It is bound to violate human rights and have devastating effects on people, as the Shi Tao saga demonstrates so dramatically.

The problem with both approaches is that they recognize no boundaries. Granted, one might argue that it's again simply a matter of balance, like almost everything in life. When designing guardrails, couldn't one just locate a middle-ground position between "too granular" on the one and "too general" on the other end of a spectrum—a sort of guardrail optimum, in other words?

What sounds plausible in theory turns out to be infeasible in practice. Unfortunately, optimization problems are hard. Throughout this book, we have described a wealth of instruments available in the toolbox that we can put to good use when dealing with issues of the data age. But the Swiss Army Knife quality of these tools, when combined with the growing list of problems in the digital age that deserve attention, creates another problem: It makes so many combinations possible that it becomes virtually impossible to say what the optimum use of these tools would look like.

To get a sense of how optimization problems can become quite difficult very quickly, consider one of the hardest calculation problems a computer can encounter. The story takes us back to a small book published in 1832 in Germany, an early version of a business self-help book; or as the title framed it, "how he must be and what he should do in order to . . . be sure of the happy success in his business."[22] The book was aimed at traveling salesmen, and described a situation later famously known in mathematics as the "traveling salesman problem": For a salesperson with a map of cities and roads connecting them, what's the shortest path for her to travel to every city and return home? It sounds like a relatively trivial issue, but the simplicity is deceptive—it turns out to be an extraordinarily complex problem, as there's no quick solution to calculate the many alternative routes and compare them. The math that supports solving this puzzle gets rapidly more arduous as you add new cities. The current record in figuring out this algorithmic problem, using cutting-edge twenty-first-century computing power, is limited to calculating the shortest route among just twenty-two cities.

Now, let's apply this to the problem of guardrails. The traveling salesman problem looks almost trivial in comparison to the universe of "routes" guardrails can prescribe—the combination of issues, connections, techniques, etc.—to address matters of human behavior. Whether for good or bad, no guardrail optimum can be calculated by a machine using some magical formula. It's a problem far too big for even the most powerful computers. We must accept that we can't determine what the optimum is when it comes to guardrails and decision-making.

Instead, we propose an alternative pathway—a reframing of the problem, if you will. Absent a calculable, fixed optimum of regulation, we should build capacities into guardrails that both force and enable us to continuously question and negotiate where the equilibrium is. We mentioned an illustration of this idea in the previous chapter, when we explained how ICANN was able to learn not just at the level of decision-making but also at guardrail adjustment.

A necessary precondition for such a system that embraces learning rather than a maximum approach when seeking to influence human action is *self-restraint*. Borrowing a line from John Milton's epic poem "Paradise Lost," self-restraint is "*[t]he rule of not too much.*"[23] It's moderation, in thought and action.

Rooted in ancient Greek philosophy, self-restraint was described by Plato and Aristotle as one of the Athenian virtues. Roman philosophers advocated for the similar idea of temperance as a virtue, as opposed to love of pleasure. A millennium later, Thomas Aquinas referred to temperance as a cardinal virtue. Another five hundred years after that, German philosopher Immanuel Kant made the case that temperance is a core element of any human being's potential, linking the notion of moderation to self-control and calm deliberation. Over the centuries, self-restraint has been praised in philosophical and religious thought—and most recently celebrated in the positive psychology movement. What sounds lofty at first also has immense practical relevance in the context of human decision-making. Quite literally, self-restraint can tip the scale for peace over war.

Why Self-Restraint Matters

On September 26, 1983, Russian duty officer Stanislav Petrov single-handedly saved the world from a nuclear war through an act of self-control and calm deliberation. In the early hours, the Soviet Union's early warning systems went off, indicating that the United States had launched a missile strike. Petrov was the responsible duty officer. It was his job to pass on this computer-generated notification of attack to the military command and political leadership. And he knew what would be likely to happen if he did: The Soviet military would retaliate immediately with a nuclear attack on the United States. Petrov suspected, from various clues, that the notification might be a false alarm caused by a glitch in the system. In what he later described as a 50:50 chance, he decided not to send the report up the chain of command—an act of moderation that saved the world from a nuclear disaster.[24]

The practical value of self-restraint in high-stakes decision-making was also demonstrated by a briefing given by Defense Secretary William Perry on June 16, 1994, to US president Bill Clinton and his National Security Council. It was thought that North Korea might imminently attack South Korea, and Perry had asked military staff to come up with scenarios to defend South Korea. One option involved a preemptive surgical strike against one of North Korea's nuclear facilities. Perry exercised self-restraint by choosing not to share that plan with Clinton, because— as he later described—he concluded that it was too likely to start a war with unimaginable consequences for the Korean peninsula.[25]

Petrov and Perry—two extraordinary individuals with a deep sense of humility—exercised self-restraint by not passing on information that was intended to serve as a basis for likely decisions with potentially disastrous human consequences. They lived up to the virtue of temperance in the spirit in which Immanuel Kant framed it. Both stories demonstrate how acts of self-restraint influence future decisions. Most important from a design perspective, they point to a crucial possible feature concerning guardrails for human decision-making. Luckily for humanity, the policies and procedures of the Soviet military didn't specify exactly the time frame in which the duty officer had to report a system alarm. Similarly, institutional practices afforded Perry a level of discretion and responsibility in his role as Defense Secretary. It was these guardrail features that enabled the protagonists to exercise self-restraint.

Looking back, it was perhaps just good fortune that Petrov and Perry thought they had some leeway to exercise self-restraint. However, as we look forward and imagine future guardrails for human decision-making in a world full of discontinuities, we should take seriously the lessons offered by these stories. In addition to nurturing the virtue of self-restraint in people, we should pay closer attention to how we can design guardrails that offer spaces and mechanisms for self-restraint in support of better decision-making. The bad news is that despite a two thousand plus–year history of exploring the virtues of human temperance, no comprehensive blueprint has emerged that demonstrates how to design such systems. The good news is that we might find at least some starting points by way of inspiration when looking at the law.

One of the biggest design challenges for the law is how to maintain legitimacy over time—and one of the biggest risks is overplaying its own power. In a long evolutionary process, the legal system has developed various mechanisms—think of them as an equivalent to fuses—to mitigate the risk of overreach. A particularly vivid illustration of both what's at stake and an important type of self-restraint involves a story of power struggles in the early period of US democracy.

Inspiration from Law

The US election in 1800 was fought between incumbent president John Adams of the Federalist Party and challenger Thomas Jefferson, who favored decentralization of power from the federal government toward the states. Jefferson won the election, but Adams would still be president for a few weeks before Jefferson was inaugurated. In that time, the outgoing Federalist Congress made a bold move to try to preserve the party's legacy by sabotaging the legislative agenda of Jefferson's party. It passed a law to create new circuit judgeships, and outgoing president John Adams proceeded swiftly to fill the positions. By the time Jefferson took office, all of the formalities for these "midnight appointments" were completed except for one final step, which required that some documents signed by the president were delivered to the appointees.

Jefferson ordered his Secretary of State, James Madison, to withhold the documents. William Marbury, a Federalist Party leader from Maryland, was among the individuals President Adams had tried to appoint. When he did not receive the documents, he decided to bring an action against Madison in the US Supreme Court.

The Marbury case created a serious dilemma for the Supreme Court, which itself was a manifestation of federal power—the very issue over which Jefferson and Adams were disagreeing. Indeed, the Supreme Court was seen at the time as "the last Federalist stronghold of the national government."[26] On the one hand, the law passed by the outgoing administration was clear—it imposed an obligation on Madison to deliver the documents to Marbury. If the court didn't recognize that, it would lose credibility. On the other hand, the Justices worried that if they instructed Madison to deliver Marbury's commission, and he ignored them, in practice there would be nothing they could do about it. The federal judiciary would look completely powerless.

Chief Justice Marshall found an unexpected way out of the dilemma: In a clever move, he relied on the legal system's built-in capacity for self-restraint. The Court found that Marbury's appointment indeed created a right protected by law and that withholding his commission was violating this right. However—and here the self-restraint kicks in—the Chief Justice also found that the Supreme Court didn't have the power to direct Madison to deliver the commission, because a piece of legislation that seemingly authorized the Court to do so was inconsistent with the Supreme Court's authority as detailed in the US Constitution.

Against this backdrop, the Chief Justice embraced the opportunity to address a fundamental question that had been lurking in the shadows for some time: Was a law enacted by Congress that turns out to be inconsistent with the Constitution valid or not? Marshall's response was twofold: He concluded that such a law was invalid, and—even more consequential with respect to the Supreme Court's power—that courts were the appropriate bodies to decide whether or not a law enacted by Congress was in conflict with the US Constitution.

Marbury is one of the Supreme Court's landmark cases.[27] The Chief Justice's genius in using self-restraint as a power move to defuse a tricky political dilemma has been widely acknowledged in legal scholarship and beyond.[28] But the story also reveals a strategic dimension that sheds light on the promise of self-restraint as a design of future guardrails for human decision-making. By self-imposing limits on how far guardrails reach, by narrowing down from within the system the contexts to which the instruments in the toolkit apply, the legitimacy and effectiveness of the guardrail system itself can be maintained or at times even enhanced. Conversely, if guardrails push too far—for instance by embracing too many contexts and issues—it runs the risk of losing the legitimacy that's at the core of the power it needs to "steer." Viewed from that angle, self-restraint *is* a form of power.

As surprising as Chief Justice Marshall's move was, self-restraint is part of the very fabric of law—it's central to what makes law such a special type of guardrail. The rule of law itself is the most fundamental overreach-protector. It has been around as a core principle at least since the ancient Greeks. As with most legal concepts, it has many meanings and serves various functions—but at its core is the demand "that people in positions of authority should exercise their power within a constraining framework of well-established public norms."[29] For instance, the rule of law requires that law operates through a set of norms that are available as public knowledge, or prohibits the law from overreaching through backward extension in time.

Despite its deep philosophical anchoring, self-restraint should not be taken for granted as a matter of practice: Law is an extraordinarily powerful tool that can be—and some argue often is—instrumentalized by those in control. The temptation to accumulate excessive power by (mis-)using the law is not limited to nondemocratic states as in the Shi Tao case. Legal scholars in the United States are currently sounding the alarm that the conservative majority on the Supreme Court has started to throw overboard some of the self-restraining norms that have counterbalanced the Court's vast power since *Marbury*. The lack of practiced self-restraint leads to a shift of power away from Congress, the administration, the states, and the lower courts toward what might be the advent of an "Imperial Supreme Court," with serious risk of damaging core democratic principles.[30]

Both the present-day threats and the long history of law make clear that self-restraint is a guardrail design principle that needs normative commitment, constant improvement, and actual practice. In the course of four thousand years of the law's development, legal actors have recognized again and again both the magnitude of its power and the risk of overreach, leading to the emergence of a diverse set of distributed mechanisms to prevent it from becoming all-encompassing. Current proposals in response to the power grab by conservative Supreme Court justices, such as changes to the number and tenure of justices on the Court and limiting its subject matter jurisdiction, stand in this long-term tradition.[31]

Wealth of Mechanisms

Law's continuous quest to restrain its own power, encapsulated in the principle of the rule of law, can serve as a lodestar when designing systems of guardrails that aim for a viable rather than an optimum level of control when it comes to guiding human decisions. One of law's most remarkable features is that the mechanisms of self-restraint are distributed across various domains, including substantive and procedural norms, and across the entire hierarchy of norms, all the way from local ordinances up to the level of the constitution. To compensate for the impossibility of determining an exact optimum of regulation, the legal system's embrace of a broad range of self-restraining techniques means the quest for the appropriate choice always remains a work in progress.

The wealth of self-restraint mechanisms embedded into law serves a variety of purposes in support of better human decision-making. When courts exercise juridical self-restraint, it is not only to secure their legitimacy over time and keep democratic principles intact: By narrowing down the aspects of a case on which it decides, a court limits the extent to which future courts will be bound by the precedent it sets. This reflects a principle of good decision-making familiar from cybernetics: Make decisions today in ways that leave open the greatest number of options for decisions in the future as circumstances might change.[32]

Other self-restraining mechanisms in law are designed to prevent geographic overreach, including the concept of jurisdiction. Personal jurisdiction, for instance, refers to rules that help determine whether a court has the power to make a decision regarding the party being sued in a case. Legislators have voluntarily created norms that limit the jurisdictions of their courts—an act of self-restraint that's particularly significant in the age of globalization. The EU, for instance, passed detailed regulations to provide legal certainty to Europeans who are traveling or doing business in the EU but beyond the borders of their home countries.[33] The Internet has added another layer of complexity, given that it connects so many people, places, and spaces. And again, the law responds to these changes by offering a sophisticated set of built-in norms and practices to continuously "negotiate" its reach. In functional terms, the concept of personal jurisdiction also ensures that courts with local knowledge adjudicate a case—another safeguard aimed at bolstering good decision-making.

Law also embraces mechanisms of self-restraint to learn from alternative decisions. Federalism, a form of governance in which the same territory is controlled by multiple levels of government, is a case in point. Higher levels of government exercise self-restraint to leave room for lower levels, such as states or cities, to govern issues of local concern. By limiting its own power, government at higher levels accepts diversity within the system, which in turn can serve as a test bed for how to deal with challenges down the road. In the realm of public policy as one form of decision-making—in areas such as education, health, or policing—federal states can serve as real-world laboratories in which different responses to common problems can be developed and tested.[34] These learnings may then become a source of guardrail innovation, as we will discuss later in this book.

Moving Target as a Feature

Let's sum up. The Internet has made the world a smaller place, at least in some ways: Billions of people—and even things—are connected across national boundaries, languages, and time zones. Social media make us feel connected, for good or ill. But this feeling of being a citizen of a shared global village is misleading in other ways. When it comes to information and decision-making, context matters hugely. Whether or not information is helpful when making a decision depends on it. The firefighter in the Kaprun drama was able to quickly assess a situation for which he was trained to make the right decision and run in the right direction—a move that saved his and his followers' lives. No matter whether looking at life-or-death situations or problems of social media regulation, contextuality poses a fundamental challenge to any system that seeks to influence information and decision-making, as guardrails necessitate some levels of abstraction and generalization.

As we've discussed in this chapter, the mainstream strategies to deal with what we called the "oil and water" problem are prone to fail. If a guardrail becomes more and more contextual and seeks to address every constellation, it ends up losing its steering power altogether given the universe of contexts out there. Conversely, if it moves into the other direction and generalizes too much to absorb any and all context, it destroys freedom instead of safeguarding it. The crucial question then becomes, Where is the optimum between these extremes? Bad news first. It turns out that such an optimum is impossible to calculate—the number of issues and ways to go about them, given the depth of the guardrail toolbox, is far too large to develop an algorithm that would produce a magical outcome to show us where the optimum is situated. The good news, however, is that we can sidestep the dilemma.

The key is self-restraint. The age-old guardrail mechanism called "law" teaches us that self-restraint can serve to avoid guardrail over-reach. It's one way to prevent either "too much" or "too little" context-awareness. As we look out for next-generation guardrail schemes that help us deal with the realities of an increasingly discontinuous world, the law—with its deep reservoir of instruments and techniques of self-restraint—can serve as a source of inspiration.

But it's not only the richness of tools and techniques that can inspire us as we seek to design effective guardrails in the light of ever-changing contexts. It's also how these mechanisms are situated with the guardrail system of "law" itself. Ultimately, it's the combination of diversity and distribution of such built-in mechanisms that's so powerful. Taken together, it forces *and* helps us to keep working toward a dynamic equilibrium of any attempts at steering human action. The fact that the optimum remains a moving target that can never be reached is a feature, not a bug. It enables innovative approaches to the seemingly never-ending onslaught of hard challenges in the decision context. As the next chapter will show, it is precisely this diversity, built up over the course of civilization, that offers hope when addressing some of the most difficult upcoming challenges of the digital age.

8

RANGE

Guardrails are boundaries. They mark out the space within which we can live our lives based on our decisions and in pursuit of our hopes and dreams. Our everyday life experiences may suggest that a guardrail is something that is set in stone—quite literally, in some cases. We might instinctively associate the idea with something rigid like the steel railings along the side of the highway that aim to lessen the severity of a crash by deflecting the vehicle back to the road and slowing it down. These steel guardrails are designed to withstand the impact of a 10,000-pound load moving at 4 miles per hour.

Some of the metaphorical guardrails we've been talking about in this book—not made out of steel, but rather created in the minds of software developers or lawyers—are also generally conceived as being inflexible. Have you ever tried to change the way your computer works? Not a chance, unless you're a programmer. Similarly, the prospects of success are fairly low when arguing that a speed limit is just a flexible number as one is stopped by a cop.

But, as with other instances we mentioned, the reality is more nuanced. Different types of guardrail systems are used on different types of highway, for instance; they can be mapped on a spectrum ranging from rigid (concrete barriers) to semi-rigid (beam guardrails) to fairly adaptable (cable barriers). Adaptability is also an important design feature when it comes to guardrails in the gestalt of computer code. In the world of software development, programs and interfaces are increasingly designed so that they are responsive to different contexts and user preferences. Check out your favorite news website on the laptop and then on your mobile phone to experience the magic of adaptive design. Legal guardrails, too, are less rigid than one might believe—and not just in the sense of how questionable lawyers in popular TV shows "bend the rules" for their clients in the courts. For decades, legal theorists have distinguished among different types of norm guardrails based on their elasticity.[1] Rules, standards, or principles are labels for boundaries that have distinct degrees of flexibility in terms of how they seek to steer human behavior.

The opportunity before us is to embrace the fact that we can actively shape the design of the guardrails that guide our decisions and lives, whether made out of steel, programmed on computers, or born out of social interactions as in the case of law. In the preceding chapters, we made the case for why it is so important and urgent to concentrate on design principles of future guardrail systems. If we are accurate with our observation that we must make decisions as individuals and as groups in and for a world that is increasingly complex and marked by discontinuity, we should think hard about what sets the boundaries for decision-making over the decades to come.

We have reasoned that principles for guardrails can go beyond narrowness, rigidity, and predictability. We contended that guardrails could be configured to open up diverse pathways in human decision-making by bolstering the diversity of information that inspires human decisions. We suggested that, as the contexts of our decisions begin to shift in the digital space, society would benefit from guardrails that embrace and support decisional variability—an inherently human capability that cautions against delegating decision-making too quickly to machines for the sake of efficiency. We asserted that guardrails could make decisions be reversible by default, rather than set in stone—or in the blockchain, for that matter. The discontinuities that come with the big challenges of our time, from climate change to public health and social justice, will require us to course-correct with increased frequency, and guardrails need to be designed to allow for such plasticity. Diversity, variability, and plasticity aren't replacements for narrowness, rigidity, and immutability. They simply, yet powerfully, capture the broad spectrum of what's possible—the solution space for guardrails fit for purpose in the light of the challenges of our time.

Choosing suitable guardrails from the solution space is challenging, but we identified three design principles that can help: individual empowerment, anchorage in the social, and the facilitation of learning. Then, in the previous chapter, we proposed that any set of guardrails aimed at improving human decision-making in the age of discontinuity needs to be aware of its own limitations and incorporate mechanisms to constrain its reach. Only guardrails that are both flexible and have in-built mechanisms to tame their own power will be able to safeguard human flourishing in the long run.

Our proposals are intended as starting points for a broader debate. The reality of human decision-making is multifaceted and often messy, and so are the mechanisms, processes, and institutions that shape and guide them. Confronted with an ever-growing list of challenges and evolving contexts of decision-making, there is no one-size-fits-all guardrail that magically combines all the qualities we desire. We should not hold out hope for a magic wand, perhaps a technical one, that will solve everything. Instead we need to accept—no, embrace—a wide range of guardrail models and systems: more tropical forest than English lawn, metaphorically speaking.

The good news is that we don't need to start from scratch—we can build on past experiences and existing foundations. Our discussion of guardrail features has already pointed us toward a deep cultural reservoir of possible mechanisms and techniques that can be used to build next-gen frameworks for decision-making. The stories in previous chapters have highlighted both inherently social and highly technical elements that might be combined, mixed, and mashed to embrace qualities such as individual empowerment, social linkage, the ability to learn and evolve, and self-imposed constraint. Some of the guardrails that guide our individual and collective decision-making today already include some of the qualities we propose for tomorrow's world. Our job is to perceive and amplify them as we come up with future-proofed guardrails and processes and institutions to operationalize them.

This chapter expands on the theme of flexible guardrails and their operationalization by putting the spotlight on a range of models and experiments that illustrate the breadth and depth of existing mechanisms. It features four case studies from different domains and geographies that shed light on some practical aspects of designing, implementing, and operating innovative guardrails. Along the way, we will discuss both successes and failures of the "art and science" of guardrail-making. These experiences may help us to flesh out the idea of iterative, adaptive, and flexible guardrail-making and illustrate how they can be put into practice to support decision-making in the human context.

As already noted, no guardrail is perfect in the sense of combining all desirable qualities in an ideal fashion. As with the stories in previous chapters, each of the case studies in this chapter embodies a specific mix of the qualities we're interested in. From a design perspective, we consider this blended nature of guardrail systems to be an advantage. It gives us a sense of the degrees of flexibility when putting guardrails into the wild. And it reveals the wealth of approaches in response to distinct contexts and needs for guiding human decisions. Taken together, the following case studies offer an opportunity to learn from past experiences while inviting us to use our imagination as we figure out viable responses to the ever-changing decision-making problems the future has in store.

Progressing Security

Russia's invasion of Ukraine in 2022 started in cyberspace, weeks before the first armed forces crossed the border and pictures of tanks and dead civilians started flooding social media feeds across the globe. In mid-February, US deputy national security advisor for cyber and emerging technology, Anne Neuberger, took the stage at a White House briefing. She warned that large and widespread cyberattacks against major Ukrainian banks and the government could set the stage for even more disruptive cyberattacks accompanying the invasion of Ukraine's sovereign territory.[2]

What in hindsight is remarkable about Neuberger's briefing is not only that her prediction was correct, but also that a top US security official communicated, in almost real time, details about cyberattacks and their Russian origins to the public. Neuberger had previously served as a high-ranking official at the traditionally super-secretive NSA. Her press conference was representative of a remarkable shift in the lead-up to the war in Ukraine toward sharing information gathered by various intelligence services more openly than before, in front of open microphones, and on the record.

Also unusual was the speed at which US officials and their UK and Ukrainian counterparts were able to attribute the cyberattacks publicly. While many details concerning the process of intelligence gathering remain confidential, the events around the press conference make clear that multiple national security agencies, private cybersecurity firms, and local and international networks were involved in documenting and analyzing the attacks.[3] An important node in the web of information flows was an agile organization known as Ukraine's Computer Emergency Response Team (CERT). At the time of Neuberger's press briefing— just a few dozen hours after the incidents—Ukraine's CERT released a detailed technical analysis of the cyberattacks based on information collected from a variety of sources.[4] Thanks to rapid coordination among different actors, both behind the scenes and on public stages, it was possible to orchestrate effective cyberdefense measures to fend off serious harm to the nation's critical infrastructure.

These incidents demonstrate the importance of information sharing and coordinated action to enable swift, reasoned, and competent decision-making in response to threats—and not only during times of war. Cybersecurity requires that both known and unknown threats are identified on an ongoing basis and that responses can be mobilized quickly to contain and neutralize them.

Cybersecurity, unfortunately, is a wicked problem that won't be resolved anytime soon. The challenge is fundamental and connected to a kind of "birth defect" of the Internet. Simply put, the inventors of the Internet didn't anticipate that it would become the technical backbone of a globally interconnected society, used to store everything from personal information to corporate secrets and national assets. That meant they didn't see the need to design it with cybersecurity requirements in mind. The underlying systems suffer structurally from technical security vulnerabilities—although humans are often the weakest link (believe it or not, the word "password" still ranks among the ten most popular passwords!).

Given that the Internet doesn't have security baked into its DNA, it's been a mission impossible to make it bullet-proof against attacks like the ones carried out by the Russians against Ukraine—or many others, though Russian hackers are both notorious and extremely skilled. As cybersecurity has morphed from a niche issue to one of the top security priorities of the most powerful nations in the world, societies have tried to find pathways to a more secure Internet. The hope that market forces could help address the challenge has gone unrealized, as in the case of so many public good challenges (like clean air or water). And cybersecurity policy hasn't been much help either, as it mostly relied on deterrence through guardrails in the form of criminal law, which is nearly impossible to enforce when attackers are very difficult to identify and often reside in another country.

The challenge is amplified by the complexity of the socio-technological system we call the Internet, with its distributed nature and global reach, interlinking billions of individuals, organizations, and even things such as baby monitors and cars—each potentially creating vulnerabilities that could affect the security of the overall system. It adds up to a nearly insurmountable collective action problem, especially in cases when a rapid response is needed. There's simply no easy answer to the cybersecurity challenge—except perhaps pulling the proverbial plug on the Internet itself, which of course is a non-starter.

Some of the most effective efforts to bolster cybersecurity have not tried to create a coherent national or international legal framework, or a single set of universally accepted guardrails. Rather, they have resorted to the types of networked information sharing and coordination mechanisms highlighted in the Ukraine incident to facilitate the evolution of suitable guardrails through information, experimentation, and mutual learning. Ukraine's CERT—the agency designed to address cybersecurity incidents, threats, and vulnerabilities through information sharing and coordination among private and public sectors—is a case in point.

A first working prototype of such a coordination center was launched in the United States in 1988, when the Morris worm took down 10 percent of the Internet. The original version of CERT was hosted at the US Department of Defense–sponsored Software Engineering Institute at Carnegie Mellon University, with the support of the Defense Advanced Research Projects Agency (DARPA). It was designed to serve as a focal point for the computer security concerns of all Internet users when an incident occurred.[5] In practical terms, anyone who experienced a security problem could call the CERT hotline to understand what happened and figure out how to handle it.[6]

The Morris worm was just the beginning. Cybersecurity incidents—from simple cases of password hacking to more sophisticated attacks, such as distributed denial of service—became more pervasive. CERT's initial approach was reactive, helping users to deal with problems after the fact. But something else was needed to better manage risks before they materialized. Working with partners from industry, government, and academia in response management and coordination, CERT decided to expand its mission and add proactive measures to its scope of activities. It started to disseminate information about threats and vulnerabilities to help users make decisions about how better to protect themselves. It also began to publish its own guardrails in the form of recommended practices to reduce the potential of an attack.

This innovative model proved to be both an instant and lasting success. While the national US-CERT is now a branch of the Department of Homeland Security, the global coordination center remains part of Carnegie Mellon University (CMU), and the two work closely together. Internationally, it inspired and informed the launch of similar coordination centers around the world, with more than fifty countries including Ukraine running their own version of national CERTs at the present time.[7] The CMU Center also serves as an international hub for the sharing of best practices among these organizations and similar programs, setting standards and drafting policies in an ever-changing threat environment. In the parlance of this book, the network of CERTs are in the business of facilitating and promoting adaptive guardrails that bolster decision-making on cyber matters.

This networked approach to building capacity to respond to the increasingly sophisticated cyberattacks has inspired large enterprises, both at the national and international level, to set up in-house cybersecurity teams, some of which also use the CERT acronym. The company-level groups are typically connected to national CERTs and often used as sources to collect information on incidents and as points of contact to share alerts in case of an attack, and best practices to better defend against them.[8]

The thickening, interlinked web of cybersecurity units additionally includes industry-led platforms for information sharing, such as McAfee's Cyber Threat Alliance or Meta's ThreatExchange, and ad hoc technical groups formed in response to emerging threats. These groups bring together experts from companies, anti-virus vendors, domain name registries, and academia to address threats such as worms and botnets. When, in the late aughts, a malware called "Conficker" brought millions of computers under its control and threatened critical infrastructure, for instance, an informal group of cybersecurity experts from these loosely tied networks—later dubbed the Conficker Working Group—came together in what was described as an unprecedented act of coordination and collaboration to enable swift decisions from all parties to block the infected computers from reaching others and causing more harm.[9]

Success stories notwithstanding, the distributed CERT model—connecting many local and international efforts with varying acronyms—isn't perfect. Scholars have criticized the lack of standards for sharing data, which creates a problem of data consistency and reliability across geographies and over time. Others have pointed to lack of attention for privacy risks when these entities share data.[10] These criticisms show that much work still needs to be done at the implementation level.

From the conceptual vantage point of guardrails, however, we submit there's much to be learned from the CERT approach to global governance. It is not an exogenous institution imposed top-down, but deeply embedded in social realities and practices. There is no World Cyberse-curity Agency trying to negotiate a global cybersecurity treaty. Instead, the guardrail model combines several design principles of the solution space discussed in chapter 6, including keeping guardrails rooted in the social by bringing together diverse societal actors across the public and private sectors in a distributed manner.[11]

The guidance, best practices, and other resources that emerge from these collaborative dynamics channeled by CERT, in turn, are intended to empower individuals to make better cybersecurity decisions—whether to prevent or respond to specific threats or incidents. While most of the decisions and actions are ultimately taken across the distrib-uted nodes of the network, the guardrails weave these interventions together toward a coordinated approach to cyber resilience as a shared societal objective. The CERT approach is also emblematic of learning. From the Morris worm to the war in Ukraine, CERTs have learned from new threats and, above all, from each other. The learned information is shared widely and quickly, as the Neuberger briefing illustrates.

Taken together, the design principles that motivate the CERT model offer a source of inspiration. They show how adaptive and learning ap-proaches can create rough alignment among a set of diverse actors worldwide, and enable rapid information sharing to support distributed yet coordinated decision-making in response to the global challenges of our time. Following these principles can succeed beyond the online world, as the following case illustrates.

Guardrailing Flows

"West Africa: Ghana and Burkina Faso Discuss Energy Crisis," read the headline of an article published in March 1998 on the AllAfrica news portal. It offered cursory coverage of a meeting between high-ranking government officials from the two neighboring countries.[12] By all accounts, the unassuming headline underplayed the magnitude of the problem. Water levels in the Volta River had fallen to a new record low, impacting hydroelectric power production and triggering a power shortage in Ghana. It led to a serious dispute between Ghana and

Burkina Faso, which garnered the attention of leading international organizations.

For generations, the Volta River Basin has been a lifeline for millions of people living in Ghana, Burkina Faso, and four other nations, including some of the world's most disadvantaged. Since pre-antiquity, the region's inhabitants have derived benefits from the river and its freshwater ecosystem, including fish, drinking water, irrigation for agriculture, and wood for fires and construction materials such as poles and timbers. Things started to change dramatically in the 1990s, after years of population growth and increased economic activities had led to overexploitation of the river's resources. In addition to these dynamics, climate change put the Volta River Basin in critical condition due to increased temperatures and massive changes in rainfall patterns.

The enormous development challenges across the Volta River Basin had been known for decades, as was the need for a collaborative response to the dramatic threats resulting from climate change. But due to a mix of local politics, national rivalries, and lack of capacity in some of the poorest countries, exactly the opposite happened. Instead of working together to take care of their shared natural resources, some of the neighboring countries entered into a race to maximize their use of those resources. The ecological and socioeconomic consequences for more than 20 million people were disastrous.

But there was at least one upside to the natural disaster of 1998 that led to the emergency diplomatic meeting between Ghana's and Burkina Faso's government officials. It made abundantly clear that *something* needed to change, and quickly. As Ghana's president J. J. Rawlings put it at the meeting, "the old ways of divide and rule must stop. The legacies of the cold war must give way to genuine collaboration."[13] Collaboration yes, but how?

The path toward enhanced cooperation was far from straightforward. In addition to anger and frustration resulting from years of competition over river resources, both countries were burdened by a colonial past with a legacy of French and English governance systems upsetting indigenous structures and resulting in divergent rules on how to manage water resources.[14] Neither country had a single authority in charge of water resource management. Instead, several government agencies used water resources without clear roles, responsibilities, or processes to coordinate among themselves—let alone with agencies in other countries. It was a real mess. Given the lack of coherent national frameworks, coming up with a coordinated transnational approach was a Herculean task.

An international coalition of nongovernmental organizations provided an important impulse to overcome this fragmented approach. They promoted a set of guardrails for the Volta Basin based on a process known as Integrated Water Resources Management (IWRM).[15] This is not a uniform concept: It is subject to different interpretations—a feature from a social and learning perspective. One particularly influential IWRM approach, developed by the Global Water Partnership, is organized around four goals: an approach to water resource management that is holistic, participatory, inclusive, and value-oriented. This framework helped address two of the most pressing challenges in the aftermath of the 1998 disaster: the urgent need for more coordination and for better decision-making.

The IWRM approach offers a model for cooperation with concrete guidance on implementation in the form of a process template, with an emphasis on stakeholder participation, and a "toolbox" of management instruments. It is a manifestation of what in the literature is known as a "multistakeholder model" (in fact, it often features as a case study in this line of work). The framework was not only theoretical. It worked in practice. It enabled coordination among previously siloed actors at the national level in Ghana and Burkina Faso. Even more important, it set the stage for transboundary water cooperation. Embracing the spirit of the framework, and with the support of international and donor organizations, Ghana and Burkina Faso entered a joint declaration in which both countries acknowledged the common environmental and water issues and expressed their willingness to collaborate on integrated management of the shared water resources.

One important milestone in the efforts to improve cooperation was a joint project called PAGEV (Projet d'Amélioration de la Gouvernance de l'Eau dans le bassin de la Volta), which launched a few years after the Ghana energy crisis with the support of the International Union for

Conservation of Nature and the Water Governance Project. PAGEV was designed to create institutional capacity for consultation and coordination on water governance. It helped to put into practice the IWRM approach's multilevel and participatory decision-making processes by involving a broad range of stakeholders, from grassroots committees and villages to national authorities and committees.[16]

In doing so, it changed the course of tens of thousands of people's lives. By bringing together a diverse group of actors from various backgrounds, it unlocked flows of information in all directions that helped decision-makers to make better and more informed choices.[17] It brought together communities that had accumulated, over decades, a broad range of experiences in dealing with scarce resources. By enhancing information diversity, it strengthened decision variability and enabled more iterative and agile decision-making under the rapidly changing environmental circumstances.

The IWRM approach provided Ghana, Burkina Faso, and other Volta River Basin countries with a high-level blueprint for managing water resources in a way that would enhance economic and social welfare equitably and without compromising the sustainability of the ecosystem.[18] As they became more used to cooperation and information exchange, Ghana and Burkina Faso agreed on more and finer-grained guardrails. "The Code of Conduct for Sustainable and Equitable Management of the Water Resources of the Volta Basin" outlined a framework for decision-making and action across areas including environmental flows, integrated strategies, harmonization of laws and policies, good environmental practices, and steps toward a multilateral convention. It also outlined mechanisms for international assistance and conflict resolution in case of conflicts, including diplomatic negotiations.[19]

These guardrails offered the basis for a diverse group of stakeholders to come together, share information and knowledge, and iteratively arrive at difficult decisions in pursuit of a common goal. While not without its flaws, the IWRM approach has become the dominant model for water management around the world today. Over the years, international organizations and independent researchers have assessed the complex multistakeholder approach in the Volta River Basin, drawing nuanced lessons about the critical role of context-aware guardrail systems in peacefully managing a complex challenge in a collaborative manner across boundaries, organizations, and individual stakeholders.

From the perspective of a guardrail solution space, these efforts illustrate again how decisional empowerment, social anchoring, and mutual learning can go hand in hand when dealing with complex and pressing governance challenges. The emphasis on multistakeholder processes helped to socially embed the initiative, connecting various actors affected by the governance challenge. This in turn enabled learning, especially from the decades of experience of various local communities. It offers another real-world illustration of how guardrail design proposed in the previous chapters can help deal with the kind of life-and-death governance challenges that, unfortunately, are expected to only worsen as the climate crisis deepens.

Squaring Circles

When US tech company Yahoo! put the final nail in the coffin of its China business in 2021, no one was surprised. With its core services banned for years and the Beijing office closed since 2015, the decision was largely symbolic.[20] Yahoo! launched in China in 1999, when the company was dominating the early Internet, with a bunch of services including email and instant messaging. From the outset, the business struggled against fast-growing local competitors. Yahoo! executives in the United States recognized the need for a local management team to navigate tricky Chinese waters, and started to build local partnerships. Unlike some other US technology companies at that time, Yahoo! decided early to take a conciliatory approach toward the powerful Chinese government and pledged to self-censor its services in China.

While this led to some headway on the business front, things went south when it was revealed that the company had turned over to the Chinese government the identity of local writer, journalist, and human rights activist Shi Tao. As mentioned earlier, he used a Yahoo! email account to send a message to a pro-democracy website abroad, leaking an official document in which journalists were ordered not to report about an upcoming anniversary of the Tiananmen massacre.

The direct involvement of an American company in the arrest of a Chinese pro-democracy activist created serious backlash in the United States. Executives from Yahoo!'s US headquarters were grilled during hearings of congressional committees.[21] People felt outrage that Yahoo! had violated core American values of fairness and justice for the sake of making money in China. Yahoo! had faced a collision between two very different sets of guardrails: local laws in one of the world's largest and fastest-growing economies, and fundamental rights protected under US and international human rights law. Without any obvious middle ground, the company had to choose which set of rules to play by.

Deeply troubled with the way Yahoo! and other Western firms "resolved" this ethical dilemma, some US politicians thought the best way to get back on track was to superimpose new guardrails. The Global Online Freedom Act (GOFA) was introduced in Congress in 2006.[22] It threatened to prohibit any US business from cooperating with officials in Internet-restricting countries to effect potential censorship of online content. It would have made it impossible for tech companies like Yahoo!, Google, or Facebook to operate in China. Bringing together an unlikely coalition of actors, the bill gained momentum in Congress but triggered skepticism in the world of industry and academia, where it was seen as a case of extremely inflexible guardrails. The bill resembled more an act of politics than an attempt at sound policymaking, and as such it worked well—it turned up the heat in the boardrooms of global tech companies, prompting them to act.

Confronted with the PR disaster and the threat of legislation, a small group of companies met in early 2006 to discuss alternative and more flexible ways to deal with the tricky problem of the clash between Chinese and US laws and the values each set of guardrails represented. One idea was to create an industry code of conduct—a more agile and bottom-up type of guardrails than the proposed new law. The companies agreed that it was worth a shot, and their executives decided to get some help by teaming up with folks from academia and civil society who had been engaged in similar discussions.

Creating an industry-wide set of guardrails was far from a walk in the park. Representatives of fiercely competing companies—who blamed each other for the PR nightmare—suddenly found themselves sitting around a conference table in San Francisco. They were tasked with finding common ground on hard questions related to dealing with some of the most powerful repressive regimes in the world. When and how should companies challenge the application of local guardrails? Under what circumstances would it be better to avoid conflicts by not offering certain products and services? What about transparency and accountability mechanisms? Then the group needed to build trust with longtime critics and human rights activists to get them on board with their answers to these questions.

Against all odds, and after more than two years of intense deliberation, the diverse group of stakeholders agreed on a path forward that led to the launch of what is now known as the Global Network Initiative (GNI).[23] At one level, GNI is a sophisticated set of guardrails that help companies to make difficult choices regarding online privacy and freedom of expression when faced with government pressure to hand over user data, remove content, or restrict information flows. The GNI framework consists of a set of core principles, implementation guidelines, and an independent assessment framework. The guardrail on privacy, for instance, requires that participating companies protect users from government demands inconsistent with internationally recognized laws and standards—which would have prevented Yahoo! landing Shi Tao in prison. While aiming to offer decisional guidance at any given moment, the drafters of the GNI framework also recognized that guardrails need to be adaptive over time: Consequently, the implementation guidelines are subject to periodic reviews and revisions with the explicit aims of learning from actual experience, adjusting to evolving circumstances, and incorporating feedback from diverse stakeholders.

As a matter of practice, the GNI norms for responsible company decision-making require that the company board, senior officials, and other key decision-makers will be fully informed about the guardrails set forth in the GNI framework and the best ways to advance them. In other words, the guardrails are designed to enhance the diversity of information leading up to an executive decision. They require executives to think about the risks and potential harms to users, employees, and other stakeholders—rather than just financial and business considerations—before entering markets in which human rights are compromised. In some cases, this might mean not entering a lucrative market. In others, it might mean exiting it—as Yahoo! did in China. The framework acknowledges that there is no "one size fits all" approach when doing business in challenging business environments, a manifestation of self-restraint.

The dilemmas that triggered the initiative remain critical today, as governments around the globe continue to enact laws that conflict with international human rights. While GNI's success in guiding corporate behavior remains contested, given the mixed track record of many technology companies, insiders familiar with the inner workings of the participating companies confirm that the GNI guardrails have shaped decision-making by corporate executives over the past decade. The GNI has also become a trusted platform for mutual learning among companies, governments, and international organizations that share a commitment to support freedom of expression and privacy rights.[24]

By connecting a diverse group of actors to share experiences, address ethical dilemmas, and discuss open questions—often in near-real-time—the GNI informs decisions that may impact billions of people's lives. Connecting people in a digitally networked world is also the subject of this chapter's final case study.

There's a Page for That

With its roughly 23,000 words and 470 footnotes, the entry on the Beatles is recognized as one of the best articles created by the Wikipedia community, a vibrant and—for outsiders—somewhat hard-to-describe crowd of about 127,000 volunteers who regularly edit pages on the popular online encyclopedia.[25] The making of the article on the best-selling music act of all time even made headlines in the *Wall Street Journal*, albeit for a reason that seemed hardly newsworthy. The *WSJ*'s article was headlined: "Editors Won't Let It Be When It Comes to 'the' or

'The.'"[26] It featured an eight-years-long heated debate among Wikipedia editors over whether the word "the" should be upper- or lowercased when referring to the band mid-sentence. In other words, should it be "the Beatles" or "The Beatles"?

The question is impossible to answer objectively. The Beatles' record companies, biographers, and even the band itself were inconsistent in the spelling of the name. Neither existing evidence nor editorial policies indicated a right or wrong way. Trademark arguments slightly pointed toward uppercase spelling, while lowercase would be more readable. Perhaps because of the lack of a clear answer, the dispute among the editors about "t" versus "T" on the Talk page of the article became so contentious that some Wikipedians were banned from participating in it.

The matter was finally referred to a mediation process, which in turn was informed by a community poll. According to the historic records of the proceedings, ninety-three editors who commented during the process supported "the Beatles," while forty-seven editors were in favor of "The Beatles." This was a surprisingly clear verdict, with 65 percent in favor of the lowercase "t." With some small clarifying tweaks and caveats, the case was closed.[27]

The question of how to spell a word mid-sentence in an online encyclopedia (even of a band like, well, THE Beatles) admittedly sounds like a trivial matter in the grand scheme of things. But the structural issue behind the seemingly silly controversy is a fundamental one. Wikipedia is the world's largest reference website, with more than 58 million articles in more than three hundred languages, and one of the most popular information resources on the web, with more than 1.7 billion unique-device visitors per month.[28] Young people in particular—despite the warnings of teachers, parents, and other adults—use it as the everyday go-to virtual place to gather information for homework, catch up on major events, form political opinions, and prepare for life decisions, small and large.[29]

What makes Wikipedia such a success—and, above all, very different from good old and now out-of-print encyclopedias like Britannica—is the fact that it is written collaboratively by amateurs.[30] Essentially anyone with Internet access can contribute to Wikipedia by adding words, references, or images—unless they are banned for having tried to damage

Wikipedia, or the editing of an article is restricted to prevent disruption or vandalism. Because of this, Wikipedia's breadth is incomparable. Articles are often added or updated within minutes after an event occurs, instead of being on hold until a next edition is printed.

Wikipedia's biggest advantage is also the root cause of its biggest challenge. Because almost everyone can edit articles, irrespective of their qualifications, it is much more vulnerable to misinformation, errors, and debatable content than traditional encyclopedias written by subject-matter experts with formal credentials. But this challenge also contains the seed of its own solution: So many people use Wikipedia all the time, and the threshold to contribute and fix things is so low, that misinformation and errors can be corrected much more quickly than in a top-down editorial model à la Britannica. Wikipedia harnesses the knowledge of many to sort out quality issues over time.

It seems like a kind of magic—but it was clear from the outset that the magic might not happen without guidance and oversight. Within the first few months of Wikipedia's operation in 2001, the question of how to build a *reliable* encyclopedia to which everyone can contribute became the main governance challenge that asked for some sort of guardrails. Wikipedia co-founder Jimbo Wales had already come up with a few bold principles when the website launched. "This community will continue to live and breathe and grow only as long as those of us who participate in it continue to Do The Right Thing," Wales wrote. "Doing The Right Thing takes many forms, but perhaps most central is the preservation of our shared vision for the neutral point of view policy and for a culture of thoughtful, diplomatic honesty."[31]

Building on Wales's ideas from the bottom up, the Wikipedia community has since developed much more detailed guidance—in terms of solution space, a true embodiment of a socially anchored guardrail system. At present, its guardrail system contains a total of more than two hundred pages clustered into groups such as "behavioral guidelines," "content guidelines," "deletion guidelines," "editing guidelines," etc. In the spirit of Wikipedia's approach, these policies and guidelines are not set in stone but continue to evolve and adjust where issues arise. Proposed changes to Wikipedia's policies and processes are often tried out on a temporary basis in a sort of experimental set-up, with a limited scope of application—especially for changes where consensus has not fully formed yet.[32] The combination of relentless community involvement, experimentation, and consensus-oriented learning make Wikipedia a particularly rich case from the perspective of guardrail design we discussed in chapter 6.

A wealth of studies over the last two decades have assessed the reliability of Wikipedia articles, with mixed findings. Perhaps unsurprisingly, given the complexity and breadth of the project, results have often been inconsistent. While Wikipedia's increasing reliability has generally been acknowledged, critics point out that its editing model facilitates systemic biases; the majority of Wikipedia's editors, for instance, are male. Non-neutral editing in the biographies of living people is flagged as another area where Wikipedia is struggling with information quality, despite all the guardrails it has put in place.

The question of whether Wikipedia's quality can *really* match the Britannica of yesteryear is in some ways comparing apples and oranges. The two types of encyclopedia are motivated and guided by very different visions, missions, and principles. No matter what our opinions are on the merits of Wikipedia (full disclosure: we're fans and frequent users), unlike its traditional, commercial counterparts it offers billions of people across the globe an incredible wealth of knowledge with minimal entry barriers and free of costs beyond the fees to obtain Internet access.

Wikipedia is an illuminating case study of the theory and practice of guardrail-making. It empowers everyone with Internet access to contribute information that has the potential to support decisions made by millions of users. We already highlighted social anchoring as one of its key design qualities when it comes to the creation, testing, and adoption of various sorts of guidelines. Wikipedia's guardrails are born out of and administered by its community and evolve based on mutual learnings, considering a shared mission and basic commitment.

Wikipedia is also a treasure trove of self-restraint. Its editorial process has no fewer than ten overlapping types of safeguards, ranging from community-level controls—through the tens of thousands of volunteer editors—to fine-grained editorial panels and processes for dispute resolution, mediation, third-party opinions, and requests for comments and consultations with the wider community, as in the case of the poll about the spelling of "the Beatles." This system of checks-and-balances signals one thing very clearly: No single person is in control of what has become one of the most popular information sources on the Internet. Even Jimbo Wales, who as co-founder was empowered to override the outcomes of this elaborate editorial oversight process, publicly waived his right and vowed to be himself bound in the event of a ruling of an arbitration committee.[33]

If it were nothing else, Wikipedia is a formidable complex guardrail system that embraces and puts into practice several of the principles and design qualities proposed in this book.

From Principles to Practice

The four stories in this chapter have each featured remarkable governance organizations that bring together distinct communities under varying operational models. In their different ways, they have developed and deployed a variety of flexible guardrails to address hard governance challenges of our time. Taken together, we hope they illustrate that the challenge of putting into practice seemingly abstract design principles can find inspiration in diverse lived experiences with a wide variety of guardrails.

The case studies also exemplify how the key design principles we laid out in chapter 6 can be employed to search the solution space. Confronted with diverse real-world governance problems—making the Internet more secure, allocating scarce resources peacefully, conducting business in countries with repressive regimes, or iteratively writing a reliable encyclopedia—people made guardrails that could empower individuals and communities to make better decisions. They came in different forms and shapes, including agreements and operating principles (Volta River), industry standards and frameworks (GNI), operational manuals, recommendations, and best practices (CERT), and community-driven policies and guidelines (Wikipedia).

We observed various ways to anchor guardrails socially by developing them collaboratively among heterogeneous and sometimes unlikely groups of partners: government officials, indigenous communities, business stakeholders, and international nonprofits (Volta River); industry competitors, human rights activists, and investors (GNI); security experts, vendors, IT professionals, and government officials (CERT); and experts and amateur enthusiasts (Wikipedia). In each case these "norm entrepreneurs" committed to develop guardrails with the shared objective of supporting good decision-making.[34]

Last, in all the examples, guardrails were designed in ways that enable the exchange of information and keep open opportunities for learning from each other. By striking a careful balance between offering concrete decision guidance and leaving open enough space for adjustment, they allow for both specific "tweaks" and modifications across time and contexts, and for longer-term evolution in light of changing circumstances, practical experiences, and better knowledge. Along similar lines, mechanisms of self-restraint not only shield against power misuses, but can be understood as an acknowledgment that guardrails are not absolute, but open to change.

Taken together, the wealth of models, mechanisms, and techniques in just these four stories—many more, of course, could be added—suggests that operationalizing the design principles for guardrails proposed in this book (as well as the inspiration provided by often overlooked guardrail qualities such as information diversity and decisional reversibility) is not only possible but has already been done with creativity and dedication. As we seek to create novel governance schemes that help us to address the challenges ahead, our lack of imagination might be the main barrier we need to overcome. After all, guardrails are made, not found.

This chapter has illustrated the various roles organizations and their communities can play when designing, implementing, and operating flexible guardrails. The guiding question of the next chapter is what role technology could and should play as we create guardrails for the future.

9

MACHINES

Crystal Marie and Eskias McDaniels never anticipated ending up in the news when they decided to move from Los Angeles to Charlotte, North Carolina. Their plan was simple: Take out a mortgage to buy a nice house at a reasonable price in a great neighborhood with a nearby playground for their young son.

The McDaniels were good people; they kept promises, valued honesty. More to the point—given that nowadays what matters for getting a mortgage is no longer subjective human trust, but hard data—they both had reputable jobs, each earning six-figure salaries, and very good credit scores. And indeed, when they applied for a mortgage, prequalifying was a walk in the park.[1] They came with all the credentials that should make the purchase of a home as hassle-free as such a transaction can be.

But just a few days before movers were scheduled to pick up the household in LA, the trouble started. Crystal Marie and Eskias received an entirely unexpected phone call from the assigned loan officer at their California-based mortgage company. Bad news. When the officer forwarded the application internally to the underwriting department, it was denied. The algorithm the company used to make a final decision on whether to offer the mortgage had deemed the McDaniels to be too risky. Had there been some kind of technical glitch? The officer checked the details and forwarded the application again, and again—more than a dozen times—and each time the computer said no.

The problem? As we saw in chapter 4, it is not always easy to figure out exactly why an algorithm is making the decisions it does. But the most likely explanation boiled down to the simple fact that the McDaniels family is Black.[2]

What the McDaniels experienced is a case of mortgage lending discrimination. And they are not alone. A recent study of mortgage approval algorithms found that lenders were 80 percent more likely to deny Black applicants than white applicants with similar financial characteristics. The data also showed that Latino, Native American, and Asia Pacific Islander applicants were similarly vastly more likely to be rejected than white people.

This bias in assessing mortgages has far-reaching implications. Home ownership is linked to better educational trajectories in children, higher civic engagement rates, better healthcare outcomes, and lower crime rates in communities. The data could not be clearer: Keeping home ownership rates low among minority households contributes to the shocking racial wealth gaps in the United States.

In this and many similar cases, the media were quick to place all the blame on the machine. The algorithms we have put in charge make bad decisions, they said. If only we reverted to human decisions, it would be fine. But, as should be obvious by now, it is not that simple. Earlier we made the case that what type of guardrail mechanism we deploy—conventional or technical—matters less than what qualities these guardrails incorporate. We must resist the temptation to think of technology as a shortcut that can avoid the need to grapple with hard issues in designing good guardrails. But that leaves another question: Assuming we get the design principles right, what place should technology occupy in society's guardrail toolbox?

This brings us to a second temptation. If good guardrails are deeply social, rather than purely technical, we could be enticed to relegate technology to an issue of implementation—a conceptual afterthought, playing only a supporting role after the social dynamics have run their course. That too, though, would be wrong. Technology is not something that happens outside social processes—it does not suddenly drop from the sky; its design is the result of social interactions. We have to *include* crafting and using technological tools among the factors we consider when creating guardrails. The goal is, of course, to develop technological tools that accept and embrace the socially anchored position that guard-rails occupy and play their part to facilitate that.

To understand the subtleties of what's at play when seeking to integrate technology into guardrail structures, we'll first look at a fascinating guardrail initiative set up some two decades ago before returning to our present day's mortgage lending problem. By examining two seemingly unrelated application areas, we hope to distill some cross-cutting insights about the role of technology as we set out to create guardrails for the future.

Creating a Commons

Copyright law gives creators of art, literature, and music exclusive control over who can use their works, and how. But what if they don't want that control? What if, instead, they want everyone to be able to use their work? For that the work needs to become part of the "public domain." This happens automatically when copyright restrictions expire, after a defined period that differs across jurisdictions and types of work. But deliberately choosing to put your work in the public domain earlier is surprisingly hard.

The late singer-songwriter Woody Guthrie offers a case in point. Guthrie became a towering figure in American folk music, writing more than a thousand songs and ballads in which he expressed some of America's biggest problems, hopes, and fears in the lead-up to and aftermath of World War II. He inspired generations of both musicians and political activists, with much of his work focused on American socialism and anti-fascism. Guthrie believed in the power of music to affect politics, often performing with a guitar that bore the label "This machine kills fascists." He wanted others to perform his songs, and spread his ideas, as widely as possible.

Guthrie made his feelings clear when listeners to his radio show in LA started to request the words to his recordings. He mailed a small songbook to his fans with the following statement printed on it: *"This song is Copyrighted in U.S., under Seal of Copyright #154085, for a period of 28 years, and anybody caught singin' it without our permission, will be mighty good friends of ourn, cause we don't give a dern. Publish it. Write it. Sing it. Swing to it. Yodel it. We wrote it, that's all we wanted to do."*[3]

Try as he might, however, Woody could not easily free his music from the legal reach of copyright. His most famous song, "This Land Is Your Land"—written in 1940, and still one of the most famous folk songs in the United States—has kept coming up in copyright disputes even decades after his death. For instance, during the 2004 presidential election campaign a company called JibJab used the song in a parody video mocking the candidates, George Bush and John Kerry. The video went viral and the company was taken to court by a business organization that claimed to be the copyright owner of the song. To try to avoid a similar fate, a rock band went to court in 2016 to get a judicial declaration that the song is free from copyright and in the public domain.[4]

In theory, copyright law gives every creator the right to control their creative works. This means, for instance, that making copies of an original work is often prohibited, unless the copyright holder grants us permission to do so. Copyright permits some flexibility in *how* exactly these rights are exercised. As Woody Guthrie tried to do, copyright holders can decide to give broad permissions on how their work can be used by others. They can choose to reserve some of the rights they are given by default, and sign away others. The problem is that, historically, there hasn't been an easy and efficient way to do this and communicate it to the public.

Copyright law is an intricate web of guardrails that emerged over hundreds of years. Little about it is intuitive. To navigate this tricky terrain, artists in the pre-Internet age who wanted to share their creations more widely often had to pay for the advice of a specialized lawyer. Determining the scope of copyright protection, defining the permissible uses, and coming up with the legal language to capture the creator's choices could be a costly exercise in terms of money, time, and energy.

The costs accumulated not only on the part of the creators willing to share their works, but on others wishing to use them. Copyright law requires—with some exceptions, such as fair use—that anyone who wants to use a work needs to ask the copyright holder. The transaction costs involved in making and granting such requests created significant barriers to content sharing even if the parties were in theory perfectly aligned. The net result of these dynamics was not only disappointing at the individual level. It was also bad for society at large. Hindering creators from governing their own work according to their preferences limited the collective reservoir of creative content from which others could draw—a reservoir that is at the core of human flourishing, collective learning, and societal development.

Then along came the Internet and the World Wide Web, which offered unprecedented opportunities for sharing materials online at costs close to zero. Never in the history of humankind has it been easier for artists, educators, researchers, and others to share their work, with global reach. Many of today's most powerful platforms—from YouTube to Meta to TikTok—rely heavily on content created by users like you and me. But the advent of this global network amplified some dilemmas of copyright law. Almost everything on the Internet—even reading a text—involves making copies, which likely triggers copyright law one way or another. And as digital technologies made it easier for people to share copyrighted works illegally, threatening business models based on exclusive rights to content, large corporations successfully lobbied for copyright protections to be tightened up. Digital tools enabled new, contract-like agreements to establish additional controls over the flow of information—think about terms of service, or click-wrap licenses—as well as new technical measures to prevent people from accessing and copying content.

The result was a power struggle between the promise of a more robust public domain and more legal and technical guardrails to control content. But in this struggle, which was briefly foreshadowed in chapter 7 in the context of the DMCA, a new space opened up for creators and users to reimagine how digital technology could be leveraged to make the existing copyright system more flexible. What if a novel type of platform could be built to strengthen the public domain by dramatically lowering the transaction costs involved in licensing? The main protagonist in addressing this question was cyberlaw professor extraordinaire Lawrence Lessig, who we met earlier in this book.

Lessig wanted to lower the effort needed to put works into the public domain.[5] So he and his collaborators developed a web application that helped people to make informed licensing decisions and communicate their choices to the world at minimal cost. Technically, the application not only offers a set of standard licenses to choose from, but also automatically translates the selected license into a machine-readable form that helps search engines and other apps to identify the work by its terms of use. Using a language that machines can understand makes it easy for other Internet users to find such licensed materials online.[6] For instance, a click on "Tools" in the Google images search bar allows one to sort the search results according to different usage rights. Similarly, the machine-readable license allows YouTube users to locate videos that are licensed for easy reuse.

The result was a nifty technical solution that retrofits flexible but unwieldy copyright law with a simple and easy to use interface. And it worked. It has decreased the effort needed for creators to contribute their works to the public domain and users wanting to use them. Because it does the job so well, and because it is the outwardly visible interface of the system, it's easy to mistake the web application for the idea itself—and hence to see this as an example for a shift from social to technical guardrails. But that would be like listening to a piece of music composed for a new instrument, and thinking that the instrument is responsible for the music—ignoring the input of the composer.

The real innovation wasn't technical. The first step was to reduce the complexity of licensing. Recall that copyright law is very flexible: It gives creators wide latitude in how they craft their licenses. But too much flexibility can make it costly to draft licenses that reflect exactly what a creator wants. The key is to come up with the right set of possible options that can then be reflected in standardized licensing agreements. Lessig and his team focused on just a few salient dimensions: whether a work can be adapted and changed; whether it can be used in derivative works, and also for commercial purposes; and whether the creator wants to be attributed as such. In doing so, they took the universe of conceivable license agreements down to just eight options initially. They knew this would not please everybody. But, they reckoned, it would cover most of the standard cases of creators wanting their works to become freely accessible. Taking a page from the book of Steve Jobs, they did not want to satisfy all, but perfect the setup for their core audience.

Without this conceptual focus on what matters for most, the technical application would not have been possible. The foundation of the solution was carefully shaping the guardrails expressed in the standard licensing terms. The technical tool simply built on it by making it fast and easy to select from among the license options.

But that alone was not enough. Lessig realized that for the idea to take off, it would require further social anchorage. So he teamed up with Harvard students and fellows to launch a nonprofit organization called Creative Commons. Its task was to create and maintain a global community of users and supporters of the new licensing options that would turn Creative Commons from a legal and technical solution into a social movement. It worked extremely well. When Creative Commons announced its service in late 2002, various organizations and influencers quickly pledged support.[7] Within a year, the organization counted one million linkbacks to the novel licenses; two years later it was five million. Each linkback could contain many different creations, as in the case of websites such as Wikipedia, which uses Creative Commons licenses.[8]

As much as Creative Commons leveraged the idea of guardrails and the power of networked technology, it also created a *social space* for people from diverse backgrounds and ideologies to make common cause on issues such as free culture, open educational content, open data, and copyright reform. Creative Commons developed into a global phenomenon—a vibrant community of creators, activists, scholars, librarians, academics, and users with diverse interests, united in their efforts to build a more robust public domain.[9] It has more than a hundred affiliated organizations around the world, and one estimate in 2019 put the number of CC-licensed works online at nearly two billion.[10]

Creative Commons licenses have evolved over the last couple of decades, from version 1.0 to the current version 4.0. The newer versions resulted from extensive discussions with stakeholders—including from the Majority World—and listening to a wide variety of feedback, as well as looking at data on what kind of licenses seemed most attractive for users. Hence, Creative Commons made additional licensing options available and adjusted some existing terms. For instance, after realizing that well over 90 percent of CC users wanted their works to be attributed to them, attribution became a standard feature in version 2.0.[11] Meanwhile, version 4.0 added a new option to drop attribution from adaptations of a work, reflecting authors' concern that they would be associated with adaptations that they can't control.[12]

Also, some CC licensing terms were clarified based on feedback from users that they were too ambiguous. In addition, as Creative Commons became a global movement, licenses were also changed to address moral rights more explicitly—an especially strong concern in Europe. But all this iterative learning that's reflected in the evolution of licenses has not diluted or distracted Creative Commons from its original goals— including to keep things simple. Case in point: Version 4.0 aims to capture most cases with only six different license types, further narrowing the initial focus rather than seeing licensing options mushroom over time.

Before any new version was issued, drafts were circulated and debated. Version 4.0 emerged after public discussion of four drafts, each incorporating feedback and responding to critiques of the previous draft. Creative Commons has employed technical tools to facilitate social interaction among stakeholders: Meetings were held online, and blogs and discussions are stored in a Creative Commons wiki, along with a comprehensive repository of how the licenses evolved, with comparisons of their various elements. The wiki also includes a growing library of case studies of how Creative Commons licensing has been used in a wide spectrum of contexts and circumstances around the world, underscoring how this digital tool helps individual creators to make licensing decisions that are linked to larger societal debates about the public domain. Creative Commons has, in effect, become a governance system—a set of guardrails that includes processes and institutions, as well as technical tools.

Despite its many successes, Creative Commons hasn't been able to address all the broader challenges of building the public domain.[13] Its reliance on copyright law, for instance, has been criticized by advocates of information freedom who want to limit the legal enclosure and ever-expanding commodification of creative works. And while it has offered

some counterbalance to the overwhelming lobbying power of commercial interests, it has still not been able to stop the expansion of intellectual
property rights over time, and hasn't propelled fundamental copyright
law reform projects that might carry the promise of a new social com-
promise between copyright owners and users of works.[14]

From another perspective, however, these criticisms can be seen as
Creative Commons taking a pragmatic approach that displayed remarkable self-restraint—deliberately abstaining from attempting to reform
the copyright system as a whole, as some critics implored them to do.
As we have seen, it also embodies the design principles we enumerated
earlier: empowering individuals by making it easier for creators to make
licensing choices; anchoring their efforts in social processes; and ensuring learning at all levels—from the creators, who can peruse material
such as case studies and FAQs to help them in their decisions, to the
Creative Commons community as they actively sought and used feedback to inform revisions of their standard licenses.

What interests us for the purpose of this chapter in particular is how
Creative Commons approached technical tools. It did not see these
tools as negating traditional forms of guardrails. But neither did it relegate such tools to a conceptual afterthought—rather, the opposite. In
every direction and at every level, Creative Commons actively employed technical tools not only to facilitate their mission, but also to
bolster their guardrails' design principles. They used online collaboration tools to co-create important documents and prepare draft revisions, and online communication tools to run discussion forums and
involve a wide stakeholder community. They operated web repositories,
blogs, and social media to reach out to their constituencies and provide
them with suitable information. And they developed an Internet infrastructure, from the web app to the standard licensing markup codes, to
turn human-readable licenses into machine-readable ones that could be,
for instance, easily discoverable for search engines. Technology played
an integral and facilitating part within the system of social guardrails
that we call Creative Commons.

There's little doubt that Woody Guthrie would have been a fan of
Creative Commons, as a platform and movement. It illustrates the kind

of opportunity space that can be shaped when technological affordances are strategically embedded in an institutional and human context to open novel avenues for exploration and collaboration in support of human agency. With a normative view on technology, though, Creative Commons is more than an illustration; it can quite usefully be employed as a conceptual template for how to embed technology in guard-rail processes. With this in mind, let's return to the thorny problem of lending discrimination introduced at the beginning of this chapter.

It's the Machine—or Is It?

People have been lending money to others for ages. For borrowers and lenders alike, it has always been both a source of power and an exposure to risk. It was not only the merchants in Venice, as Shakespeare told us, who required promises from personal guarantors to pay in case of default. Banks, meanwhile, managed risk by spreading it across multiple parties. But until well into the twentieth century, the decision of whether to grant a loan was still made in significant part based on personal connections and subjective criteria.

The result was, unsurprisingly, biased. Bank managers offered loans to those they trusted, who—it turns out—were socioeconomically much like them. The mortgage and loan industry was perpetuating existing hierarchies and inequalities in society, hardening widespread discrimination.

After World War II, greater demand for credit especially in the United States and Europe required faster, more accurate, and fairer decision-making than human loan officers were able to manage. The solution was to speed up and objectify loan decisions through a more scientific and standardized "scorecard system." In contrast to the loan officer's spotty and often-biased assessment of applicants' past behavior and likely future performance, the new system promised a fast, objective, color-blind, and nondiscriminatory way to guide loan decisions. It was based on an analysis of eight to twelve variables with some predictive value, resulting in a single score for each applicant.[15] Within a decade, multiple such scorecard models had entered the mass market and become more generic. Crucially, the decision algorithms started to tap into the steady flows of data from national credit bureaus, which enabled lenders to assess credit risks at a much more granular level and without any prior experience with a particular customer.

Seeing that this approach seemed able, encouragingly, to broaden access to mortgages for minorities and underserved communities, in the 1960s and 1970s the US government passed laws prohibiting discriminatory loan assessments. The Fair Housing Act (1968) and the Equal Credit Opportunity Act (1974) are examples of such anti-discrimination laws. They were intended to outlaw exactly the type of bias we saw Crystal Marie and Eskias McDaniels experience in the story that opened this chapter.[16]

In parallel, credit scoring evolved. The first general credit bureau risk score was introduced in 1989 and is widely known as the FICO score—still, today, the standard measure of consumer risk in the United States. Developed initially for credit marketing and account approval, FICO scores made an entry into mortgage lending half a decade later when Freddie Mac and Fannie Mae—two powerful home mortgage companies created by the federal government to promote homeownership in the United States—established guardrails requiring the use of the FICO system.[17]

FICO scores improved many aspects of the decision-making process in the financial industry.[18] Following the law, they also did not use race or gender as input variables. But, unfortunately, that did not eliminate discrimination. In fact, reliance on FICO scores scaled up problems inherent in this type of credit scoring.[19] For instance, for decades, it privileged those living in the "right" zip codes, further ossifying geographic segregation of American cities. In the versions currently used by most lenders, FICO scores reward traditional credit—to which people of color have less access than white individuals. It ignores factors like on-time payments for rent, cell phone bills, and utilities, but penalizes those who fall behind. It lowers the score for medical debt even if it has been paid. It does not capture what would count as responsible financial behavior in under-resourced communities. The list goes on.[20]

In short, while the algorithm itself cannot and does not use race or other prohibited classifications as input, the model is regarded as unfair and biased against minorities and underserved borrowers. Unsurprisingly, a meta-analysis of studies examining discrimination in housing and mortgage lending shows that racial gaps in loan denial declined only slightly between 1976 and 2016, and gaps in mortgage costs did not change at all over the course of roughly forty years.[21]

It's as if the lending industry has been built on discriminatory decision-making that it can't get rid of, even if it tries. Researchers have analyzed potential flaws in the methodology and offered suggestions for change.[22] The company behind FICO released updated versions of the algorithms that address at least some of the issues. Technical entrepreneurs tout alternative credit scoring systems that are supposedly less prone to discrimination.[23] But as valuable as these efforts are, they do not address the root problem: the naïve belief that a technical tool—calculated scorecards—could act as a guardrail to individual lender decision-making that solves a deeply social problem.

Simple credit scoring systems use a limited number of variables, some of which turn out to be proxies for ethnicity. In ways that reflect centuries of discrimination and marginalization, people of color often have their ethnicity reflected in the places they live, the schools and universities they attend, even the products they buy. Credit scoring can be utterly devoid of using ethnicity directly as an input variable, and still be shockingly discriminatory. The culprit isn't simply technology. Whether we like to admit it or not, racial discrimination is systemic and deeply embedded in the social reality of America. Much like Creative Commons, credit scoring is a system of guardrails in which social processes, institutions, and technical tools interact with each other—and this can sometimes happen in challenging and unexpected ways. Choose a few socio-demographic variables to assess creditworthiness, and you end up incorporating and perpetuating racial bias. To effectively counter such discrimination requires a more comprehensive set of guardrails than any single technology can offer.

As technology has proved unable to "fix" discriminatory decision-making in money lending, calls have grown for stronger and more targeted enforcement of existing legal rules—including from high-ranking government officials in the responsible agencies.[24] Early in his term, President Joe Biden took executive action to strengthen anti-discrimination housing policies.[25] US lawmakers have also looked for ways to remove barriers to accessing financial services that are known to be linked to race and ethnicity.[26] This return to social guardrails makes much sense. Everything we know about racial, ethnic, and gender discrimination tells us that it is a social problem that requires a more comprehensive system of guardrails to solve, rather than a technical Band-Aid. Creative Commons understood this—that's why they focused on conceptual clarity and paired their technical implementation with a learning institutional framework, all thanks to technology deeply anchored in social structures.

This does not deny technology a significant role—quite the contrary. By seeing technical tools as a powerful way to support social guardrails, but not as a panacea to replace them, we are not raising unrealistic expectations. Instead we are positioning technology as one, albeit important, piece in the puzzle of a comprehensive solution.

Applying the Creative Commons template normatively to the money lending space suggests that only when we understand the deep roots of the problem in social mechanisms and structures can we hope to devise a framework of social guardrails to address the issue of discriminatory lending decisions. Creative Commons used technology to facilitate and empower precisely the social guardrail systems its creators identified as necessary. A closer look at algorithmic bias reveals how this could be done to improve money lending decisions, and much more.

Algorithmic Bias Revisited

Algorithmic bias describes a situation in which systemic and repeatable errors result in outputs that benefit or disadvantage certain individuals or groups more than others without justified reasons for the unequal impact. Bias is inherently human and, of course, existed in society long before the rise of digital technology—but ubiquitous personal data and unprecedented processing power has put the problem on steroids. With conventional algorithms, bias was hard coded—and thus often deliberate and, at least in principle, transparent. Modern algorithms, however, as we explained in chapter 4, are frequently the result of machine learning from vast amounts of training data. This algorithmic bias mirrors bias already present in the training data, or results from a misconfiguration or misapplication of machine learning tools, or both. Its stealth makes it extremely hard to detect.

The potential danger of algorithmic bias runs deep and far. Headlines focus on easily understandable cases, from school admissions to job hiring to mortgage applications, as with the McDaniels. But a growing body of empirical evidence finds significant prejudices based on factors such as gender, race, ethnicity, and religion in areas as diverse as search engine results, social media, election outcomes, natural language processing, facial recognition software, risk assessment tools in the criminal justice system, and healthcare tools. As these technical systems profoundly affect the lives of millions of people, overcoming algorithmic bias is absolutely crucial.

It is also fundamentally challenging—both to identify the concrete nature of the bias in any particular algorithmic setting and to select appropriate measures to redress it. While the selection of learning methods is also scrutinized, the initial focus is on the choice of training data. It may be incorrectly collected, wrongly filtered and constrained, or perhaps resting on erroneous human decisions, but it represents at some level a reflection of reality, especially social reality. Identifying problems in the data is less a purely technical task than a cognitive, conceptual, and social one. It needs human thinking and social deliberation.

The same is true for remedying algorithmic bias once the cause has been identified. Training data can be amended, by injecting data from a different source, or by deliberately altering them to be "unbiased." At one level, this is a technical task of data handling and manipulation. But it entails choices about goals and constraints, and necessitates that we realize the conceptual consequences of such choices. The important decisions involve seeing what the data reflect and understanding how they are cross-linked.

We find ourselves in need of robust *social* guardrails on how to design and implement algorithms that learn from data: from what data are collected and how they relate to the phenomenon we want to capture, and features we want to avoid, to how data are understood, cleaned, constrained (what data points are omitted), and prepared for machine learning, to how we test the validity of the algorithm that results. Much like the shrinkage of the intellectual space to share creative works that was the root problem Creative Commons chose to address, the biased algorithms reflect a bigger, deeper, and more systemic issue that necessitates a broader social response to address it. Applying the Creative Commons template, technology could—if employed well—be an integral element of a comprehensive solution. Here is how.

Technologies of Redress

Because a data-trained AI system is a black box, it is unclear at the outset whether its decisions are biased or not. To know, we need to peek inside. But we can't easily do that directly. This is where technical tools come into play. They can help us explain the behavior of AI systems, even without fully pushing aside the veil of ignorance about the systems' exact inner workings. Even though the systems remain "black boxes," we can still get sufficient insight into them to grasp whether they are likely biased or not.

Such technical tools afford us the ability to evaluate and test data-trained algorithms. It's the algorithmic-age equivalent to the microscope or the telescope—it lets us "see" things we otherwise would not see. And it turns out that we can use these tools not just to diagnose the problem, but also to help remedy it, by reducing or eliminating some of the biases we identify.

Over the past few years, computer scientists have developed technical strategies to achieve these feats. Some focus on "fair representation" in the training data. Others use tools from machine learning to "regularize" the process of model building by assigning a penalty to undesirable model attributes.[27] Taking this a step further, a team at the University of Oxford suggested the use of "counterfactuals" to help explain the inner workings of the black box.[28] By exploring what changes in input data would lead to different outcomes, we can start to comprehend the path of action we should take, giving us agency and control without needing to understand the inner workings of the system. This is well aligned with our design principles of individual empowerment and learning. Several large software and cloud computing providers, such as Microsoft, Google, and AWS (Amazon's cloud computing subsidiary), have introduced tools that incorporate this approach.

Importantly, though, these tools can be used only once we choose a desired outcome, which brings us back to questions of goals and aims, and the need for debate and social anchorage. It forces us to pick the policy dimensions we care about. We may want to eliminate all bias—that is, all differences between analytical results and factual reality—in comprehensive training sets, but in practice that's impossible. What is feasible is to focus on eliminating specific dimensions of bias, say ethnicity or gender. Which dimensions we select is a normative question that precedes the use of technical tools.

One approach is to generate synthetic data that captures accurately some selected dimensions in the actual training data, but carefully reweights others to undo specific biases—or perhaps introduce a bias that's desired.[29] The AI system is then trained on the synthetic data and never exposed to the possibly sensitive actual training data. Some industry sources suggest that by the late 2020s, more than half of training data sets will be based on such synthetic data generation.[30]

Still other technical tools are becoming available, offering new ways to help identify or reduce a particular bias. But they will all need to support, rather than try to replace, a system of social guardrails that normatively define what decisional deformations we find unacceptable. Applying the example of Creative Commons, we need to settle on appropriate guardrails to lessen certain biases and develop the technical tools to make it happen—then frequently evaluate whether the tools need adjusting to avoid unintended consequences. With this strategy, technical tools become deeply embedded in the social processes and turn into integral elements of the comprehensive system of guardrails we need.

The cases of Creative Commons and algorithmic bias together show that the key to defining the role of technology is less the choice of a particular technical tool or its concrete application and closer to how it is *embedded* in the overall guardrail processes and structures. This task is, rightly, attracting increasingly wide attention.

Positioning Technology

Linking the use of technical tools with social structures and mechanisms necessitates a sharp understanding of what tools can and cannot achieve. It requires a clear definition of the interface between technology and social structures, including resolving questions of agency and control. It also entails a sufficiently defined focus for technical tools to deliver what is expected from them. This means tools must be well understood and evaluated as fit for purpose. And we must equally expect a clarity of design and process from the social structures that make up the system of guardrails, as well as a functioning interface. More challenging but also potentially more useful would be socio-technical setups that are capable of iteration, adaption, and learning—so that the system of guardrails not only helps individual decision-makers to improve but also the system itself to evolve and progress as experience accrues and contexts become clearer.

These necessities have had process and systems approaches penetrate into computer science as well as practical software and hardware design, prompting a shift in attention from purely technical issues to ones more at the interface of the social and the technical. Some of these approaches are comparatively conventional, utilizing process standardization; others are more innovative, even actively reaching out to experts in science and technology. But regardless of their ambition and originality, the various approaches share an open acknowledgment of the need to understand and craft technology's role within a larger social system and that system's specific qualities and needs.

We see examples of such a more socio-technical approach already in the context of identifying and combating discriminatory bias in AI. The influential US National Institute of Standards and Technology (NIST), for instance, released a road map toward a standard for identifying, understanding, managing, and reducing bias. It offers a broad overview of the different sources of bias—from systemic and human to statistical and computational—and maps out both procedural and practical guidance on how to deal with the issue across the entire life cycle of AI, from design and development to deployment. The NIST report highlights human factors, including societal and historical biases within organizations, as well as challenges related to implementing a "human-in-the-loop" approach. NIST not only offers a helpful framework to identify bias, but also lists tools and techniques that are available to address the different types of bias, emphasizing a holistic, socio-technical approach.[31]

Leading tech companies similarly have created guidelines, checklists, and frameworks to test for and reduce bias in AI systems. Some have entered partnerships with other stakeholders to develop collaborative platforms to help customers identify and mitigate unfairness in AI systems. One example, provided by a professional service firm in collaboration with a large tech vendor, is an interactive web-based assessment tool that creates risk profiles and risk scores of AI systems to catch possible fairness issues with machine learning models along the system's life cycle.[32] Initial use cases include tests with mortgage adjudication data to improve the fairness of loan decisions by reducing the kind of bias that afflicted the McDaniels.[33]

Engineers have teamed up with ethicists and social scientists to establish organizations that help others tackle the social dimension of embedding technology within a workable and effective guardrail system. For instance, the Algorithmic Justice League was founded by Ghanaian-American-Canadian computer scientist and digital activist Joy Buolamwini, whose research at MIT Media Lab uncovered racial and gender bias in popular AI systems. It challenges bias in decision-making software and highlights the social implications of AI, including the threats it poses to civil rights and democracy, through activities such as research, artwork, storytelling, and advocacy to raise public awareness, shape policies, and give voice to affected individuals and communities.[34] AI4ALL is another well-respected nonprofit organization, which seeks to address the bias problem in AI by developing a diverse and inclusive pipeline of

talent through education and mentorship in underrepresented communities.[35] These and related efforts are indicative of the solution—or,
perhaps better, *opportunity*—space in front of us.

This opportunity space is enlarged and improved as engineers learn
more about social structures, and those on the social side—organizers,
policymakers, social science experts, the media, even the public at
large—start to understand more about the role, functioning, and limitations of technical tools. In doing so, we (re)discover that we are all craf-
ters and guardians of guardrails all the time. Knowing more is often
empowering, conceptually as well as practically.

Of course, we are only in the early stages of this shift toward a more
thoughtful and deliberate embedding of technical tools in a system of
social guardrails. More research is necessary: the understanding of dependencies and causalities, the development of better processes, the
establishment of suitable institutions, and the incorporation of appropriate practices in organizational and societal culture. But we have no
doubt that progress is possible if we want—and that it is what we need.

At a time when the digital frontier advances so dramatically, the biggest challenge ahead remains both conceptual and deeply practical. As
we seek to embrace and incorporate increasingly powerful technical
instruments such as AI to make future guardrails more efficient and
robust, it is essential to clearly demark the limits of what we can expect
from these tools—and what not. Like when designing guardrails themselves, we need to integrate technical tools with self-restraint in mind.
As the stories in this chapter have illustrated, technology can help in
myriad ways to shape and operate guardrails, as long as we avoid "boil-
ing the ocean" with it and remain crystal clear and specific about exactly
what problem we aim to solve.

The Sum of It All

Years ago, on the island of Kalimantan, the government suggested land
use that disregarded the traditional rights and practices of local communities. Negotiations between the government and these local communities ensued. But as local communities defined their geographic

boundaries according to their traditional knowledge, they could not delineate their territory using longitude and latitude on a Western Cartesian map, and talks stalled.

NGOs then intervened to facilitate discussions, introducing GPS and a geographic information system to translate the communities' traditional knowledge of boundaries into information the government could comprehend and vice versa. By creating common informational ground, this socio-technological intervention ultimately led to better decisions about land use.[36] It's yet another example of how technical tools don't necessarily have to be hugely sophisticated to make a difference—rather, they have to be cleverly positioned within the social system.

In earlier chapters we detailed how technical guardrails produce troubling outcomes when they reflect the wrong qualities, disregarding the fundamental design principles we identified. As we hope this chapter makes clear, this doesn't suggest technical tools are useless in the context of guardrails—quite the opposite. But the technical guardrails must be understood as valuable elements of social systems of guardrails, not as substitutes. In the end, all guardrails are socially constructed, and some benefit greatly from technical tools embedded in them. It is our task to ensure that we utilize the capabilities technical tools offer and organize their interplay, as the final chapter argues, with the other instruments when reimagining guardrails in support of human decision-making for the decades to come.

10

FUTURES

More than three decades ago, writer Neal Stephenson imagined a fully immersive virtual world in his sci-fi novel *Snow Crash*. He called it the Metaverse.[1] Today a good part of the digital industry is banking it's the next big thing. Large tech firms and venture capitalists invested more than $120 billion in the metaverse in the first five months of 2022. Some predict it will generate $5 trillion in value by 2030—which would give it equivalent economic power to Japan, the world's third largest economy.[2] Currently the metaverse is at a transition point from rapid innovation and tech enthusiasm to massive commercialization. If the pattern of previous cycles of tech innovation holds, the next phase will be a form of anarchy during which the governance structure of the metaverse is up for grabs.[3] Stephenson predicted as much. In *Snow Crash* he has a media magnate say: "Watching government regulators trying to keep up with the world is my favorite sport."[4]

We may not buy into the metaverse hype. But the idea of a metaverse is a useful *metaphor* for the more general idea of the next frontier: the notion that societies continue to evolve in ways both anticipated and disruptive, that technologies will play a decisive role in these dynamics, and that new needs and opportunities for guardrail-making will emerge. Viewed from such an angle, the metaverse is a placeholder to address the fundamental questions of our shared vision for society's future operating system, including the guardrails we want to put in place to guide our individual and collective decisions. As much as cyberspace forced us to think about how to govern ourselves in a globally networked space thirty years ago, the metaverse offers us another chance to reimagine the guardrails that form part of the next social contract.[5]

Saintly Rules

There's much we can learn from the recent past and across domains for coming up with guardrails for emerging virtual spaces such as the metaverse, as the numerous examples of guardrails referred to in earlier chapters exemplify. But we can go even farther back in time for guidance in imagining the future. Just consider one of the most successful guardrail architects in human history: Saint Benedict of Nursia, born in 480 CE and remembered as the founder of Western monasticism.

In today's language, we can think of Saint Benedict as a serial entrepreneur who founded a dozen monasteries and served as their abbot. Even more significantly for our context, he drafted the key principles that have governed the lives of monastic communities in the Western hemisphere ever since. Bringing to bear his extensive experience as a monk and abbot, paired with his deep understanding of both the promises and risks of monastic life, he built upon earlier rules to draft a formidable set of guardrails for decision-making and governance that has become known as the Rule of St. Benedict. It has guided the monastic way of life over the past 1,500+ years—and counting.[6] Consisting of a prologue and seventy-three chapters, the Rule offers guidance about the essential monastic virtues of humility, silence, and obedience as well as directives for daily living. It includes specific instructions regarding the care of the sick, reception of guests, recruitment of new members, and journeys away from the monastery, among other things. But the secret of the Rule's success is that St. Benedict embraced uncertainty. While many of the norms are quite specific, they are made flexible by introducing numerous exceptions, offering the abbot significant discretion, and anticipating changing contextual circumstances.

The Rule of St. Benedict is only one—albeit impressive—set of guardrails from ancient times that is thick in formulation and flexible in application. In the first chapter, we explained the difference between thin and thick rules—that is, between rules with little flexibility and room for interpretation that must be accepted and are enforced at face value, and rules that are adaptable and adjusted to suit specific contexts.[7] St. Benedict's Rule is an example of the latter, while smart contracts and algorithms are often samples of the former. Models we have of the world constrain our decisions, but they tend to be thick rules, in need of contextualization and interpretation. Laws can straddle a wide spectrum, depending on how abstractly or concretely they are formulated. But because laws require interpretation, some flexibility is built into all of them. As historians have pointed out, over recent centuries guardrails have trended toward the thin, rigid, and specific rules that run counter to the principles we propose in this book.[8]

Technology may, as we mentioned, have exacerbated that shift. Information flow and decision governance issues have mutated significantly over the past few decades. Both at the surface and more structurally, these changes have challenged the effectiveness of the predominantly social guardrails that steered our decisions in the pre-Internet age. In response to this vacuum—and fueled by an accelerating stream of exciting technological innovations, including advances in AI—many societies have been tempted to look to "tools born digital" for solutions to the new decision challenges. To be sure, technology can and should play an important role in the guardrail context, as discussed in chapter 9. But below the surface, the shift from mostly social to increasingly technocentric guardrails has been accompanied by a deeper and more troublesome development: These forces pull us toward guardrails that run the risk of narrowing the flow of information and the variety of decisions, and deepening path dependencies in our decision processes.

We don't propose turning back the clock when addressing the most complex governance challenges of our time. But we think it is worthwhile to resist the impulse to increasingly rely on narrow, rigid, and immutable guardrails. The guardrail qualities we suggest for the age of the metaverse share some of the key attributes that have made the Rule of St. Benedict so successful over the past 1,500 years: *diversity*, *variability*, and *plasticity*. Our broader, more important message though is that we should look beyond narrow interventions aimed at addressing a specific governance problem, especially when we need to imagine different futures and how to govern our decisions within them. That is why we put forward over-arching design principles, such as learning and self-restraint.

Granted, the challenge of coming up with guardrails for our times is daunting. But there is also some good news. While the governance challenges we face have gotten harder since the time of St. Benedict, the toolbox of guardrail-making has expanded as well. Guardrails to steer the daily life of monks in a monastery were limited to a narrow arsenal of organizational and communicative measures. In contrast, today we have a wealth of sophisticated social, organizational, and technical approaches and techniques at our fingertips. We introduced this reservoir as *solution spaces* in chapter 6 and offered a series of illustrative use cases in chapters 8 and 9, showing how guardrails can encompass a variety of social, organizational, and technical instruments to address governance problems through decisional empowerment, social anchoring, and learning.

These instruments can be used, tailored, tweaked, and—most important—arranged and combined in novel ways when designing and putting into practice guardrails aimed at decision-making. When tackling problems of bias in AI in a field such as health, for instance, guardrails must address the social context and organizational practices, and consider the best techniques available along the entire life cycle of AI systems. To address ecological sustainability issues in emerging economies, to take another example, we need to develop guardrails that tap into the knowledge of local communities and unlock the promise of green technologies. When dealing with interoperability issues in the metaverse, guardrails should not only focus on the technical and data layers, but also consider business models, corporate policies, and IP law. In one context after another, the solution spaces offer a universe of potential guardrails and instruments that can be used to build and implement them—to empower humans, individually and collectively, and facilitate learning.

Moments of discontinuity—when experience and expertise cease to work[9]—can pose a real challenge to guardrails that served well in the past. The recent pandemic is a sobering case in point. Although think tanks and expert groups who look at global risks had been warning for years about pandemics as one of the biggest societal threats, the world was largely unprepared for COVID-19. Confronted with a previously unknown virus, decision-makers did not have much of a playbook to act upon. Existing guardrails meant to offer decision guidance turned out to be either outdated, given today's messy realities of globalization, or based on assumptions that proved not to hold. The result: A maze of ever-changing and sometimes contradictory rules about social distancing, isolation, quarantine, vaccination, travel restrictions, etc.

Even guardrails that embrace the qualities we detailed may hit functional limits when confronted with decision problems related to events that mark larger junctures in human history, such as the COVID-19 pandemic or the war in Ukraine. Looking at the current landscape of global risks—including climate, global health, and geopolitics—it is not unreasonable to expect that we may experience more such dramatic inflection points in the future, and likely at an accelerating pace. While some carefully designed guardrails can be helpful in times of crisis, and—as the Rule of St. Benedict shows—have a long shelf life, others will need to be overhauled in moments of tectonic shift. Investing in creating a systemic capacity to learn and adapt when guardrails need an overhaul is just as important as designing guardrails with the flexibility to accommodate changing circumstances and incorporate new data and knowledge. Whether in moments of evolution or revolution, it is essential that guardrails are designed with *learning* in mind.[10]

An Issue of Power

As guardrails seek to influence the decisions of others, they are always expressions of *power*. Kings and emperors, religious elites, and states have used guardrails to establish and legitimize power—from the Rule of St. Benedict to COVID-19 public health measures. Formal laws as well as community norms convey power as they aim to shape the behavior of people. The same goes for envisioning the rules of the game for the metaverse, or an equivalent vision of the future. Conversations about the role of standard-setting organizations that not only set technical guardrails but also make and break business models illustrate how guardrails and questions of power are deeply interwoven.

Guardrails not only signify power, they also rearrange it. From food labels in grocery stores to anti-bias rules in the housing market, guardrails empower some decision-makers while constraining others for the greater good. The rich history of law spanning cultures, continents, and different legal traditions is full of stories that show not only how heavy-handed rulers may be able to exercise power through law, but also how the same rulers find that their laws can eventually be turned back against them.[11] The history of modern American legal thought, from critical legal studies to postcolonialism, offers analysis and critique of the different power structures and dynamics baked into and exercised through the law, its institutions, and actors.[12] Contemporary scholarship in cyberlaw and platform regulation offers perspectives on power shifts involving large tech companies and their strategic use of guardrail systems that combine legal and algorithmic means of control.[13]

In short: The narrative about how guardrails have been used as tools of power captures a significant slice of the history of humankind. In this book, however, we have not been analyzing these shifts in power. As we stated in the first chapter, we have been looking at guardrails as a means to an end. We have offered qualities and design principles to make guardrails more effective as a means, but we have not pondered ends, beyond the overarching importance of human flourishing. And yet, our normative perspective for guardrails also has consequences for the question of power reflected in guardrails. Two are particularly noteworthy.

First, we suggest that whatever power is being expressed and reconfigured through guardrails needs to be limited and contextual. This is inherent in the design principles of learning and self-restraint. When guardrails aim to cover everything in detail, with little flexibility, they risk losing their value as reality evolves. In contrast, through self-restraint and learning, guardrails keep open socially desirable avenues for pluralistic decision-making while also offering the possibility to critique and contest power mechanisms in ever-changing circumstances.

Second, as we argue for thick guardrails, we see power vested in processes, institutions, practices, and culture rather than substantive rules alone. We think this produces better decisions in a changing world—but, more fundamentally, it also reflects our conviction that guardrails without social anchorage suffer from a lack of legitimacy that ultimately undermines their effectiveness. We of course appreciate that shifting to ever more detailed guardrails, devoid of flexibility, comes from a desire to limit how much power is in the hands of corruptible humans. But, as we hope we have clarified in this book, we do not think such a strategy can work in the long run. Guardrails *are* social constructs—take the human element out of the equation and they will fail.[14] There is no shortcut to avoid facing and confronting the messiness of human involvement, nor should there be.

Agents of Our Futures

As we draft these final paragraphs, the world is deep in crisis mode. Headlines about record temperatures, severe water and energy shortages, a possible next pandemic in the making, and the threat of escalating military confrontation in Europe and Asia hit us with a breathtaking cadence. Humanity's central challenge arises with new urgency: How can we imagine and build a better world, a better future for our children? Much boils down to what theory of change one has in mind. While far from offering a silver bullet or even a comprehensive blueprint, we have suggested how suitably designed guardrails can guide humans toward better decision-making.

In considering the role of guardrails, we affirm the importance of individual choice and human volition. Guardrails can guide us, but they ought not and cannot decide for us. This is both a blessing and a curse. The latter because we cannot escape responsibility for the trajectory that humanity takes. And the former because without volition we would not have agency. It's the human condition: to decide as individuals yet be anchored in society. The guardrails we wrote about in this book link one with the other—and good guardrails embrace and deepen this link, while appreciating the limitations of all human decisions and the potential for learning, progress, and evolution this entails.

And yet, we will fail if our guardrails do not reflect the human ability to dream. Guardrails can, as Fernanda Pirie says of laws, "make a social vision concrete and explicit, holding it up for others to see."[15] It is in this spirit that we invoke the metaverse as a metaphor for the next frontier in society's evolution. Ambiguous as it is, it offers the much-needed rhetorical space for reimagination and creativity. We hope that our readers—and everyone in governments, companies, and communities tasked with confronting some of humanity's biggest challenges—will embrace this timely opportunity to think about and experiment with smarter guardrails to work toward better, fairer, and more sustainable futures. The stakes, as we all might agree, could not be higher.

ACKNOWLEDGMENTS

We thank our Princeton University Press editors: Chuck Myers, for being excited about the project initially; Eric Crahan, who took over; and finally, Bridget Flannery-McCoy and Alena Chekanov—their infectious enthusiasm encouraged us to dash to the finish line. We gratefully acknowledge PUP's copyeditor, Karen Verde. We also thank the three anonymous reviewers for their thoughtful feedback. On our end, we owe a significant debt to Andrew Wright, who deftly and with an outstanding sense for nuance and detail edited our initial draft, and to Phil Cain, who made sure the facts were checked. All remaining errors are of course ours.

We also gratefully acknowledge the committees, groups, and fora advising on governance of information issues that we had the privilege to serve in over the years. This includes the German Digital Council and its leadership, the inimitable Katrin Suder, and the Republic of Colombia's AI Expert Mission led by the incomparable Sandra Cortesi.

Urs thanks: his students at Harvard Law School and now at the Technical University of Munich; staff, fellows, and faculty at Harvard's Berkman Klein Center for Internet & Society for two decades brimming with conversations and research collaborations where technology and society intersect; Martha Minow for being a lodestar; the founding members of the global Network of Internet & Society Research Centers, who have guided international explorations and helped diversify frames; the new team at the TUM School of Social Sciences and Technology, particularly Constanze Albrecht for research support, intellectual engagement, and for teaching the art of seeking new answers to familiar questions; and John Palfrey for many years of unwavering transatlantic partnership in a world marked by discontinuity.

Viktor thanks: his students over the years in the "Law & Internet" course at the University of Oxford (with a special shout-out to the 2022/23 group); his Oxford college, Keble, for continuing support; his departmental colleagues Ralph Schroeder and Richard Susskind for enlightening conversations; Fred Cate; Paul Schwartz and the participants of his data privacy seminar at Berkeley for their feedback; Alexander Somek; Paul B. Stephan; colleagues at the University of Graz law school for their support and continuing conversation; many (and too many to list) colleagues and friends in Europe, the Americas, and Asia, for decades-long conversations about the essence of governance in the information age.

If humanity stands a chance to get out of the challenges, it's only through learning from and with others—especially when this entails re-evaluating one's own biases and going beyond one's comfort zone. Because such learning is so crucial, we dedicate this book to two individuals, who not only taught us, but instilled in us the desire to always dig deeper in our understanding and to appreciate a multitude of perspectives. They stand in for all teachers who did similarly.

To write a book takes a huge amount of energy—for us at least, despite being repeat offenders. Hence, unsurprisingly, the biggest debt we owe is to our loved ones, who have come to accept and appreciate us for what we concede we are—addicts to ideas, even if that means spending hours in front of a screen.

NOTES

1. Decisions: How We Decide and Why It Matters: Human Agency and Changing the World

1. The full accident report by the German Federal Bureau of Aircraft Accident Investigation can be found here: "Investigation Report," German Federal Bureau of Aircraft Accidents Investigation, July 1, 2002, https://www.bfu-web.de/EN/Publications/FinalReports/2002/Report _02_AX001-1-2_Ueberlingen_Report.pdf?__blob=publicationFile&v=1.

2. The term "guardrails" has been used in the governance context before, including for climate change policy as well as sustainability; for the former see, e.g., IPCC FAQ, https://www .ipcc.ch/sr15/faq/faq-chapter-1/, and the latter, e.g., WBGU, *Human Progress Within Planetary Guard Rails* (Berlin: WBGU, 2014), https://www.idos-research.de/uploads/media/wbgu_pp8 _en.pdf.

3. See, e.g., Brian Wansink and Jeffrey Sobal, "Mindless Eating: The 200 Daily Food Decisions We Overlook," *Environment and Behavior* 39(1): 106–123 (2007); Jim Sollisch, "The Cure for Decision Fatigue," *Wall Street Journal*, June 10, 2016; Grant A. Pignatiello, Richard J. Martin, and Ronald L. Hickman, Jr., "Decision Fatigue: A Conceptual Analysis," *Journal of Health Psychology* 25(1): 123–135 (2020).

4. For an overview of the evolution of decision analysis, see James S. Dyer and James E. Smith, "Innovations in the Science and Practice of Decision Analysis: The Role of Management Science," *Management Science* 67(9): 5364–5378.

5. See, e.g., Lionel Casson, *Libraries in the Ancient World* (New Haven, CT: Yale University Press, 2001).

6. See Wayne A. Wiegand, *Part of Our Lives: A People's History of the American Public Library* (Oxford, UK: Oxford University Press, 2017); Matthew Battles, *Library: An Unquiet History* (New York: Norton, 2015); also John Y. Cole, *America's Greatest Library: An Illustrated History of the Library of Congress* (Lewes, UK: Giles, 2018).

7. Article I, Section 8, Clause 8 U.S. Constitution.

8. See, e.g., Kenneth Cukier, Viktor Mayer-Schönberger, and Francis de Véricourt, *Framers: Human Advantage in an Age of Technology and Turmoil* (New York: Dutton, 2021).

9. Cukier et al., *Framers*, 46–48.

10. *Pars pro toto* see Daniel Kahneman, *Thinking Fast and Slow* (London: Allen Lane, 2011); Daniel Kahneman and Amos Tversky, *Choices, Values, and Frames* (Cambridge, UK: Cambridge University Press, 2000).

11. See, e.g., Sam Harris, *Free Will* (Florence, MA: Free Press, 2012); for a detailed overview of the debate, see Robert Kane, *The Oxford Handbook of Free Will*, 2nd ed. (Oxford, UK: Oxford University Press, 2011).

12. Cf., e.g., 15 CFR § 908.12—Public Disclosure of Information. See also Paul M. Healy and Krishna Palepu, "Information Asymmetry, Corporate Disclosure and the Capital Markets: A Review of the Empirical Disclosure Literature," *SSRN Electronic Journal* (2001); Mark H. Lang and Russell J. Lundholm, "Corporate Disclosure Policy and Analyst Behavior," *Accounting Review* 71(4): 467–492 (1996), https://www.jstor.org/stable/248567.

13. James B. Stuart, "Did Elon Musk Violate Securities Laws with Tweet about Taking Tesla Private?," *New York Times*, August 8, 2018.

14. See, e.g., Timothy D. Lytton, "Signs of Change or Clash of Symbols? FDA Regulation of Nutrient Profile Labeling," *Health Matrix* 19(2): 217 (2010), https://papers.ssrn.com/sol3/papers.cfm?abstract_id=1510283; Joshua Dhyani, "Science-Based Food Labels: Improving Regulations & Preventing Consumer Deception Through Limited Information Disclosure Requirements," *Journal of Science and Technology* 26 (2016).

15. For the US context, see, e.g., Archung Fung, Mary Graham, and David Weil, *Full Disclosure: The Perils and Promise of Transparency* (New York: Cambridge University Press, 2007).

16. Such reporting, however, is challenging, given multiple and often competing standards and rating frameworks; for a glimpse at the conundrum, see Michael O'Leary and Warren Valdmanis, "An ESG Reckoning Is Coming," *Harvard Business Review*, March 4, 2021, https://hbr.org/2021/03/an-esg-reckoning-is-coming; ESG reporting nevertheless remains crucial and may not negatively impact economic performance; for empirical research suggesting a correlation between economic performance and ESG commitment, see Michael L. Barnett and Robert M. Salomon, "Beyond Dichotomy: The Curvilinear Relationship Between Social Responsibility and Financial Performance," *Strategic Management Journal* 27: 1101–1122 (2006).

17. See Wendy Ginsberg, *The Freedom of Information Act (FOIA): Background, Legislation, and Policy Issues* (Washington, DC: Congressional Research Service, 2014); for an analysis see Margret B. Kwoka, *Saving the Freedom of Information Act* (Cambridge, UK: Cambridge University Press, 2021); more generally see also Fung et al., *Full Disclosure*.

18. Ralph Nader, *The Ralph Nader Reader* (New York: Seven Stories Press, 2000).

19. Examples include § 240 of the German Criminal Code; New York Consolidated Laws, Penal Law—PEN § 135.60; and the California Code, Civil Code—CIV § 52.1, among many others.

20. For an overview of the function of "Latin notaries," see, e.g., Ezra N. Suleiman, *Private Power and Centralization in France: The Notaries and the State* (Princeton, NJ: Princeton University Press, 1987).

21. See, e.g., in Belgium: "Legislation Concerning Euthanasia in Belgium," Drze.de, https://www.drze.de/in-focus/euthanasia/modules/belgium-loi-relatif-a-leuthanasie; in Switzerland: "The Various Forms of Euthanasia and Their Position in Law," Federal Office of Justice, https://www.bj.admin.ch/bj/en/home/gesellschaft/gesetzgebung/archiv/sterbehilfe/formen.html; in Austria: "New Law Allowing Assisted Suicide Takes Effect in Austria," BBC News, https://www.bbc.com/news/world-europe-59847371; in the Netherlands: "Euthanasia, Assisted Suicide and Non-Resuscitation on Request," Government of the Netherlands, https://www

.government.nl/topics/euthanasia/euthanasia-assisted-suicide-and-non-resuscitation-on
-request.

22. In the United States, such cooling-off periods exist for contracts agreed with consumers in their homes; see FTC, 16 CFR Part 429, online at https://www.ecfr.gov/current/title-16 /part-429.

23. These include statutory cancellation periods for consumer contracts in many US states; for instance, in California such cancellation periods apply to contracts with anything from dance studios and dating services to insurance, telephone, and seminar sales; for a summary with further pointers, see State and Consumer Services Agency of California, *Consumer Transactions with Statutory Contract Cancellation Rights*, January 2010, online at https://www.marincounty .org/-/media/files/departments/da/consumer-guides/k6.pdf.

24. Ray Fisman and Tim Sullivan, *The Inner Lives of Markets: How People Shape Them—And They Shape Us* (New York: Public Affairs, 2016); on how a "lex mercatoria" matters in Internet times, see, e.g., Joel R. Reidenberg, "Lex Informatica: The Formulation of Information Policy Rules through Technology," *Texas Law Review* 76(3): 553–593 (1997).

25. Richard H. Thaler and Cass R. Sunstein, *Nudge—the Final Edition* (New Haven, CT: Yale University Press, 2021).

26. For an ethical argument against nudging, see, e.g., Tom Goodwin, "Why We Should Reject 'Nudge'," *Politics* 32(2): 85–92 (2012); Adrien Barton and Till Grüne-Yanoff, "From Libertarian Paternalism to Nudging—and Beyond," *Review of Philosophy and Psychology* 6: 341–359 (2015); for an empirical argument, see, e.g., Karen Yeung, "Nudge as Fudge," *Modern Law Review* 75: 122–148 (2012).

27. See, e.g., Paco Underhill, *Why We Buy: The Science of Shopping—Updated and Revised for the Internet, the Global Consumer, and Beyond* (New York: Simon & Schuster, 2008).

28. Paco Underhill, *Call of the Mall: The Geography of Shopping by the Author of Why We Buy* (New York: Simon & Schuster, 2004).

29. Paul Resnick and Richard Zeckhauser, "Trust Among Strangers in Internet Transactions: Empirical Analysis of Ebay's Reputation System," in M. R. Baye, ed., *The Economics of the Internet and E-commerce* (Amsterdam: Elsevier, 2002), 127–157.

30. See, e.g., Microsoft's Software Development Lifecycle, https://www.microsoft.com/en -us/securityengineering/sdl.

31. See, e.g., Gunnar Folke Schuppert, *The World of Rules: A Somewhat Different Measurement of the World* (Frankfurt/Main, Germany: Max-Planck-Institut für Rechtsgeschichte und Rechtstheorie, 2017).

32. Gillian Hadfield, *Rules for a Flat World: Why Humans Invented Law and How to Reinvent It for a Complex Global Economy* (Oxford: Oxford University Press, 2016).

33. There is debate about the exact mechanisms of cultural evolution. For a persuasive view, see, e.g., Joseph Henrich, *The Secret of Our Success: How Culture Is Driving Human Evolution, Domesticating Our Species, and Making Us Smarter* (Princeton, NJ: Princeton University Press, 2016); for an academic treatment of the debate, see Tim Lewens, "Cultural Evolution," *Oxford Academic*, online edition (2015).

34. See, e.g., Guillaume P. Chossière, Robert Malina, Akshay Ashok, Irene C. Dedoussi, Sebastian D. Eastham, Raymond L. Speth, and Steven R. H. Barrett, "Public Health Impacts of

Excess NOx Emissions from Volkswagen Diesel Passenger Vehicles in Germany," *Environmental Research Letters* 12(3): 1–14 (2017); Susan C. Anenberg, Joshua Miller, Ray Minjares, Li Du, Daven K. Henze, Forrest Lacey, Christopher S. Malley, Lisa Emberson, Vicente Franco, Zbigniew Klimont, and Chris Heyes, "Impacts and Mitigation of Excess Diesel-Related NOx Emissions in 11 Major Vehicle Markets," *Nature* 545: 467–471 (2017).

35. George A. Akerlof, "The Market for 'Lemons': Quality Uncertainty and the Market Mechanism," *Quarterly Journal of Economics* 84(3): 488–500 (1970).

36. Friedrich Kratochwil, *Rules, Norms and Decisions: On the Conditions of Practical and Legal Reasoning in International Relations and Domestic Affairs* (Cambridge: Cambridge University Press, 1989), 11.

37. Being targeted by social guardrails for decision-making is therefore not only a constraint, but also a privilege of being taken seriously; see Hannah Arendt, *The Origins of Totalitarianism* (New York: Harcourt Brace Jovanovich, 1973).

38. See https://en.wikipedia.org/wiki/GPT-3.

39. There is robust debate over what a Google engineer, or Google, knows or doesn't. Google's John Mueller has denied that Google does not know (although he has not said whether only the sum of all engineers know how it works), but others have said that Google sources dispute such a view, at least when interpreted in a comprehensive manner. See, e.g., Barry Schwartz, "Google: We Do Understand Our Highly Complex Algorithms," *Search Engine Roundtable,* May 15, 2017, https://www.seroundtable.com/google-understand-complex -algorithms-23848.html.

40. Lorraine Daston, *Rules: A Short History of What We Live By* (Princeton, NJ: Princeton University Press, 2022).

41. Viktor Mayer-Schönberger and Kenneth Cukier, *Big Data—A Revolution That Will Transform How We Live, Work, and Think* (New York: Houghton Mifflin Harcourt, 2013); John Palfrey and Urs Gasser, *Born Digital—Understanding the First Generation of Digital Natives* (New York: Basic Books, 2008).

42. Melvin Kranzberg, "Technology and History: 'Kranzberg's Laws,'" *Technology and Culture* 27(3): 544–560 (1986).

43. See, e.g., Tim Wu, *The Master Switch: The Rise and Fall of Information Empires* (New York: Alfred A. Knopf, 2010).

44. Walter Isaacson, *Steve Jobs* (New York: Simon & Schuster, 2011), 92.

45. Kenneth L. Karst, *Belonging to America—Equal Citizenship and the Constitution* (New Haven, CT: Yale University Press, 1989).

46. See "Decision on the Constitutionality of the 1983 Census Act," BVerfGE 65, 1–71, https://www.bundesverfassungsgericht.de/SharedDocs/Entscheidungen/EN/1983/12 /rs19831215_1bvr020983en.html; Spiros Simitis, "Reviewing Privacy in an Information Society," *University of Pennsylvania Law Review* 135(3): 707 (1987).

47. "The Human Flourishing Program," Harvard University, accessed August 10, 2022, https://hfh.fas.harvard.edu/.

48. Anthony Giddens, *The Constitution of Society: Introduction of the Theory of Structuration* (Berkeley: University of California Press, 1984).

2. Rules: The Governance of Cyberspace Offers a Cautious Tale of Hype, Hope, and Failure

1. For an overview of PARC's history and contribution, see Michael Hiltzik, *Dealers of Lightning—Xerox PARC and the Dawn of the Computer Age* (New York: HarperBusiness, 1999).

2. Neal Stephenson, *Snow Crash* (New York: Bantam Books, 1992).

3. Julian Dibbell, "A Rape in Cyberspace; or, How an Evil Clown, a Haitian Trickster Spirit, Two Wizards, and a Cast of Dozens Turned a Database into a Society," in Mark Dery, ed., *Flame Wars* (Durham, NC: Duke University Press, 1994), 237–261.

4. Frank H. Easterbrook, "Cyberspace and the Law of the Horse," *University of Chicago Legal Forum* 207 (1996).

5. Imre Lakatos, *Proofs and Refutations: The Logic of Mathematical Discovery*, reissue ed. (Cambridge, UK: Cambridge University Press, 2015).

6. For the legal context, see Jean Nicolas Druey, *Information als Gegenstand des Rechts* (Zürich: Schulthess Polygraphischer Verlag, 1995). More generally on the concept of information, see James Gleick, *The Information: A History, a Theory, a Flood* (New York: Pantheon Books, 2011).

7. Rohan Samarajiva, Electronic Public Space, Presentation, University of Salzburg, June 1995.

8. William J. Mitchell, *City of Bits—Space, Place, and the Infobahn* (Cambridge, MA: MIT Press, 1995).

9. On markets as coordination mechanisms, see, e.g., Charles E. Lindblom, *The Market System—What It Is, How It Works, and What to Make of It* (New Haven, CT: Yale University Press, 2011).

10. See, e.g., DataRPM, *Anomaly Detection & Prediction Decoded*, https://www.progress.com /docs/default-source/datarpm/progress_datarpm_cadp_ebook_anomaly_detection_in_6 _industries.pdf?sfvrsn=82a183de_2; other sources suggest up to 73 percent of data in enterprises is unused; for a discussion of these figures, see Jeff Barrett, "Up to 73 Percent of Company Data Goes Unused for Analytics," *Inc.*, April 12, 2018, https://www.inc.com/jeff-barrett /misusing-data-could-be-costing-your-business-heres-how.html.

11. He writes about this in *Code: And Other Laws of Cyberspace* (New York: Basic Books, 1999), 3.

12. Lawrence Lessig, *The Future of Ideas—The Fate of the Commons in a Connected World* (New York: Random House, 2001).

13. Lawrence Lessig, *Free Culture: How Big Media Uses Technology and the Law to Lock Down Culture and Control Creativity* (New York: Penguin, 2004).

14. James Boyle, "The Second Enclosure Movement and the Construction of the Public Domain," in *Copyright Law*, 1st ed. (London: Routledge, 2017), 63–104.

15. See, e.g., Robert C. Allen, *Enclosure and the Yeoman* (Oxford: Clarendon Press, 1992); for a historical comparison, see James Boyle, "The Second Enclosure Movement," 63–104.

16. Jerry Frug, "The Geography of Community," *Stanford Law Review* 48(5): 1047–1108 (1996).

17. Lawrence Lessig, "The Zones of Cyberspace," *Stanford Law Review* 48(5): 1403–1411 (1996).

18. For the community standards benchmark in obscenity cases, see *Miller v. California*, 413 U.S. 15 (1973); for a history of the rule of juries in defamation cases, see the famous case of John Peter Zenger, accused of libel and represented by Andrew Hamilton, detailed in Richard Kluger, *Indelible Ink: The Trials of John Peter Zenger and the Birth of America's Free Press* (New York: Norton, 2016).

19. See, e.g., Brian Z. Tamanaha, *Legal Pluralism Explained—History, Theory, Consequences* (New York: Oxford University Press, 2021).

20. Tamanaha, *Legal Pluralism Explained*, 116–127.

21. An early netiquette framework is "Netiquette Guidelines," RFC 1855 (1995), https://www.rfc-editor.org/rfc/rfc1855.

22. David D. Clark, "A Cloudy Crystal Ball—Visions of the Future," Presentation, MIT Laboratory for Computer Science, July 1992, https://groups.csail.mit.edu/ana/People/DDC/future_ietf_92.pdf. David D. Clark acted as chief protocol architect and chaired the Internet Activities Board during the 1980s.

23. David R. Johnson and David Post, "Law and Borders: The Rise of Law in Cyberspace," *Stanford Law Review* 48(5): 1367–1402 (1996).

24. Jack Goldsmith and Tim Wu, *Who Controls the Internet? Illusions of a Borderless World* (New York: Oxford University Press, 2006).

25. Communications Decency Act of 1996 (CDA), Pub. L. No. 104–104 (Tit. V), 110 Stat. 133 (Feb. 8, 1996), codified at 47 U.S.C. §§223, 230. For how it came into being, see, e.g., Jeff Kosseff, *The Twenty-Six Words That Created the Internet* (Ithaca, NY: Cornell University Press, 2006).

26. For an illustrative case, see Jonathan Wallace and Mark Mangan, *Sex, Laws, and Cyberspace—Freedom and Censorship on the Frontiers of the Online Revolution* (New York: Henry Holt, 1996).

27. Directive 2000/31/EC of the European Parliament and of the Council of 8 June 2000 on certain legal aspects of information society services, in particular electronic commerce, in the Internal Market ("Directive on electronic commerce"), *Official Journal L* 178, 17.7.2000, 1–16.

28. Directive 95/46/EC on the protection of individuals with regard to the processing of personal data and on the free movement of such data, *Official Journal L* 281, 23.11.1995, 31–50.

29. See, e.g., Chris Reed, "How to Make Bad Law: Lessons from Cyberspace," *Modern Law Review* 73: 903–932 (2010).

30. This includes, e.g., the Communications Decency Act of 1996 (CDA) mentioned earlier.

31. Lawrence Lessig, *Republic, Lost: How Money Corrupts Congress—and a Plan to Stop It* (New York: Twelve, 2015).

32. Francis Cairncross, *The Death of Distance—How the Communications Revolution Will Change Our Lives* (Boston, MA: Harvard Business School Press, 1997).

33. "GDPR: US News Sites Unavailable to EU Users under New Rules," *BBC News*, https://www.bbc.com/news/world-europe-44248448.

34. Alan M. Turing, "Computing Machinery and Intelligence," *Mind* 49 (1950): 433–460; but see also John von Neumann, *First Draft of a Report on the EDVAC* (June 30, 1945), https://web.mit.edu/STS.035/www/PDFs/edvac.pdf.

35. John Palfrey and Urs Gasser, *Interop: The Promise and Perils of Highly Interconnected Systems* (New York: Basic Books, 2012).

36. See, e.g., Barbara van Schewick, *Internet Architecture and Innovation* (Cambridge, MA: MIT Press, 2010), 57–81; Marjory Blumenthal and David D. Clark, "Rethinking the Design of the Internet: The End-to-End Arguments vs. the Brave New World," *ACM Transactions on Internet Technology* 1: 70–109 (2001); Jerome H. Saltzer, David P. Reed, and David D. Clark, "End-to-End Arguments in System Design," *ACM Transactions on Computer Systems* 2(4): 277–288 (1984).

37. For an overview, see Tarleton Gillespie, "Engineering a Principle: 'End-to-End' in the Design of the Internet," *Social Studies of Science* 36(3): 427–457 (2006).

38. See, e.g., Ronald J. Deibert, "Dark Guests and Great Firewalls: The Internet and Chinese Security Policy," *Journal of Social Issues* 58(1): 143–159 (2002).

39. Lawrence Lessig, *Code: And Other Laws of Cyberspace* (New York: Basic Books, 1999).

40. Others similarly worried about the declining role of the state; see, e.g., for the area of information privacy, Paul Schwartz, "Internet Privacy and the State," 32 *Connecticut Law Review* 815 (2000); suggesting an enduring role of the nation-state, see Jack Goldsmith and Tim Wu, *Who Controls the Internet? Illusions of a Borderless World* (Oxford: Oxford University Press, 2006).

41. Shoshana Zuboff, *The Age of Surveillance Capitalism: The Fight for a Human Future at the New Frontier of Power* (New York: Public Affairs, 2019).

42. Julie E. Cohen, *Between Truth and Power—The Legal Construction of Information Capitalism* (Oxford, UK: Oxford University Press, 2019).

43. For a good overview of the interface of technology and society (and thus guardrails) as well as undercurrents of determinism, see Claude S. Fischer, *America Calling: A Social History of the Telephone to 1940* (Berkeley: University of California Press, 1992). For a comprehensive overview of that interface, see Merritt Roe Smith and Leo Marx, eds., *Does Technology Drive History? The Dilemma of Technological Determinism* (Cambridge, MA: MIT Press, 1998).

44. These thoughtful perspectives include Brett Frischmann and Evan Selinger, *Re-Engineering Humanity* (Cambridge: Cambridge University Press, 2018); Jamie Susskind, *The Digital Republic* (London, UK: Bloomsbury, 2022); and Joshua A. T. Fairfield, *Runaway Technology—Can Law Keep Up?* (Cambridge, UK: Cambridge University Press, 2021).

3. Falsities: Two Ways to Approach the Problem of Misinformation

1. For a history of disinformation from the early twentieth century to today, see Thomas Rid, *Active Measures: The Secret History of Disinformation and Political Warfare* (New York: Farrar, Strauss & Giroux, 2020).

2. David Wise, *Cassidy's Run—The Secret Spy War over Nerve Gas* (New York: Random House, 2000).

3. Jeffrey Kluger, "Accidental Poisonings Increased after President Trump's Disinfectant Comments," *Time*, May 12, 2020, https://time.com/5835244/accidental-poisonings-trump/.

4. Souroush Vosoughi, Deb Roy, and Sinan Aral, "The Spread of True and False News Online," *Science* 359: 1146–1151 (2018).

5. See Adrienne Goldstein, "Social Media Engagement with Deceptive Sites Reached Record Highs in 2020," *GMF*, https://www.gmfus.org/news/social-media-engagement-deceptive-sites -reached-record-highs-2020.

6. Amy Watson, "Online Sharing of Fake News U.S. 2019," *Statista*, https://www.statista.com /statistics/657111/fake-news-sharing-online/.

7. "Community Standards Enforcement," Transparency Center, accessed August 9, 2022, https://transparency.fb.com/data/community-standards-enforcement/fake-accounts /facebook/#content-actioned.

8. Elisa Shearer and Amy Mitchell, "News Use across Social Media Platforms in 2020," *Pew Research Center's Journalism Project* (2021), https://www.pewresearch.org/journalism/2021/01 /12/news-use-across-social-media-platforms-in-2020/.

9. See, e.g., Dylan de Beer and Machdel Matthee, "Approaches to Identify Fake News: A Systematic Literature Review," *Integrated Science in Digital Age* 136: 13–22 (2020).

10. For a treatise on the various misinformation efforts online, see, e.g., Joan Donovan, Emily Dreyfuss, and Brian Friedberg, *Meme Wars: The Untold Story of the Online Battles Upending Democracy in America* (London, UK: Bloomsbury, 2022).

11. See, e.g., James Lamond, "The Origins of Russia's Broad Political Assault on the United States," *Center for American Progress*, October 3, 2018, https://www.americanprogress.org/article /origins-russias-broad-political-assault-united-states/; see also Scott Detrow, "What Did Cambridge Analytica Do During the 2016 Election?" *NPR*, March 20, 2018, https://www.npr.org/2018 /03/20/595338116/what-did-cambridge-analytica-do-during-the-2016-election; "Cambridge Analytica and Facebook: The Scandal and the Fallout So Far," *New York Times*, April 4, 2018, https://www.nytimes.com/2018/04/04/us/politics/cambridge-analytica-scandal-fallout.html.

12. House of Commons, Digital, Culture, Media and Sport Committee, "Disinformation and 'fake news': Final Report," *HC* 1791 (2019), https://publications.parliament.uk/pa /cm201719/cmselect/cmcumeds/1791/1791.pdf.

13. See, e.g., Emily Chen and Emilio Ferrara, "Tweets in Time of Conflict: A Public Dataset Tracking the Twitter Discourse on the War Between Ukraine and Russia," March 14, 2022 (preprint) arXiv:2203.07488 [cs.SI]; Hans W. A. Hanley, Deepak Kumar, and Zakir Durumeric, "Happenstance: Utilizing Semantic Search to Track Russian State Media Narratives about the Russo-Ukrainian War on Reddit," May 28, 2022, accepted to ICWSM 2023, arXiv:2205.14484 [cs.SI].

14. Fabio Rugge, "Confronting an 'Axis of Cyber'?: China, Iran, North Korea, Russia in Cyberspace," *Library OAPEN*, http://library.oapen.org/handle/20.500.12657/23931.

15. See, e.g., Edward Lucas, Jake Morris, and Corina Rebega, "Information Bedlam: Russian and Chinese Information Operations During COVID-19," Center for European Policy Analysis, March 15, 2021, https://cepa.org/information-bedlam-russian-and-chinese-information -operations-during-covid-19/; and Ben Dubow, Edward Lucas, Jake Morris, "Jabbed in the Back: Mapping Russian and Chinese Information Operations During COVID-19," Center for European Policy Analysis, December 2, 2021, https://cepa.org/jabbed-in-the-back-mapping -russian-and-chinese-information-operations-during-covid-19/.

16. See, e.g., Sam Harris, *Lying* (Los Angeles, CA: Four Elephants Press, 2013).

17. Hannah Arendt, *On Lying and Politics* (New York: Library of America, 2022), 11; Karl Popper, *The Logic of Scientific Discovery* (London: Routledge, 2002).

18. See, e.g., on Jefferson Merrill Peterson, *The Jefferson Image in the American Mind*, rev. ed. (Charlottesville and London: University of Virginia Press, 1999); see also David G. Post, *In Search of Jefferson's Moose—Notes on the State of Cyberspace* (Oxford: Oxford University Press, 2009), 186–206; on Benjamin Franklin, see Walter Isaacson, *Benjamin Franklin: An American Life* (New York: Simon & Schuster, 2004).

19. See, e.g., in the field of medicine, Jill A. Hayden, Danielle A. van der Windt, Jennifer L. Cartwright, et al., "Assessing Bias in Studies of Prognostic Factors," *Annals of Internal Medicine* 158: 280–286 (2013); in the social sciences see, e.g., Alec P. Christie et al., "Quantifying and Addressing the Prevalence and Bias of Study Designs in the Environmental and Social Sciences," *Nature Communications* 11: 6377 (2020); Annie Franco, Neil Malhotra, and Gabor Simonovits, "Publication Bias in the Social Sciences: Unlocking the File Drawer," *Science* 345: 1502–1505 (2014); Philip M. Podsakoff, Scott B. MacKenzie, and Nathan P. Podsakoff, "Sources of Method Bias in Social Science Research and Recommendations on How to Control It," *Annual Review of Psychology* 63: 539–569 (2012).

20. Timothy Garton Ash, *Free Speech—Ten Principles for a Connected World* (New Haven, CT: Yale University Press, 2016).

21. In addition to public sources, this is based on personal conversation with Maria Windhager by one of the authors in 2022.

22. On what hate speech is and how it comes about, see Matthew Williams, *The Science of Hate: How Prejudice Becomes Hate and What We Can Do to Stop It* (London: Faber & Faber, 2022).

23. *Eva Glawischnig-Piesczek v. Facebook Ireland Limited*, Judgment of the Court (Third Chamber) of 3 October 2019—Request for a preliminary ruling from the Oberster Gerichtshof, Case C-18/18, https://curia.europa.eu/juris/liste.jsf?num=C-18/18.

24. Danielle Keats Citron, *Hate Crimes in Cyberspace* (Cambridge, MA: Harvard University Press, 2014).

25. *Oberschlick v. Austria*, 19 EHRR 389 91/29 (1995).

26. See, e.g., in Germany, Gesetz zur Verbesserung der Rechtsdurchsetzug in sozialen Netzwerken (Netzwerkdurchsetzungsgesetz—NetzDG), BGBl I 3352 (2017), § 4 Bußgeldvorschriften.

27. YouTube, *Copyright Transparency Report 2022*, https://storage.googleapis.com/transparencyreport/report-downloads/pdf-report-22_2022-1-1_2022-6-30_en_v1.pdf.

28. Google Transparency Report, https://transparencyreport.google.com/copyright/overview.

29. On the fragmentation debate, see, e.g., Tim Maurer and Robert Morgus, "Stop Calling Decentralization of the Internet 'Balkanization'," *Slate*, February 19, 2014, https://slate.com/technology/2014/02/stop-calling-decentralization-of-the-internet-balkanization.html.

30. Sarah T. Roberts, *Behind the Screen: Content Moderation in the Shadows of Social Media* (New Haven, CT: Yale University Press, 2021).

31. Sarah Feldman, "How Does Facebook Moderate Content," *statista*, March 13, 2019, https://www.statista.com/chart/17302/facebook-content-moderator/.

32. Maggie Fick and Dave Paresh, "Facebook's Flood of Languages Leave It Struggling to Monitor Content," *Reuters*, April 23, 2019, https://www.reuters.com/article/us-facebook-languages-insight/facebooks-flood-of-languages-leaves-it-struggling-to-monitor-content-idUSKCN1RZ0DW.

33. "A Focus on Efficiency: A Whitepaper from Facebook, Ericsson and Qualcomm," September 16, 2013, https://internet.org/efficiencypaper, p. 7.

34. Josh Sklar as told to Jacob Silverman, "I Was a Facebook Content Moderator. I Quit in Disgust," *New Republic*, May 12, 2021, https://newrepublic.com/article/162379/facebook-content-moderation-josh-sklar-speech-censorship.

35. Dirk Meissner, "Canadian Press Names Kamloops Unmarked Graves Discovery Canada's News Story of the Year," *CBC*, December 16, 2021, https://www.cbc.ca/news/canada/british-columbia/canadian-press-story-of-the-year-unmarked-grave-discovery-1.6288978.

36. "Oversight Board Overturns Meta's Original Decision: Case 2021-012-FB-UA," https://oversightboard.com/news/326519182635025-oversight-board-overturns-meta-s-original-decision-case-2021-012-fb-ua/.

37. *Google Spain SL and Google Inc. v. Agencia Española de Protección de Datos (AEPD) and Mario Costeja González*—Request for a preliminary ruling from the Audiencia Nacional, Judgment of the Court (Grand Chamber), 13 May 2014, Case C-131/12, https://eur-lex.europa.eu/legal-content/EN/TXT/?uri=CELEX%3A62012CJ0131.

38. Theo Bertram et al., "Five Years of the Right to Be Forgotten," https://storage.googleapis.com/pub-tools-public-publication-data/pdf/acb2ee7bae98250e41590012f8cd305df9b86d94.pdf.

39. See Google Transparency Report, https://transparencyreport.google.com/eu-privacy/overview.

40. Guy Rosen, "Community Standards Enforcement Report, Third Quarter 2021," https://about.fb.com/news/2021/11/community-standards-enforcement-report-q3-2021/.

41. See *Lloyd Corp. v. Tanner*, 407 U.S. 551 (1972) and *Pruneyard Shopping Center v. Robins*, 447 U.S. 74 (1980).

42. See, e.g., Ronan Ó Fathaigh, Natalie Helberger, and Naomi Appelman, "The Perils of Legally Defining Disinformation," *Internet Policy Review* 10(4), https://ssrn.com/abstract=3964513; for an overview of various viewpoints and perspectives in the academic debate, see Knight First Amendment Institute at Columbia University, "Lies, Free Speech, and the Law" (2022), https://knightcolumbia.org/events/symposium-lies-free-speech-and-the-law.

43. Tom Simonite, "Facebook Is Everywhere; Its Moderation Is Nowhere Close," *WIRED*, October 25, 2021, https://www.wired.com/story/facebooks-global-reach-exceeds-linguistic-grasp/#:~:text=Human%20reviewers%20and%20AI%20filters,nuances%20in%20different%20Arabic%20dialects.

44. Anil Gupta and Nuel D. Belnap, *The Revision Theory of Truth* (Cambridge, MA: MIT Press, 1993).

4. Bias: Why We Can't Expect AI to Solve Deep-Rooted Flaws in Human Decision-Making

1. Kenneth Cukier, Viktor Mayer-Schönberger, and Francis de Véricourt, *Framers: Human Advantage in an Age of Technology and Turmoil* (New York: Dutton, 2021).

2. Daniel Kahneman, *Thinking Fast and Slow* (London: Allen Lane, 2011).

3. Cukier et al., *Framers*; Farnham Street, *The Great Mental Models Vol. 1* (Ottawa: Latticework Publishing, 2019).

4. See, e.g., for accessible works on behavioral economics and cognitive biases in decision-making, Dan Ariely, *Predictably Irrational, Revised and Expanded Edition: The Hidden Forces That Shape Our Decisions* (New York: Harper, 2009); Michelle Baddeley, *Behavioral Economics—A Very Short Introduction* (Oxford: Oxford University Press, 2017); Philip Corr and Anke Plagnol, *Behavioral Economics: The Basics* (London: Routledge, 2018).

5. Ben Smith, "How TikTok Reads Your Mind," *New York Times*, December 5, 2021, https://www.nytimes.com/2021/12/05/business/media/tiktok-algorithm.html.

6. Atul Gawande, *The Checklist Manifesto: How to Get Things Right* (New York: Metropolitan Books, 2010).

7. Atul Gawande, "The Checklist," *The New Yorker*, December 10, 2007, accessed August 8, 2022, https://www.newyorker.com/magazine/2007/12/10/the-checklist.

8. For an overview of rule-based AI, see, e.g., Rolf Pfeifer and Christian Scheier, *Understanding Intelligence* (Cambridge, MA: MIT Press, 1999).

9. For an early technical treatise, see, e.g., Kevin Murphy, *Machine Learning—A Probabilistic Perspective* (Cambridge, MA: MIT Press, 2012).

10. Alex Davies, *Driven—The Race to Create the Autonomous Car* (New York: Simon & Schuster, 2021), p. 83.

11. David Silver et al., "Mastering the Game of Go with Deep Neural Networks and Tree Search," *Nature* 529: 484–489.

12. Frank Pasquale, *The Black Box Society—The Secret Algorithms That Control Money and Information* (Cambridge, MA: Harvard University Press, 2015); for an early account, see Viktor Mayer-Schönberger and Kenneth Cukier, *Big Data—A Revolution That Will Transform How We Live, Work, and Think* (New York: Houghton Mifflin Harcourt, 2013), 178–180; a later, often cited paper is Sandra Wachter, Brent Mittelstadt, and Chris Russell, "Counterfactual Explanations Without Opening the Black Box: Automated Decisions and the GDPR," 31 *Harvard Journal of Law & Technology* 842–887 (2018).

13. Derek E. Bambauer and Michael Risch, "Worse than Human?," 53 *Arizona State Law Journal* 1091 (2022), https://papers.ssrn.com/sol3/Papers.cfm?abstract_id=3897126.

14. Mayer-Schönberger and Cukier, *Big Data*, 180–182.

15. This is apparently different from obeying rules, where people seem to prefer process over outcome; see, e.g., Tom R. Tyler, *Why People Obey the Law* (Princeton, NJ: Princeton University Press, 2006).

16. Sandra Wachter, Brent Mittelstadt, and Luciano Floridi, "Transparent, Explainable, and Accountable AI for Robotics," *Science Robotics* 2(6): 1–2 (2017).

17. A popular rendition of the danger of AI bias can be found, e.g., in Cathy O'Neil, *Weapons of Math Destruction: How Big Data Increases Inequality and Threatens Democracy* (New York: Crown, 2016).

18. The incompleteness of data is a more fundamental and conceptually challenging issue; see David J. Hand, *Dark Data—Why What You Don't Know Matters* (Princeton, NJ: Princeton University Press, 2010).

19. For insights into how even presumably raw training data can be biased, see, e.g., Lisa Gitelman, ed., *"Raw Data" Is an Oxymoron* (Cambridge, MA: MIT Press, 2013).

20. See, e.g., Robert C. Allen, *The British Industrial Revolution in Global Perspective* (Cambridge: Cambridge University Press, 2009), 157–181.

21. See, e.g., Alison Gopnik, *The Philosophical Baby: What Children's Minds Tell Us about Truth, Love and the Meaning of Life* (New York: Farrar, Straus and Giroux, 2009).

22. Alison Gopnik, "Let the Children Play, It's Good for Them!," *Smithsonian Magazine*, July 2012.

23. Margot Lee, *Hidden Figures: The American Dream and the Untold Story of the Black Women Mathematicians Who Helped Win the Space Race* (New York: William Morrow, 2017).

24. John F. Kennedy, *Profiles in Courage* (New York: Harper & Row, 1964).

25. Charles Edward Lindblom, *The Market System: What It Is, How It Works, and What to Make of It* (New Haven, CT: Yale Nota Bene, 2002).

5. Doubt: Incomplete Information and the Problem of Irreversibility

1. "Self-Driving Cars Stuck in Neutral on the Road to Acceptance," Ellen Edmonds, AAA Newsroom, March 5, 2020, https://newsroom.aaa.com/2020/03/self-driving-cars-stuck-in -neutral-on-the-road-to-acceptance/.

2. "Our Robophobia," Andrew Keane Woods, *Lawfare* (blog), February 19, 2020, https:// www.lawfareblog.com/our-robophobia.

3. "Self-Driving Cars: Road to Deployment," US House of Representatives, accessed August 8, 2022, https://docs.house.gov/meetings/IF/IF17/20170214/105548/HHRG-115-IF17 -Wstate-PrattG-20170214.pdf.

4. The trolley problem as a modern moral dilemma was detailed first in Judith Thompson, "Killing, Letting Die, and the Trolley Problem," *Monist* 59: 204–217 (1976).

5. See the website of the "Moral Machine" Project, http://moralmachine.mit.edu.

6. See, e.g., Johannes Himmelreich, "Never Mind the Trolley: The Ethics of Autonomous Vehicles in Mundane Situations," *Ethical Theory and Moral Practice* 21(3): 677 (2018).

7. "Our History—eBay Inc.," eBay, https://www.ebayinc.com/company/our-history/.

8. The problem of not knowing who one was interacting with was encapsulated brilliantly in a cartoon by the *New Yorker*, showing a dog at a computer terminal captioned with "On the Internet, nobody knows you're a dog"; see Glenn Fleishman, "Cartoon Captures Spirit of the Internet," *New York Times*, December 14, 2000.

9. Adam Cohen, *The Perfect Store: Inside eBay* (London: Piatkus, 2002), 24.

10. Christopher Avery, Paul Resnick, and Richard Zeckhauser, "The Market for Evaluations," *American Economic Review* 89(3): 575 (1999).

11. Lian Jian, Jeffrey MacKie-Mason, and Paul Resnick, "I Scratched Yours: The Prevalence of Reciprocation in Feedback Provision on eBay," *The B E Journal of Economic Analysis & Policy* 10: 20 (2010).

12. See, e.g., Yuanyuan Wu et al., "Fake Online Reviews: Literature Review, Synthesis, and Directions for Future Research," *Decision Support Systems* 132: 113280 (2020).

13. Nick Wingfield, "Court Issues Warrant for Arrest of Alleged eBay Scam Artist," *Wall Street Journal*, March 4, 2002, https://www.wsj.com/articles/SB101501488412044200.

14. Mohamed S. Abdel Wahab, M. Ethan Katsh, and Daniel Rainey, "A Look at History," in *Online Dispute Resolution: Theory and Practice: A Treatise on Technology and Dispute Resolution* (The Hague: Eleven International Pub, 2012), 23.

15. Ethan Katsh, Janet Rifkin, and Alan Gaitenby, "E-Commerce, E-Disputes, and E-Dispute Resolution: In the Shadow of 'eBay Law'," *Ohio State Journal on Dispute Resolution* 15(3): 711 (2000).

16. Based on conversation with SquareTrade co-founder and long-time CEO Steve Abernethy with one of the authors, as well as supporting documents.

17. Colin Rule, "Designing a Global Online Dispute Resolution System: Lessons Learned from eBay," *University of St. Thomas Law Journal* 13(2): 368 (2017).

18. Rule, "Designing a Global Online Dispute Resolution System."

19. Nick Szabo, "Unenumerated," August 24, 2008, http://unenumerated.blogspot.com /2006/11/wet-code-and-dry.html.

20. Don Tapscott and Alex Tapscott, *Blockchain Revolution: How the Technology Behind Bitcoin Is Changing Money, Business, and the World* (New York: Portfolio, 2016); more nuanced, Kevin Werbach, *The Blockchain and the New Architecture of Trust* (Cambridge, MA: MIT Press, 2018).

21. Reid Hoffman, "The Future of the Bitcoin Ecosystem and 'Trustless Trust'—Why I Invested in Blockstream," *LinkedIn*, https://www.linkedin.com/pulse/20141117154558-1213-the -future-of-the-bitcoin-ecosystem-and-trustless-trust-why-i-invested-in-blockstream.

22. Werbach, *The Blockchain and the New Architecture of Trust*, 29.

23. See, e.g., Oliver D. Hart, "Incomplete Contracts and the Theory of the Firm," *Journal of Law, Economics, & Organization* 4: 119 (1998). In the smart contracts context, see Kevin Werbach and Nicolas Cornell, "Contracts Ex Machina," *Duke Law Journal* 67: 313 (2017); Jeremy Sklaroff, "Smart Contracts and the Cost of Inflexibility," *University of Pennsylvania Law Review* 166: 263 (2017).

24. Quinn DuPont, "Experiments in Algorithmic Governance: A History and Ethnography of 'The DAO,' a Failed Decentralized Autonomous Organization," in Malcolm Campbell-Verduyn, ed., *Bitcoin and Beyond: Cryptocurrencies, Blockchains, and Global Governance* (London: Routledge, 2018), 157–177.

25. DuPont, "Experiments in Algorithmic Governance," 162–165.

26. Mark A. Lemley, "The Benefit of the Bargain," Stanford Law and Economics Olin Working Paper No. 575, August 2022, Last revised August 9, 2022, https://papers.ssrn.com/sol3 /papers.cfm?abstract_id=4184946.

27. Werbach, *The Blockchain and the New Architecture of Trust*, 126.

28. See, e.g., Robert E. Scott and George G. Triantis, "Incomplete Contracts and the Theory of Contract Design," 56 *Case Western Reserve Law Review* 187 (2005); for its wide-ranging implications, see Philippe Aghion and Richard Holden, "Incomplete Contracts and the Theory of the Firm: What Have We Learned over the Past 25 Years?," *Journal of Economic Perspectives* 25: 181–197 (2011).

29. Phil J. McConnaughay, "Rethinking the Role of Law and Contracts in East-West Commercial Relations," *SSRN* (2000), p. 17, https://papers.ssrn.com/sol3/papers.cfm?abstract_id=252659.

30. Noam Chomsky, *New Horizons in the Study of Language and Mind* (Cambridge: Cambridge University Press, 2000).

31. Mireille Hildebrandt, "The Adaptive Nature of Text-Driven Law," *Journal of Cross-Disciplinary Research in Computational Law* 1(1): 1–12 (2022), https://journalcrcl.org/crcl /article/view/2.

32. Katharina Pistor, "A Legal Theory of Finance," *Journal of Comparative Economics* 41(2): 320 (2013).

6. Principles: Guardrails Should Empower Individuals, Be Socially Anchored, and Encourage Learning

1. There are numerous books on the Terra Nova Expedition; a more recent one detailing personnel and equipment choices is Diana Preston, *A First Rate Tragedy: Captain Scott's Antarctic Expeditions* (London: Constable, 1997).

2. See Peter Densen, "Challenges and Opportunities Facing Medical Education," *Transactions of the American Clinical and Climatological Association* 122: 48–58 (2011); some suggest that time span has shrunk even further in recent years—see, e.g., Breda Corish, "Medical Knowledge Doubles Every Few Months; How Can Clinicians Keep Up?," *Elsevier*, April 23, 2018, https://www.elsevier .com/connect/medical-knowledge-doubles-every-few-months-how-can-clinicians-keep-up.

3. See, e.g., Brian Tamanaha, *Legal Pluralism Explained: History, Theory, Consequences* (New York: Oxford University Press, 2021); or, for a somewhat different take, Paul Schiff Berman, *Global Legal Pluralism: A Jurisprudence of Law beyond Borders* (Cambridge, UK: Cambridge University Press, 2012).

4. Tamanaha, *Legal Pluralism Explained.*

5. Benedict R. Anderson, *Imagined Communities: Reflections on the Origin and Spread of Nationalism*, rev. ed. (London, New York: Verso, 2016), e.g., 67–82.

6. Tamanaha, *Legal Pluralism Explained.*

7. On the interface of tribal law with US national law, see Tamanaha, *Legal Pluralism Explained*, 110–115 (with many additional references).

8. Paul Schiff Berman, *Global Legal Pluralism: A Jurisprudence of Law beyond Borders* (Cambridge, UK: Cambridge University Press, 2012), 10.

9. See, e.g., the discussions in this SMART car forum online: https://www.smart-forum.de /topic/30319-abregelung-beschränkung-der-geschwindigkeit/.

10. See, e.g., Alexander Hamilton's argumentation in Federalist 83: "The friends and adversaries of the plan of the convention, if they agree in nothing else, concur at least in the value they set upon the trial by jury; or if there is any difference between them it consists in this: the former regard it as a valuable safeguard to liberty, the latter represent it as the very palladium of free government"; more generally see, e.g., Albert Alschuler and Andrew G. Deiss, "A Brief History of the Criminal Jury in the United States," 61 *University of Chicago Law Review* 867: 869–876 (1994).

11. *Dobbs v. Jackson Women's Health Organization*, 597 US 66 (2022), https://www.supremecourt .gov/opinions/21pdf/19-1392_6j37.pdf.

12. See, e.g., Sarah McCammon, "Two Months After the Dobbs Ruling, New Abortion Bans Are Taking Hold," *NPR*, August 23, 2022, https://www.npr.org/2022/08/23/1118846811/two -months-after-the-dobbs-ruling-new-abortion-bans-are-taking-hold.

13. *Gitlow v. New York*, 268 U.S. 652 (1925), https://www.loc.gov/item/usrep268652/.

14. Anthony Giddens, *The Constitution of Society: Introduction of the Theory of Structuration* (Berkeley: University of California Press, 1984), 17.

15. For more on Turing and his discovery, see Andrew Hodges, *Alan Turing: The Enigma* (Princeton, NJ: Princeton University Press, 1983).

16. See, e.g., the contributions in Sheila Jasanoff, Gerald E. Markle, James C. Petersen, and Trevor Pinch, eds., *Handbook of Science and Technology Studies*, rev. ed. (Thousand Oaks, CA: SAGE, 1995).

17. See, e.g., Joseph Henrich, *The Secret of Our Success* (Princeton, NJ: Princeton University Press, 2016).

18. See, e.g., Helena Matute et al., "Illusions of Causality: How They Bias Our Everyday Thinking and How They Could Be Reduced," *Frontiers in Psychology*, July 2, 2015, https://www .frontiersin.org/articles/10.3389/fpsyg.2015.00888/full.

19. Terence R. Mitchell, Charles M. Smyser, and Stan E. Weed, "Locus of Control: Supervision and Work Satisfaction," *Academy of Management* 18: 623–631.

20. Michael Tomasello, *A Natural History of Human Thinking* (Cambridge, MA: Harvard University Press, 2014); Michael Tomasello, *Becoming Human: A Theory of Ontogeny* (Cambridge, MA: Harvard University Press, 2019).

21. Henrich, *The Secret of Our Success.*

22. Steven Pinker, *Language, Cognition, and Human Nature—Selected Articles* (New York: Oxford University Press, 2013).

23. On the advantage of social learning see, e.g., Henrich, *The Secret of Our Success*, 8–21.

24. Jonathan Zittrain, *The Future of the Internet and How to Stop It* (New Haven, CT: Yale University Press, 2008).

25. Second chances are afforded by law through a broad range of techniques, including mechanisms for forgiveness; see Martha Minow, *When Should Law Forgive?* (New York: W.W. Norton & Company, 2019).

26. The following draws on the excellent Milton L. Mueller, *Ruling the Root: Internet Governance and the Taming of Cyberspace* (Cambridge, MA: MIT Press, 2002), 175–184; on Tamar Frankel, "Accountability and Oversight of the Internet Corporation for Assigned Names and Numbers (ICANN)," https://papers.ssrn.com/sol3/papers.cfm?abstract_id=333342 (2002); Tamar Frankel, "The Managing Lawmaker in Cyberspace: A New Power Model," https://papers .ssrn.com/sol3/papers.cfm?abstract_id=288544 (2001); and conversations with Tamar Frankel in 2002, partially videotaped and with one of the authors. See also "IFWP Chair Chides ICANN As 'Entirely Inappropriate'," *TechMonitor*, November 1, 1998.

27. Shoshana Zuboff, *The Age of Surveillance Capitalism: The Fight for a Human Future at the New Frontier of Power* (New York: Public Affairs, 2019).

28. Katharina Pistor, *The Code of Capital* (Princeton, NJ: Princeton University Press, 2019).

29. See, e.g., Roberto Mangabeira Unger, "The Critical Legal Studies Movement," 96 *Harvard Law Review* 561–675 (1983).

30. Tamanaha, *Legal Pluralism Explained.*

7. Self-Restraint: How to Avoid the Governance Trap of Too Much Context-Awareness, or Not Enough

1. Carina Schwab, Peter-Paul Hahnl, 20 Jahre Kaprun-Unglück: Ein langer Weg zurück, 11. November 2020, *salzburg.ORF.at*, https://salzburg.orf.at/stories/3075130.

2. *GC, AF, BH, and ED v. Commission Nationale de l'Ínformatique et de Libertes (CNIL)*, Premier ministre, and Google LLC, C-136/17, Judgment of the Court (Grand Chamber) of 24 September 2019, https://curia.europa.eu/juris/liste.jsf?num=C-136/17.

3. Article 6(1)(c) to (e) of the Directive 95/46 of the European Parliament and of the Council of 24 October 1995 on the protection of individuals with regard to the processing of personal data and on the free movement of such data. *Official Journal L* 281/31, 1995.

4. *Google v. Agencia Española de Protección de Datos (AEPD) and Mario Costeja González*, Case C-131/12, https://eur-lex.europa.eu/legal-content/EN/TXT/?uri=CELEX%3A62012CJ0131.

5. "Sex on the Internet—When Bavaria Wrinkles Its Nose, Must the Whole World Catch a Cold?" *The Economist*, January 6, 1996, 18.

6. German Civil Code (BGB) § 327e.

7. Daniel Martin Katz, Corinna Coupette, Janis Beckedorf, and Dirk Hartung, "Complex Societies and the Growth of the Law," *Scientific Reports* 10(1) (2020), https://www.nature.com/articles/s41598-020-73623-x.

8. "Guidance for Industry: Food Labeling Guide," U.S. Food and Drug Administration (FDA), accessed May 21, 2023, https://www.fda.gov/regulatory-information/search-fda-guidance-documents/guidance-industry-food-labeling-guide.

9. Directive 2019/2161 of 27 November 2019 amending Council Directive 93/13/EEC and Directives 98/6/EC, 2005/29/EC, and 2011/83/EU of the European Parliament and of the Council as regards the better enforcement and modernization of Union consumer protection rules, *Official Journal L* 328/7.

10. See, e.g., Christopher T. Marsden, *Internet Co-Regulation: European Law, Regulatory Governance and Legitimacy in Cyberspace* (Cambridge, UK: Cambridge University Press, 2011).

11. Ina Fried, "Exclusive: Microsoft to Grow Legal Team amid Global Tech Regulation," Axios, June 29, 2021, https://www.axios.com/2021/06/29/microsoft-legal-team-expands-regulation.

12. See, e.g., Rohit Supekar, "How *The New York Times* Uses Machine Learning to Make Its Paywall Smarter," https://open.nytimes.com/how-the-new-york-times-uses-machine-learning-to-make-its-paywall-smarter-e5771d5f46f8; AWS Retail Editorial Team, "In the News: How Amazon Is Using Machine Learning to Eliminate 915,000 Tons of Packaging," January 29, 2021, https://aws.amazon.com/blogs/industries/how-amazon-is-using-machine-learning-to-eliminate-915000-tons-of-packaging/; "Zurich Insurance to Acquire Conversational AI Company AlphaChat," December 16, 2021, https://www.insurancejournal.com/news/international/2021/12/16/645962.htm.

13. Directive (EU) 2019/790 of the European Parliament and of the Council of 17 April 2019 on copyright and related rights in the Digital Single Market and amending Directives 96/9/EC and 2001/29/EC, *Official Journal L* 130/92, 2019.

14. Regulation (EU) 2021/784 of the European Parliament and of the Council of 29 April 2021 on addressing the dissemination of terrorist content online, *Official Journal L* 172/79, 2021.

15. "The Strengthened Code of Practice on Disinformation 2022," https://ec.europa.eu/newsroom/dae/redirection/document/87585.

16. Digital Millennium Copyright Act (1998), 112 Stat. 2860.

17. "Hours of Video Uploaded to YouTube Every Minute as of February 2020," https://www.statista.com/statistics/259477/hours-of-video-uploaded-to-youtube-every-minute/.

18. See, e.g., Maayan Perel (Filmar) and Niva Elkin-Koren, "Accountability in Algorithmic Copyright Enforcement," 19 *Stanford Technology Law Review* 473 (2016).

19. "Unfiltered: How YouTube's Content ID Discourages Fair Use and Dictates What We See Online," Electronic Frontier Foundation, https://www.eff.org/document/unfiltered-how -youtubes-content-id-discourages-fair-use-and-dictates-what-we-see-online.

20. See, e.g., William W. Fisher III, "Reconstructing the Fair Use Doctrine," 101 *Harvard Law Review* 1659 (1988); Pamela Samuelson, "Unbundling Fair Uses," 77 *Fordham Law Review* 2537 (2009); Matthew Sag, "Predicting Fair Use," 73 *Ohio St. Law Journal* 47 (2011).

21. Neil Gough, "Chinese Democracy Advocate Is Freed After 8 Years in Prison," *New York Times*, September 8, 2013, p. 13, https://www.nytimes.com/2013/09/08/world/asia/shi-tao -chinese-democracy-advocate-is-released-from-prison.html.

22. Unknown Author, *Der Handlungsreisende wie er sein soll und was er zu thun hat, um Aufträge zu erhalten und eines glücklichen Erfolgs in seinen Geschäften gewiß zu sein* (Ilmenau: Voigt, 1832).

23. John Milton, 1608–1674, *Paradise Lost* (London, New York: Penguin Books, 2000).

24. Pavel Aksenov, "Stanislav Petrov: The Man Who May Have Saved the World," *BBC News*, September 26, 2013, https://www.bbc.com/news/world-europe-24280831.

25. Jamie McIntyre, "The Last Korean Meltdown: Bill Clinton on the Brink of War," *Daily Beast*, November 24, 2010, https://www.thedailybeast.com/articles/2010/11/24/the-last -korean-meltdown-bill-clinton-on-the-brink-of-war.

26. *Marbury v. Madison*, 5 US 137 (1803), https://www.law.cornell.edu/supremecourt/text /5/137.

27. Richard A. Posner, "The Meaning of Judicial Self-Restraint," 59 *Indiana Law Journal* 14 (1983).

28. For more details, see recently also Lawrence Lessig, *Fidelity & Constraint—How the Supreme Court Has Read the American Constitution* (New York: Oxford University Press, 2019), 19–35.

29. Jeremy Waldron, "The Rule of Law," in Edward N. Zalta, ed., *The Stanford Encyclopedia of Philosophy* (2020), chapter 2, https://plato.stanford.edu/archives/sum2020/entries/rule-of -law/.

30. Mark A. Lemley, "The Imperial Supreme Court," *SSRN*, July 28, 2022, https://ssrn.com /abstract=4175554.

31. See, e.g., Presidential Commission on the Supreme Court of the United States, *Final Report*, December 2021, https://www.whitehouse.gov/wp-content/uploads/2021/12 /SCOTUS-Report-Final-12.8.21-1.pdf.

32. John Steinbruner, *The Cybernetic Theory of Decision* (Princeton, NJ: Princeton University Press, 1974).

33. This is based on the four "freedoms" (of goods, persons, services, and capital) in the Consolidated version of the Treaty on the Functioning of the European Union—Protocols— Annexes—Declarations annexed to the Final Act of the Intergovernmental Conference which adopted the Treaty of Lisbon, signed on 13 December 2007, *Official Journal C* 326, 26/10/2012 P. 0001–0390.

34. For a recent overview and critique, see Charles Tyler and Heather Gerken, "The Myth of the Laboratories of Democracy," 122 *Columbia Law Review* 218–224 (2022).

8. Range: Four Case Studies That Illustrate the Art and Science of Making Innovative Guardrails

1. From the vast body of literature and only as an illustration of the breadth of variations on the theme, see, e.g., Ronald Dworkin, *Law's Empire* (Cambridge, MA: Harvard University Press, 1986); Duncan Kennedy, "Form and Substance in Private Law Adjudication," 89 *Harvard Law Review* 1685 (1976); Mireille Hildebrandt, "The Adaptive Nature of Text-Driven Law," *Journal of Cross-Disciplinary Research in Computational Law* 1(1): 2022, https://journalcrcl.org/crcl/article/view/2.

2. Nicole Sganga, "White House Believes Russia Responsible for Cyberattacks on Ukrainian Banks and Defense Sites," *CBS News*, February 18, 2022, https://www.cbsnews.com/news/russia-ukraine-cyber-attacks-white-house/.

3. Sganga, "White House Believes Russia Responsible."

4. "CERT-UA," Computer Emergency Response Team of Ukraine, https://cert.gov.ua/.

5. Barbara Fraser, "Security Incidents, Threats and Vulnerabilities," *Software Engineering Institute Carnegie Mellon University* (1997), https://apricot.net/apricot97/apII/Presentations/SecurityIncidentsThreats/sld001.htm.

6. Carl Malamud and Barbara Fraser, "Geek of the Week," *Internet Talk Radio / Open Transcripts*, October 20, 1993, http://opentranscripts.org/transcript/geek-ᴑf-the-week-barbara-fraser/.

7. For a list, see https://en.wikipedia.org/wiki/Computer_emergency_response_team.

8. See, e.g., Factsheet, US-CERT: United States Computer Emergency Readiness Team, Homeland Security, https://www.cisa.gov/uscert/sites/default/files/publications/infosheet_US-CERT_v2.pdf.

9. "Conficker Working Group Lessons Learned 17 June 2010," The Rendon Group based upon work supported by the Department of Homeland Security under Air Force Research Laboratory Contract No. FA8750-08-2-0141, accessed August 9, 2022, http://docs.media.bitpipe.com/io_10x/io_102267/item_465972/whitepaper_76813745321.pdf.

10. See, e.g., Stuart E. Madnick, Xitong Li, and Nazli Choucri, "Experiences and Challenges with Using CERT Data to Analyze International Cyber Security," MIT Sloan Research Paper No. 4759–09, https://ssrn.com/abstract=1478206 (2009); Samantha Bradshaw, "Combating Cyber Threats: CSIRTs and Fostering International Cooperation on Cybersecurity," Global Commission on Internet Governance Paper Series, Paper no. 23, https://ssrn.com/abstract=2700899 (2015).

11. Advocating a similar approach in the context of international relations is Anne-Marie Slaughter, *The Chessboard & the Web: Strategies of Connection in a Networked World* (New Haven, CT: Yale University Press, 2017).

12. "West Africa: Ghana and Burkina Faso Discuss Energy Crisis," *Ghana Focus*, March 26, 1998, https://allafrica.com/stories/199803260109.html.

13. "West Africa: Ghana and Burkina Faso Discuss Energy Crisis."

14. Megan Matthews, "The Volta Convention: An Effective Tool for Transboundary Water Resource Management in an Era of Impending Climate Change and Devastating Natural Disasters," *Denver Journal of International Law & Policy* 41(2): 281 (2013).

15. See, e.g., Jan Hassing, Niels Ipsen, Torkil Jønch Clausen, Henrik Larsen, and Palle Lindgaard-Jørgensen, "Integrated Water Resources Management in Action," WWAP, DHI Water Policy, UNEP-DHI Centre for Water and Environment (2009), https://www.gwp.org /globalassets/global/toolbox/references/iwrm-in-action-unescounwwapunep-dhi-2009.pdf.

16. "Volta River Basin Ghana & Burkina Faso," IUCN, accessed August 9, 2022, https:// portals.iucn.org/library/efiles/documents/2012-010.pdf.

17. Anil Agarwal, *Integrated Water Resources Management* (Stockholm: Global Water Partnership, 2000), 31.

18. Ben Y. Ampomah, Bernadette A. Adjei, and Eva Youkhana, "The Transboundary Water Resources Management Regime of the Volta Basin," *ZEF Working Paper Series*, no. 28 (2008), https://nbn-resolving.de/urn:nbn:de:0202-20080911287.

19. See, e.g., Global Water Partnership West Africa, "Outlines and Principles for Sustainable Development of the Volta Basin," Final Report, June 2014, https://www.gwp.org /globalassets/global/gwp-waf_files/wacdep/brochure_outlines_principles_wacdep_abv _en.pdf.

20. Vincent Ni, "Yahoo Withdraws from China as Beijing's Grip on Tech Firms Tightens," *The Guardian*, November 2, 2021, https://www.theguardian.com/technology/2021/nov/02 /yahoo-withdraws-from-china-as-beijings-grip-on-tech-firms-tightens.

21. Tom Zeller, "Web Firms Are Grilled on Dealings in China," *New York Times*, February 16, 2006, https://www.nytimes.com/2006/02/16/technology/web-firms-are-grilled-on-dealings -in-china.html.

22. H. R. 4780 to promote freedom of expression on the Internet, to protect US businesses from coercion to participate in repression by authoritarian foreign governments, and for other purposes, https://www.congress.gov/bill/109th-congress/house-bill/4780/text.

23. Colin M. Maclay, "Can the Global Network Initiative Embrace the Character of the Net?," in Ronald Deibert et al., eds., *Access Controlled: The Shaping of Power, Rights, and Rule in Cyberspace (Information Revolution and Global Politics)* (Cambridge, MA: MIT Press, 2010), 88–108.

24. Global Network Initiative, "Collaborating in Changing Times," GNI Annual Report 2021, https://globalnetworkinitiative.org/wp-content/uploads/2022/07/GNI-2021-Annual -Report.pdf.

25. "Wikipedia:Wikipedians," *Wikipedia*, August 3, 2022, https://en.wikipedia.org/w/index .php?title=Wikipedia:Wikipedians&oldid=1102201036.

26. Saabira Chaudhuri, "Editors Won't Let It Be When It Comes to 'the' or 'The,'" *Wall Street Journal*, October 13, 2012, https://online.wsj.com/article/SB10000872396390444657804578 048534112811590.html.

27. "Wikipedia Talk: Requests for Mediation / The Beatles," *Wikipedia*, May 5, 2022, https://en.wikipedia.org/w/index.php?title=Wikipedia_talk:Requests_for_mediation/The _Beatles&oldid=1086388207.

28. "Wikipedia:About," *Wikipedia*, July 25, 2022, https://en.wikipedia.org/w/index.php?title =Wikipedia:About&oldid=1100365834.

29. See, e.g., John Palfrey and Urs Gasser, *The Connected Parent—An Expert Guide to Parenting in a Digital World* (New York: Basic Books, 2020), 206.

30. Wikipedia is one of the most prominent and lasting examples of socially anchored peer production enabled by the World Wide Web. For a fundamental account, see Yochai Benkler, *The Wealth of Networks: How Social Production Transforms Markets and Freedom* (New Haven, CT: Yale University Press, 2006).

31. "User: Jimbo Wales/Statement of Principles," *Wikipedia*, July 1, 2022, https://en.wikipedia .org/w/index.php?title=User:Jimbo_Wales/Statement_of_principles&oldid=1095903302.

32. "Wikipedia:Experiment," *Wikipedia*, accessed August 11, 2022, https://en.wikipedia.org /w/index.php?title=Wikipedia:Experiment&oldid=927595353.

33. "Wikipedia:Editorial Oversight and Control," *Wikipedia*, June 8, 2022, https://en .wikipedia.org/w/index.php?title=Wikipedia:Editorial_oversight_and_control&oldid =1092086563.

34. Paul B. Stephan recently highlighted the enduring role of "norm entrepreneurs" in Paul B. Stephan, *The World Crisis and International Law: The Knowledge Economy and the Battle for the Future* (Cambridge: Cambridge University Press, 2022), 268–272; on the phenomenon of "norm entrepreneurs," see Carmen Wunderlich, *Dedicated to the Good: Norm Entrepreneurs in International Relations* (Cham, Switzerland: Springer, 2020).

9. Machines: Why Technology Is Neither Anathema nor a Panacea, But a Valuable Piece in the Puzzle

1. The company's spokesperson denied that race was a factor in the decision. With the help of a real estate agent and Crystal Marie's employer, they ultimately managed to get the mortgage. For more information, see Emmanuel Martinez and Lauren Kirchner, "The Secret Bias Hidden in Mortgage-Approval Algorithms," *The Markup*, accessed August 12, 2022, https://themarkup .org/denied/2021/08/25/the-secret-bias-hidden-in-mortgage-approval-algorithms.

2. Martinez and Kirchner, "The Secret Bias Hidden in Mortgage-Approval Algorithms."

3. "Only in Oklahoma This Man Was Our Man," *Tulsa World*, accessed August 12, 2022, https://tulsaworld.com/archives/only-in-oklahoma-this-man-was-our-man/article_324f81ed -f406-566c-97f3-d82c37e3b28e.html.

4. "This Song Belongs to You and Me: Lawsuit Filed Declaring Guthrie's Classic in Public Domain," *Hypebot*, June 30, 2016, https://www.hypebot.com/hypebot/2016/06/this-song -belongs-to-you-and-me-lawsuit-filed-declaring-guthries-classic-in-public-domain.html.

5. "CC in Review: Lawrence Lessig on How It All Began," October 12, 2005, https://creative commons.org/2005/10/12/ccinreviewlawrencelessigonhowitallbegan/.

6. An example of a Creative Commons Attribution 4.0 International License, for example, would translate into <a rel="license" href="http://creativecommons.org/licenses/by/4.0/"> <img alt="Creative Commons License" style="border-width:0" src="https://i.creativecommons .org/l/by/4.0/88x31.png" /></a>
This work is licensed under a <a rel="license" href ="http://creativecommons.org/licenses/by/4.0/">Creative Commons Attribution 4.0 International License</a>.

7. "Creative Commons Unveils Machine-Readable Copyright Licenses," December 17, 2002, https://creativecommons.org/2002/12/16/creativecommonsunveilsmachinereadablecopyri ghtlicenses/.

8. "CC in Review."

9. "Creative Commons' Global Network: How We're Growing," February 23, 2018, https://creativecommons.org/2018/02/23/global-network/.

10. Creative Commons Annual Report 2019, https://wiki.creativecommons.org/images/2/20/CC_AnnualReport_2019.pdf.

11. Creative Commons, "Announcing (and Explaining) Our New 2.0 Licenses," May 25, 2004, https://creativecommons.org/2004/05/25/announcingandexplainingournew20licenses/.

12. See, e.g., https://wiki.creativecommons.org/wiki/4.0/Treatment_of_adaptations.

13. Niva Elkin-Koren, "Exploring Creative Commons: A Skeptical View of a Worthy Pursuit," in Bernt Hugenholtz and Lucie Guibault, eds., *The Future of Public Domain* (Amsterdam: Kluwer, 2006), 21–.

14. Consider, e.g., the reform proposals by Larry Lessig's faculty colleague William Fisher, *Promises to Keep: Technology, Law, and the Future of Entertainment* (Stanford, CA: Stanford University Press, 2004).

15. Hollis Fishelson-Holstine, "The Role of Credit Scoring in Increasing Homeownership for Underserved Populations," Joint Center for Housing Studies Harvard University, BABC 04–12, (2004): 4.

16. Title VIII of the Civil Rights Act of 1968 (Fair Housing Act), codified at 42 U.S.C. §§ 3601 et seq. and Equal Credit Opportunity Act, codified at 15 U.S.C. §§ 1691 et seq.

17. See Fannie Mae Letter LL09–95 to all Fannie Mae lenders from Robert J. Engelstad, "Measuring Credit Risk: Borrower Credit Scores and Lender Profiles," October 24, 1995; Freddie Mac Industry, Letter from Michael K. Stamper, "The Predictive Power of Selected Credit Scores," July 11, 1995.

18. Fishelson-Holstine, "The Role of Credit Scoring," 6.

19. To be clear, FICO is not the only element that guides much of the decision-making process of lenders that is increasingly driven by software. Underwriting algorithms are another element in the approval process that is largely automated, widely untransparent, and potentially unfair. Recent investigations into the untransparent algorithms at the heart of underwriting software used by large lenders suggest that some of the criteria used in these programs play out differently for diverse applicants based on their race or ethnicity, with likely discriminatory effects for people of color, despite the promise of color-blindness and compliance with fair lending guardrails defined by law.

20. Martinez and Kirchner, "The Secret Bias Hidden in Mortgage-Approval Algorithms."

21. Lincoln Quillian, John J. Lee, and Brandon Honoré, "Racial Discrimination in the U.S. Housing and Mortgage Lending Markets: A Quantitative Review of Trends, 1976–2016," *Race and Social Problems* 12(1): 13 (2020).

22. See, e.g., Lyn C. Thomas, "A Survey of Credit and Behavioural Scoring: Forecasting Financial Risk of Lending to Consumers," *International Journal of Forecasting* 16(2): 149–172 (2000).

23. Emre Sahingur, Allison Binns, and James Egan, "Credit Invisible No Longer: Racial Disparities in Lending," VantageScore and Morgan Stanley, June 24, 2021, accessed August 12, 2022, https://s3.documentcloud.org/documents/20986644/vantagescore-slides-june-2021.pdf.

24. Tracy Jan, "Trump Gutted Obama-Era Housing Discrimination Rules. Biden's Bringing Them Back," *Washington Post*, April 13, 2021, https://www.washingtonpost.com/us-policy/2021/04/13/hud-biden-fair-housing-rules/.

25. Cleve Wootson Jr. and Tracy Jan, "Biden Signs Orders on Racial Equity, and Civil Rights Groups Press for More," *Washington Post*, January 26, 2021, https://www.washingtonpost.com

/politics/biden-to-sign-executive-actions-on-equity/2021/01/26/3ffbcff6-5f8e-11eb-9430
-e7c77b5b0297_story.html.

26. *Gitlow v. New York*, 268 U.S. 652 (1925), https://www.loc.gov/item/usrep268652/.

27. For an overview of some such technical strategies see, e.g., Joshua A. Kroll et al., "Accountable Algorithms," *University of Pennsylvania Law Review* 165: 633–706 (2017).

28. Sandra Wachter, Brent Mittelstadt, and Chris Russell, "Counterfactual Explanations without Opening the Black Box: Automated Decisions and the GDPR," *Harvard Journal of Law & Technology* 31(2): 880 (2018).

29. "Synthetic Data: The Complete Guide," *Datagen*, accessed August 12, 2022, https://datagen.tech/guides/synthetic-data/synthetic-data/.

30. Andrew White, "By 2024, 60% of the Data Used for the Development of AI and Analytics Projects Will Be Synthetically Generated," *Gartner*, July 24, 2021, https://blogs.gartner.com/andrew_white/2021/07/24/by-2024-60-of-the-data-used-for-the-development-of-ai-and-analytics-projects-will-be-synthetically-generated/.

31. Reva Schwartz et al., "Towards a Standard for Identifying and Managing Bias in Artificial Intelligence," National Institute of Standards and Technology, March 2022, p. 2, https://doi.org/10.6028/NIST.SP.1270.

32. "EY Trusted AI Platform," EY, accessed August 12, 2022, https://www.ey.com/en_us/consulting/trusted-ai-platform.

33. "EY Platform Uses Fairlearn to Help Customers Gain Trust in AI," Microsoft Customers Stories, accessed August 12, 2022, https://customers.microsoft.com/sv-se/story/809460-ey-partner-professional-services-azure-machine-learning-fairlearn.

34. "Unmasking AI Harms and Biases," Algorithmic Justice League, accessed August 12, 2022, https://www.ajl.org/.

35. "AI4ALL," accessed August 12, 2022, https://ai-4-all.org/.

36. M. Sirait et al., "Mapping Customary Land in East Kalimantan, Indonesia: A Tool for Forest Management," http://www2.eastwestcenter.org/environment/fox/kali.html, September 30, 2003; see also Gernot Brodnig and Viktor Mayer-Schönberger, "Bridging the Gap: The Role of Spatial Information Technologies in the Integration of Traditional Environmental Knowledge and Western Science," *Electronic Journal on Information Systems in Developing Countries* 1: 1–15 (2000).

10. Futures: How to Think About the Exercise of Power as Humans Approach a New Digital Frontier

1. Neil Stephenson, *Snow Crash* (New York: Bantam, 1992).

2. "Value Creation in the Metaverse," McKinsey, accessed August 12, 2022, https://www.mckinsey.com/~/media/mckinsey/business%20functions/marketing%20and%20sales/our%20insights/value%20creation%20in%20the%20metaverse/Value-creation-in-the-metaverse.pdf.

3. See also Deborah L. Spar, *Ruling the Waves: From the Compass to the Internet, a History of Business and Politics along the Technological Frontier* (Orlando, FL: Harcourt, 2001).

4. Stephenson, *Snow Crash*, paperback ed. (New York: Bantam, 2003), 114.

5. See, e.g., "A New Social Contract for a New Era," UN Sustainable Development Goals, https://www.un.org/sustainabledevelopment/a-new-social-contract-for-a-new-era/; Tim Berners Lee, "Contract for the Web: A Global Plan of Action to Make Our Online World Safe and Empowering for Everyone," Contract for the Web, https://contractfortheweb.org/.

6. St. Benedict, *The Rule of Saint Benedict*, vintage ed. (New York: Random House, 1998).

7. Lorraine Daston, *Rules: A Short History of What We Live By* (Princeton, NJ: Princeton University Press, 2022).

8. Daston, *Rules*.

9. Alex Steffen, "Discontinuity Is the Job," *The Snap Forward*, https://alexsteffen.substack .com/p/discontinuity-is-the-job.

10. The same applies to guardrail-makers: It is our capacities for abstract thinking and communication that allow us to confront the problem of how to adapt our guardrails to new problems and circumstances head-on. See Gillian K. Hadfield, *Rules for a Flat World: Why Humans Invented Law and How to Reinvent It for a Complex Global Economy* (New York: Oxford University Press, 2017).

11. Fernanda Pirie, *The Rules of Laws: A 4,000-Year Quest to Order the World* (London: Perseus, 2021), 455.

12. See, e.g., David W. Kennedy and William W. Fisher, eds., *The Canon of American Legal Thought* (Princeton, NJ: Princeton University Press, 2006).

13. See, e.g., Julie E. Cohen, *Between Truth and Power: The Legal Constructions of Informational Capitalism* (Oxford: Oxford University Press, 2019); Brett Frischmann and Evan Selinger, *Re-Engineering Humanity* (Cambridge: Cambridge University Press, 2018); Danielle Citron, *The Fight for Privacy: Protecting Dignity, Identity, and Love in the Digital Age* (New York: Norton, 2022); Frank Pasquale, *The Black Box Society* (Cambridge, MA: Harvard University Press, 2015); Ariel Ezrachi and Maurice E. Stucke, *Virtual Competition—The Promise and Perils of the Algorithm-Driven Economy* (Cambridge, MA: Harvard University Press, 2016).

14. In this sense, guardrail design is a constructive undertaking; for a resurrection of law as a constructivist endeavor, see, e.g., Alexander Somek, *The Legal Relation: Legal Theory after Legal Positivism* (Cambridge: Cambridge University Press, 2017).

15. Pirie, *The Rules of Laws*.

INDEX